Once Upon a Trainwreck

SIMON
ELEMENT
An Imprint of Simon & Schuster, LLC
1230 Avenue of the Americas
New York, NY 10020

Some names and identifying characteristics have been changed and some dialogue has been re-created.

The authorized representative in the EEA is Simon & Schuster Netherlands B.V., Herculesplein 96, 3584 AA Utrecht, Netherlands. info@simonandschuster.nl

First Simon Element hardcover edition October 2026

Interior design by Hope Herr-Cardillo

Photos on pages 1, 8, 23, 44, 68, 90, 120, 135, and 246 by Sharon Romano. Photo on page 155 by Mike Ruiz. Photo on page 185 by Anthony Romano. Photos on pages 223 and 224 by Amelia Strauss. Photo on page 243 by Natalie Black. Photo on page 246 courtesy of the author. Photo on page 247 by Brenda Rooney.

Manufactured in the United States of America

10 9 8 7 6 5 4 3 2 1

Library of Congress Control Number has been applied for.

ISBN 978-1-6680-8221-8
ISBN 978-1-6680-8223-2 (ebook)

Once Upon a Trainwreck

The Fall and Rise of a Child Star

Christy Carlson Romano

SIMON ELEMENT
New York Amsterdam/Antwerp London
Toronto Sydney/Melbourne New Delhi

Contents

For Isabella, Sophia, and Brendan.
I love you.

Author's Note

This memoir reflects the author's life as faithfully and carefully as possible at the time of its conception. The events are drawn from the author's recollections over time and are shaped by memory, perspective, healing, and hindsight. Memory is inherently human, and others may remember certain moments differently. Where dialogue appears, it has been re-created to convey the essence of conversations rather than verbatim transcripts. Some names and identifying characteristics have been changed to protect privacy. Let this book be not only a record of self-discovery, growth, and accountability, but also a jumping-off point for future repair, deeper honesty, and the lifelong practice of choosing truth over performance.

Preface

To my fellow millennials reading this: We were promised that if we got good grades, went to college, and worked hard, we'd have houses, stable careers, and 401(k)s by thirty. Instead, we got Columbine and 9/11 in high school, student loans and drinking problems in college, three roommates and no work after the '08 financial crisis, a pandemic when we finally had babies, and the harsh realization that "adulting" is just making it up as you go along while pretending to know how to pronounce "quinoa" correctly in social settings. We're former try-hards who got burnt out experiencing one too many "unprecedented historical events" over the decades.

Whether you grew up watching me as the perfect good girl Ren Stevens, or you're here for the chaos, know this: We're all just overachievers—because our parents pressured us to live out their American dream—now navigating late-stage capitalism with little to no inheritance or savings and coexisting with dependent elderly parents or unhelpful family members who are checked out when it comes to helping with reliable childcare. While most of us admit that we have no village, we are, without a doubt, having a generational hive-mind existential crisis—and I am still a reflection of your maturity. Cue the commercial: "Disney stars are just like you . . ."

If you're reading this book wondering how a girl who had been so close to luck for a short period of time ended up as confused and humbled as you—well, that's exactly the point. We're all just taking it one day at a time together, and it's sort of tragically wonderful to know we're not alone. The only difference between me and you is that my quarter-life crisis happened on the internet. So here's to millennial culture—be you geriatric or cusper: We may not own houses, but we own our stories. And sometimes, that's enough. Proving once again to Gen Z that we "did it for the plot" before that was even a thing.

Dear Girls,

Before we dive in, you should know I still believe in magic. People have called me all sorts of things over the years (bitter, jaded, inauthentic, a try-hard). Most criticism from these strangers has been uninformed and inaccurate. Whatever they've seen in me or projected onto me, I have always been, at my core, a hopeless romantic. I believe in unconditional love. As you will learn, it is through a steadfast commitment to this personal flaw that I eventually found my superpower: resilience in a harsh world. I have fallen (sometimes publicly), and I have made the tough choice, again and again, to become a little stronger by keeping my sense of humor and pulling myself back up.

The world isn't always so kind to us as women. I want you to learn from my mistakes. I'm offering not just transparency but a collection of lessons in hindsight. I hope you take from it that you don't have to be perfect to be loved. Both of you girls are enough.

Maybe after reading this, you will know why I parented you the way I did. Or why every time we watched a parade or a fireworks show, I would ugly cry because it was all so wholesome and beautiful. Or why you couldn't do sleepovers. Or why I wanted to keep you close and protected for as long as possible. You will never get rid of me, by the way. I will spend the rest of my life building you up so that you may never forget who you are.

I love you two more than the amount of breath God will let me hold. As many mothers understand, I would kill and be killed for you. So, after I am gone, may this book be a reminder of my humanity and a comforting extension of my love for you.

1

Inner Child

1989

Age 5

"Christy, sit still! I need to fix your hair. You don't want to look like you just got out of bed."

I squirm a bit.

"Stop moving!"

Mom brushes my long straight hair back, hard, pulling it into tight braids. Mom has wavy blond hair and light eyes, not the same as me at all. I have dark eyes and hair, like Dad. The dressing room air is thick with the sharp, sweet smell of Aqua Net hair spray. Other girls and their moms hurry in and out, pulling on sequined leotards and pinning sparkly ribbons into their perfectly shiny, curled hair. I recognize some of the girls but don't really know anyone. The heat from the vanity lights is making me sweat. My mom pulls each braid tight, and I try to sit still, even though it hurts. I want to do a good job and make all the adults happy and proud, so I force myself not to cry out. I try to remember my choreography and that I need to smile (big). There's one problem, though.

"Mommy?"

"Sit still—we gotta go!"

"I need to pee," I whisper. I'm trying my best to be still as a statue while she finishes pulling my ponytail. Being still when you're five years old is not easy.

A stage manager pops their head into the dressing room. "Christy Romano! 'Le Jazz Hot!' Sixty seconds!"

"Hold your breath," says my mom as she gives me a final Aqua Net spritz and slicks back my baby hairs.

"I can hold it," I mumble.

My mom smiles. "Go get 'em." She always tells me that I'm a "good kid" because I "behave," and that my older siblings don't listen like I do. I love it when adults tell me I'm "easy to work with," because it makes me feel like I'm doing the very best job and Mom will be happy, so I rarely complain and I always pay attention. I train at The Dance Connection in East Haven, Connecticut, and my dance teacher Miss Linda loves finding songs that she thinks fit each kid's personality. When she told me I'd be doing a routine to the song "Le Jazz Hot!" from *Victor/Victoria*, I just agreed and did as I was told. She's the teacher, so she must know the best songs for little kids to dance to, right? She knows what an audience will love. Miss Linda said the song has "sass." I worked on my routine for months, and Mom always said she was proud of how hard I worked. When it was time for the competition, Mom paid for an expensive leotard, so I knew this was a big deal. I *have* to get it perfect.

I have butterflies in my stomach, but now they're fluttering even more since I have to "hold it." Mom hands me over to a stage manager who ushers me backstage and away from Mom.

"I'll be out front watching," Mom says. "Smile big."

She hurries off to find her seat, and the stage manager brings me into the pitch-black wings, where older girls in their own sparkly costumes sit in the splits or practice pirouettes. The bright stage lights make me squint, and I watch the older girls, hoping that one day I can be as pretty and as good at dancing as they are. My costume is made up of shiny red sequins.

It looks pretty, but it's itchy and tight. The stockings are hot. My stomach grumbles, and I know I need a snack. I haven't eaten much today since we've been at the auditorium for hours.

"Stand here and wait until you hear your name," says the stage manager. I see a little girl in a yellow glittery leotard crying to her mom in a corner. I wonder what she's upset about, but I can't think about her. I have to focus. Smile. Dance like I did in rehearsals. Hit my steps. Stay on beat. Win.

From the cavernous stage, a voice booms: "And now, dancing to 'Le Jazz Hot!' from *Victor/Victoria*, Christy Romano from Milford, Connecticut!"

That's my cue. I strut to the middle of the stage with my hand on my hip, fully aware that a stage light is following me. I strike a pose and wait for the music to start, and once it does, I make funny faces and thrust my hips like Miss Linda taught me to do. I "ham it up," as Mom says, for the table of judges out front. I'm not nervous; I'm having fun. Dancing onstage, I almost forget the whole world. I feel like I'm floating and watching myself dancing down below. I only remember where I am and what I'm doing when the song ends, so I give one final smile to the judges and skip offstage.

I go into the dressing room, and Mom walks in, saying I did a great job. She has a huge smile on her face, which makes me feel happy. But there's no time for snacks or anything else, because the stage manager rushes in and tells us to line up with the other girls in our age range, five through seven, for the awards announcements. Mom is truly excited; she thinks I'm going to win. "You were the best," she whispers. "I watched from the front." She gives me a hug, and I skip off backstage with the other girls, ready to hear the winners.

Once we line up under the bright lights onstage, the emcee in his black-and-white tuxedo holds a piece of paper and a microphone and begins to talk about how well we each did. All of a sudden, the urge to pee comes back. I'd forgotten all about it while I was dancing, but now it actually hurts. I'm standing in fifth position with my hands on my hips, just like the other four girls onstage with me. I'm trying my best to smile even though I'm feeling scared about needing to pee. I notice that there's cold air pumping onto the stage, making me shiver. I can't see out into the audience; I can't see my mom. My heart is beating fast.

"And our third-place dancer is . . . Renee DeFranco . . ."

I squeeze, trying my hardest to hold it.

"Second place is Lisa Moretti . . ."

Just as the emcee gets ready to announce first place, it happens. I can feel something wet and warm sliding down my itchy nude-colored dance stockings. By the time it puddles around my ankles, it is cold, blasted by the frigid air of the stage. I smile wider, hoping no one will notice the urine that has come out of my five-year-old body. I look to the wings and see the stage manager looking right at me. She looks panicked.

"And our first-place winner, best in show, is . . . Gia Rossi!"

My face, painted with Kabuki-like red lips and blue eye shadow, feels tight and hot. I try to keep smiling, but I frantically search for someone to come save me. I'm looking for someone to stop this moment from happening. I'm looking for help. I'm looking for my mom to fix this, to make me feel better. But I can't move. Once the audience notices what's happened, they look horrified, as I stand frozen in fifth position in a puddle of my own pee in front of an entire theater of people. I didn't get the red ribbon or even a blue one. My name wasn't called, and even worse, I've done this most horrible, embarrassing thing. I feel like I let everyone down, like the whole town will know me as the girl who peed onstage.

I finally find Mom in the seats, and she stares straight ahead, clapping for the winners. Even from far away, I can tell she's angry. Or maybe she's disappointed, which is even worse.

My sisters participated in the same competition the day before, and they both medaled in their age groups. I won't get the flowers or the congratulations that the winners get. Mom comes to the dressing room and rushes over to me. She pulls me to the bathroom to clean me up.

"Christy, why didn't you tell me you had to pee?" She sounds angry.

"I did," I say, but I don't think she hears me. She just cleans me up, looking disgusted as she peels off my sticky tights. We pack up my light-blue-and-pink Caboodle with all my makeup and hair ties. My head hurts from the tight braids and crusted hair spray, but I don't complain.

On the car ride home to Milford, Mom doesn't say much about my loss or what happened on the stage, and neither do I. I can tell she's disappointed, because when she's proud, she always tells me I'm a "star" or "special." Not today, though. She says Dad is making chicken cutlets and pasta and that we have school in the morning, so everyone needs to go to bed early. I stare out the window at the snow on the ground. I silently promise myself that next time, I'll do better. Next time, I'll hold it.

Dear Girls,

I didn't want to sign you up for dance class at first, Izzy. But I realized quickly that I was projecting my own issues onto the situation. I owed it to you and your baby sister, Sophia, to let you partake in the arts. I had almost forgotten how much I loved it all. It was intoxicating to receive your costume, the one with the flower crown zipped up in a white bag with your name on it. The spring performance was coming up fast, and I made sure you and your sister had extra individual coaching so that you didn't feel behind or timid onstage the next week at the big, local high school stage.

On the day, you two looked perfect. Okay, almost perfect. Aside from a tear in a stocking and a few flyaways from wrestling with you to put your coats on. Your dad was there, and Grandma Romano talked about "how Mommy started dancing when she was this age." Mimi and Papa brought flowers and drove from an hour away. We waited for the lights to dim and your little feet to tiptoe onstage. Sophia, you went first and did great, and we were so excited for you as you skipped offstage, wearing a smile.

I did my best to ignore the presence of my mom. Not because I wasn't grateful that she was alive and well. But because I could feel her eagerness for history to repeat itself in you both. Izzy, when you first came on in your Mexican dress and floral crown to dance to "De colores," I could tell you were so very aware of the many eyeballs staring at you. You held your own wonderfully. The song continued as you all turned and held your dresses in one hand. You were almost done with the full routine when . . . SLAM! You slipped and fell on your back, hard. My world stopped. There was an audible gasp from everyone in the audience.

"YOU GOT THIS, IZZY!" Your dad bolted to his feet, shouted as if he were back in the Marines, and clapped in support as you got up, visibly shaken, with tears in your eyes.

Before anyone could stop me, I was already charging to the back of the house.

History was *repeating itself, and I had to fix it. Thirty-five years later, my nervous system was still trying to protect a five-year-old girl in itchy dance tights. My mind was frozen in fear, as if something truly tragic had happened to you. When I reached you, an older dancer from the studio was comforting you. The humanity of the moment was enough to help me breathe and collect my emotions. Later that day, you told me, "I never want to go onstage again."*

Should I have ignored your plea and signed you up again to "face your fear" and build your resilience? Or should I listen to you? I sat you on my lap and said, "Okay, baby." I kissed the bridge of your button nose and held you tight. That day, I made a promise to myself: Neither one of my daughters would be pushed into anything that didn't feel good to them or that made them feel unsafe. But even as I write this, I'm uniquely haunted with knowing that this will be my plight as a parent. Which pedal to push to raise you right, the gas or the brake. That day, I learned that being a "good mom" doesn't mean creating kids who will be "tough later." It means listening to their needs first.

2

Scene, Not Heard

1990

Age 6

I'm sitting on the steps by our blue-carpeted hallway. The windows in the house are open since we rarely use AC, even in the middle of summer. Mom and Dad are downstairs, fighting about money, which makes us nervous. They always seem to be fighting about money, even though we live in this big, old farmhouse with a huge backyard. They always yell about bills or savings, but if I even complain about anything, Mom will remind us that we have a "perfect" life, and we live in a "mansion," and we're a "good family." If we're so lucky and "perfect," though, why are they always fighting?

Our light blue house has a stained-glass window in the front that says "Welcome" on it, but whoever made it didn't realize that it would read "emocleW" from the outside. Once I learned to read and saw that it was backward, I asked Mom about it. She just said it was a mistake, but Mom was proud of having the two stained-glass windows she'd found at an estate sale for an old congregation. Whenever I told people where I lived, they would say, "Oh, I thought that was a church." Whenever people said things like that, it made me feel like our house was weird, like we lived in a funhouse at a circus, with a hall of mirrors, where everything is backward and upside-down.

My sisters are both in high school, and we don't talk much. My brother is a few years older than I am. Mom calls me "the caboose" because I'm the youngest. I'm always sitting in the back of the blue Cadillac while she drives us to our lessons. We're a loud bunch, always fighting and talking over each other. One time, we were so loud, my mom angrily threw her shoe into the back seat just to quiet us down. It didn't work.

My dad has dark hair and dark eyes. All four kids look a lot like him. We call them the "Romano eyes." The same as my great-grandparents' Florence and Joseph, who came to the US on a boat from Calabria and Sicily. The next generation, my grandparents, fell in love in the Poconos one summer, got married, and worked hard and opened a bakery called Mama Romano & Six Sons. It's known all over the tri-state area for its Italian rum cakes and stuffed breads. My dad is one of the six sons. The bakery was so popular that my dad and his brothers were almost like celebrities as teenagers, or so he says. His family didn't have a lot of money growing up in Ansonia, just north of Milford, and neither did my mom's parents, really. My mom grew up in Ohio, and when she met my dad in college in Cincinnati, she fell head over heels. His family didn't accept her because she's not "of the people," which means she's not Italian. Mom said my dad was "very charming" and it didn't matter that his family didn't accept her, because they were in love and he promised her a good life together in coastal New England.

When my dad was a kid, he didn't have it easy at all. After a massive flood in his town, Pop and Grandma Romano had to release him and his brothers into foster care in hopes that the church would keep them in line as altar boys while they found a place to live. My dad never really talks about it. Tough times made him want to "strive for excellence" and never be poor as an adult. Maybe that's why my parents always fight about money. They're both scared not to have it.

Mom says my dad, unlike his brothers, is the "golden child," even though he went to law school but never actually became a lawyer. He works in the printing business in New York City, and when he finishes work, he commutes home and cooks us Italian food and tells us jokes. On the weekends, he's more fun. He'll grill steaks, make lemonade in the summer, and sometimes wrestle with me like a bear when I try to wake him up in the morning. He can be strict too, but he says he just wants to raise us right. Sometimes at night, Dad will walk up and down the hallway outside our bedrooms, snapping his belt against his hands, making his voice deep like a superhero's or a villain's, and saying, "Are you asleep? You kids better be asleep!" When he does this, I wonder if it's something he learned when he was a kid or if he's just trying to be funny. I think he's just joking with us, but it does make me listen and go to bed. He's not doing it tonight, though, because he and my mom are fighting.

"I don't know what you want me to do, Shar," Dad says downstairs. "I work hard to provide for you and the kids. I'm doing the best I can, and you need to watch your spending too."

"Well, I am not listing my home," says Mom. "I don't want people gossiping about us struggling."

"I'll figure it out," Dad says.

Mom and I never tell the rest of my family about what happened at the dance competition. I still have nightmares about it, but I never talk about it. Dad says he's proud of me, but he doesn't sign me up for everything and take me everywhere like Mom does. He does bring flowers and gives me a big hug after I perform. Soon after my accident onstage, I performed in New York at an even bigger competition: Talent America. One of the celeb judges was a show business manager named Shirley Grant. She came up to me and Mom after the show and introduced herself, telling us she was a talent manager for kids. She had long red fingernails and poofy blond hair, and she smelled like smoke. Her voice was scratchy and deep. She handed Mom a card and told her that she thought I had a good look and I could be a "triple threat." When I asked Mom what that meant on the drive home, she excitedly explained that it meant someone who could do three things well: sing, dance, and act. Judging by her smile, this was big news, happy news. I wasn't really sure what to think about that, but if Mom was happy, I was too.

I always work extra hard to memorize songs and dances, because the applause and the proud looks on adults' faces make me feel like I'm doing the right thing, like I'm not just *any* kid but a special kid who can entertain. I know how to sing the full Connie Francis song "Where the Boys Are" for my parents, and Dad loves it when I do my gangster impression: "You dirty rat, you killed my bruthuh . . ." Dad always asks me to perform at our family dinners or for my uncles for a laugh. I get embarrassed, but the bear hug I get from him afterward makes it worth it. "She's my little star," he says.

Finally, my parents stop arguing, and I hear one of them walking toward the steps, so I sprint through the hallway full of smiley family pictures and quickly shut my door and jump into bed. Mom and Dad always remind us to pray before we go to sleep, even though I'm not sure they pray except for when we go to St. Mary's Church on Sundays. I quickly make the sign of the cross and say an Our Father before closing my eyes. I add a little prayer that our family will be fine and we won't lose our home.

A few months after the competition where I met Shirley, Mom and I drive to New Jersey. Shirley's office is in the basement of her narrow brick house, and the walls are covered with glossy black-and-white pictures of showbiz kids. I recognize a few of them from TV, but most of them I don't. In the waiting room, Mom squeezes my hand extra tight. On the way over, Mom had explained that Shirley is a powerful manager who could help us kick-start my acting career, getting me into commercials and movies and plays. She represents kids like Christina Ricci and Keshia Knight Pulliam. "You know, Rudy in *The Cosby Show*," Mom tells me on the long drive down the I-95 highway from Connecticut.

While we sit and wait, the phone rings about 857 times. A woman wearing big silver earrings and a pink dress answers the calls, saying, "Shirley Grant's office," over and over in a New York accent. I've never heard a phone ring so much, and I wonder if that woman ever gets tired of saying, "Shirley Grant's office, please hold!"

"It's busy," Mom whispers. "That's a good sign."

I notice that I'm not blond or blue-eyed like most of the girls my age in the photos on the walls, but Shirley asked me here, so there must be a reason.

The woman with the big earrings stands up and walks over to us.

"Shirley is ready for you," she says with a friendly smile.

"Great," Mom answers as she grabs my hand and pulls me out of the chair. She's always guiding me around, shuffling me in and out of doors, putting her hand on my back to push my tiny body forward. We walk into the office, and Shirley stands up and shakes Mom's hand, telling us to "sit, sit." There are papers and headshots and notebooks scattered all over Shirley's desk. A lit cigarette burns in an ashtray nearby, and a package that says "Pall Mall" sits on the table. Her hair looks a little like a white helmet with some bangs in the front. She wears blue eye shadow and red lipstick, a blue suit, and lots of gold jewelry. Her bracelets clang together whenever she waves her hands around in the air, which is a lot.

"Christy! Mrs. Romano. Thanks for coming in."

We sit down, and my mom talks about my latest competition, and Shirley says how great I did.

"She's adorable!" says Shirley. "Great smile, great voice. She can dance. You're a six-year-old dynamo."

Mom wants to make sure that Shirley knows just how much of a dynamo I am. "She can do tap, ballet, modern," quickly listing off a bunch of "special skills" to impress Shirley. I smile and make sure to make eye contact, to show Shirley how good I am at listening. I sit on my hands so I don't squirm from nerves.

Mom is always taking me to voice lessons and dance classes when I'm not in school. I take voice lessons with a woman in our neighborhood who used to teach my sisters before they decided they were more interested in sports and boys. My voice teacher tells me I "have pipes," which makes me want to sing louder and do better. I love singing "Tomorrow" and getting a compliment about how much I've improved at each lesson. We record my sessions on cassette tapes, and I play them back on our large tape player to practice every day after school.

"So, Christy," Shirley says, "do you get scared when you have to talk to adults?"

"She never gets nervous," Mom says before I can answer.

"I love talking to adults!" I say brightly, which is true.

"Great, kid," Shirley says. "If you get nervous, this probably isn't the career for you. But if you can go out there and dazzle them, show them how talented you are, you'll do great."

Shirley picks up a piece of paper and shoves it at me.

"Here, doll," she says. "Read this."

I take the paper and read the lines as fast as I can: "I just love my Easy-Bake Ultimate Oven! I can make cookies, muffins, and my favorite—chocolate brownies!"

Shirley and Mom stare at me. My face starts to get hot, but I take a few deep breaths, calm myself down, and put on a big smile.

"I just love my Easy-Bake Ultimate Oven! I can make cookies, muffins, and my favorite—chocolate brownies!"

I look up from the paper.

"Try it again, kid."

I take a deep breath and imagine that I can make the world's most delicious brownies, better than any kid has ever made before. I try to really believe it, and I do it again.

"I just love my Easy-Bake Ultimate Oven! I can make cookies, muffins, and my favorite—chocolate brownies!"

Shirley grabs a few more pieces of paper and hands them to Mom.

"Great work, kid," Shirley says, and my whole body relaxes, like it had been smashed up into a tiny ball and now it was free. "I want to officially represent you, so we need to get down to business."

I can feel Mom smiling next to me. It's like the sun is shining in the room.

"You'll need to get official headshots made immediately, and I have a guy in the city you'll go to. You'll need a résumé that shows people any training you've had, plays you've done, competitions you've been in, trophies, special skills."

"Not a problem. I can type that up," Mom says confidently.

"We'll need to sign the paperwork before I send Christy out, so take it home, read it, and you can fax it back."

"Great," Mom says. She's been nodding and smiling this whole time.

"Now, Mrs. Romano, if Christy is going to succeed, she'll need to be available for auditions and callbacks at all times, and most of the work is in Manhattan. Are you working?"

"I used to work in sales at Xerox," Mom says, "but I stopped once Christy was born."

"Good, good." Shirley stands up and claps her hands together. "Christy, are you ready to get out there?"

"I am!"

"She is. We are," Mom says. If she's confident, then so am I.

Shirley explains that she will start sending me on auditions for plays and commercials and that Mom will have to make sure her schedule allows her to take me into New York "at a moment's notice." Shirley also sets us up with a dentist to get fitted for a flipper to make my teeth look good. I will have to use denture glue to push it into my mouth before auditions for a perfect smile.

"That's no problem at all," Mom says. "Christy was born to do this; she loves performing and hamming it up."

It makes me feel proud that my mom thinks I'm special.

"If they like you, you'll get a callback, which is when you go back and perform for them again so they can be a hundred-percent sure you're the one for the job," Shirley says. She stops and looks me up and down. "You seem like a booker to me."

"What's a booker?" I ask, crinkling my tiny nose, which makes Shirley laugh for some reason.

"A booker is someone who books a lot of jobs, kid. Let's hope that's you."

So right then and there, that's exactly what I want to become. *A booker.*

A few days after Shirley starts sending my headshots out, I get my first audition! In the morning, Mom helps me pick out an outfit, she pulls my hair into pigtails, and then we take the train from Milford into New York City. Taking the Metro-North into Grand Central feels exciting, with the towns rushing by outside the windows and hundreds of adults going to work or going home. I wonder if my siblings are mad that I get to miss school and ride into the city with Mom, but when I said goodbye that morning, they didn't seem like they cared much.

Once we get off at Grand Central, Mom grabs my hand, hard, and yanks me through crowds of people hurrying in every direction. The giant gold clock in the middle of the station shows the time on all sides, and the huge green ceiling is painted with golden stars and figures from astrology. Every couple minutes, a loud tapping is heard as the schedule board changes. When I stop and look up, Mom yanks my arm.

"Hurry! Let's keep moving! We need to get to the subway, Christy."

We take the 6 Train to Spring Street, and Mom pulls me up the stairs, past more crowds of people, and onto the street up above. Outside the station, the cold air hits my face like a slap. We hurry to a big office building, and Mom checks her notebook for the address.

"This is it."

We get off the elevator and step into a long hallway packed with other little girls, all about my age. Some sit on hard plastic chairs, looking nervous; others are huddled in corners with their moms, practicing their lines. I get checked in, and a distracted lady hands Mom a piece of paper with the lines I'm supposed to memorize before I go in.

"Maui Steel, you're up!"

A girl with bright blond hair hops off her chair and goes into the audition room alone. I've never met anyone named Maui, and I've never seen a girl with hair that blond. I feel a little jealous, knowing that my hair will never look like that and that blond characters are so much more popular on TV and in movies than characters with brown hair and eyes, like me. Mom helps me practice the lines while we wait.

"You know what? My skin's not only clean . . . it feels really smooth!"

I say this at least twenty-five times, trying different smiles and ways of saying each word. The audition room door opens, and Maui comes out. She looks happy, like she did a good job. I practice my lines even harder.

Finally, a woman pops her head out of the door. "Christy Romano? You're up!"

My mom hands me the paper with the lines on it and gives me a little push. "Good luck."

I smile at her even though I'm nervous. I walk into the room alone. The lights are bright in the room, and a few cameras are set up. I'm introduced to the casting director and a few other adults sitting at a long table. I give them my biggest pageant smile, and when they tell me to go ahead, I try not to look into the camera as I say my lines.

"You know what? My skin's not only clean . . . it feels really smooth! It's 'cause I use Zest! The sooner you start, the smoother you'll feel!"

When I finish, the casting director asks someone to bring Mom into the room. My stomach does somersaults, since I don't know if they're going to tell her I did amazing and I "booked it," or if they'll tell her I wasn't any good at all, which will probably make Mom disappointed and me embarrassed, like I'm not good enough. While I wait for her to come in, I just keep smiling. Mom comes in looking serious, like she's at a business meeting.

"Hello," she says.

"Mrs. Romano, Christy did great. We'll have callbacks next week, but we're asking parents to make sure that their kid will be comfortable being filmed from the back, with no shirt on, since the ad will have the little girl delivering her lines in the shower. Are you open to that? It's very tasteful and family-friendly. But this is soap, so . . ."

"I'm sure that's fine," Mom says quickly, even though I am not feeling fine about it at all. My whole body feels squirmy, like I want to run out of the room, but I stay right there, smiling.

"Great, we'll be in touch. NEXT!"

Mom takes my hand, and we leave through the long hallway, still full of girls saying the same lines over and over: "The sooner you start, the smoother you'll feel!" I know some kids run around outside naked all day long and don't care at all, but *I* care. When we go to church, they talk about modesty, and Mom always tells us to act like "ladies," so I feel uncomfortable going against any of that. I want to act and be a professional, I want to make Shirley and my parents proud, but I know one thing for sure: I don't feel great about Zest.

Bundled in our coats, Mom and I rush down the street to Grand Central. I see a shop corner window full of gleaming little crystals shaped like tiny pianos and penguins spinning on a tray. There are heart-shaped crystals and musical-note crystals, little bears, and a slice of white cake with a gold fork. I can't help but stop and stare. They're perfect!

"Christy, get moving!" says Mom. She's still holding my hand, but I'm parked in front of the crystal shop window, so she has to stop too. "What are you doing?"

"These are so pretty, Mommy," I say, pointing to the tiny cake.

"Well, if you book an audition, maybe we'll get one. Let's go! We'll miss the train, and we need to get home."

We speed-walk into Grand Central, past the giant clock, and this time I notice a horse with wings painted on the ceiling. We file onto our crowded platform and into the red line train to Milford. The whole ride home, I can't stop watching the black power lines sloping up and down as we move in and out of tunnels. I think about booking that audition, about the "congratulations" and "great jobs" I'll get from Mom and Dad. But most of all, I think about which perfect crystal I'll pick when it happens.

"You didn't book Zest," Mom says when she gets off the phone with Shirley Grant. "That girl Lacey got it. I saw her name on the sign-in sheet."

"Sorry, Mommy," I say as I look down at the kitchen floor.

"It happens," she says firmly. "Shirley has a few others for you next week. We'll try harder next time."

I feel like I'm already trying my very best every day, so I don't know what else Mom thinks I can do. I think she's trying to cheer me up, like next time will be better, but now I feel like nothing I do will be good enough.

Later that night, we're all at the table eating the chicken parm and peas and pasta Dad made. My family doesn't say much about the audition, but Dad looks at me like he's worried.

"You okay, Christy?" he asks.

I smile and tell him I'm fine, even though I feel a little embarrassed that I didn't get it.

"There will be others," he says. "It sounds like this Shirley woman knows her stuff."

Mom doesn't say much, maybe because right before dinner, they were fighting again. Dad brought us back gifts from his work trip to China—porcelain dolls for me and my sisters, and some baseball cards for my brother. I don't know why they always fight about money when we *seem* okay. They talk about school uniforms and car payments, cat food, and groceries. I don't ask any questions—I just stay quiet and try not to upset anyone, because I'm the baby.

The commercials are fun, and I like making my parents and Shirley proud, but what I really want to do is act onstage. I love walking through Times Square, and Broadway seems like the most exciting place an actor can be. I've been taking singing lessons with a coach named Bob Marks and taking every dance class I can at Broadway Dance Center when we're in the city. Bob's studio is right across the street from Carnegie Hall, and it's stuffed with books of sheet music and smells like sweet pipe smoke. He teaches me new show tunes every week for my auditions, and he makes me feel confident as a singer.

When Mom and I aren't doing auditions in a building with a long hallway and white chairs, we go to cattle calls for musicals at the Equity building. Sometimes we stand out in the street in a long line filled with other girls and their moms. Even if it's snowing or raining, we stand outside and wait. You get a number, and when they call you in, it's your shot to be a booker.

Bob Marks taught me to sing "I Don't Know How to Love Him" from *Jesus Christ Superstar* for auditions and cattle calls. The one time I sang it in an audition, though, the casting director called Mom in and said, "She shouldn't be singing this song."

"Why not?" Mom asked.

I heard the casting director when she whispered, because adults don't realize that when you whisper *right in front of a kid*, they can hear you.

"Because it's not appropriate," whispered the casting director. "It's about a *prostitute*."

"Oh, I had no idea," Mom says. "Bob just thought it would show her range."

By the time I get to a cattle call for a touring production of *Annie*, I'd booked some commercials, I'd gotten some crystals, and I knew what *not* to do. When my number is called by the casting director, number four, I shuffle onstage with all the other actors. I learn some dance steps, I sing my heart out, I act and do just what the director tells us to do.

When we finish, we wait for the casting director to call out our numbers. I'm quietly praying I get to stay.

"Numbers ten, thirteen, two, and twenty-three, STEP BACK!"

Those girls take a step to the back of the stage, and the rest of us stand there, frozen.

"Numbers four, twenty-one, six, fourteen, twenty-eight, STEP FORWARD!"

We step forward.

"EVERYONE IN THE BACK, THAT'S IT FOR TODAY!"

Cattle calls are scary, but there I am, still onstage.

When the director asks us to sing again, each on our own, I do my very best.

"OKAY. NUMBERS FOURTEEN, SIX . . . STEP BACK! Kids in the front, welcome to *Annie*!"

I can't believe it! *Annie* is one of the best musicals a kid can book. This production will be in Atlanta, so that means Mom and I will leave home and live there for a few months. Mom says, "It'll be a fun adventure," so I guess she's not worried about moving away for a little while. I wonder if my family will miss me.

Since I'm six, I'll play Molly, the littlest orphan. Mom is always telling me to be professional, and now I feel like a true pro. I know I have a lot to learn, and I'll work so hard that no one will feel let down, ever. I'll be the best singing and dancing orphan that's ever been onstage.

When we get home from the train that night, Dad is making a special dinner with meatballs, which is one of the only meals we always agree on. The whole family is proud of me. They're not even mad that Mom and I have to live in Atlanta for a few months. After dinner I do the sign of the cross and say my prayers before I go to bed. I give thanks for my family, our six cats and two dogs, for my voice being able to sing loudest that day, and for everyone being together, safe, in our house. Mostly I give thanks because I'm a booker after all. Shirley Grant is "thrilled" and says that this is "just the beginning."

Dear Girls,

Your grandparents, my parents, built their dream from scratch and wanted everything for their kids: private schools, a big house, a life that looked like they'd made it. Your grandpa was an entrepreneur who needed to be in charge, but he was bootstrapping the whole thing. He didn't come from money and neither did your grandma. When I was born, she stopped working, and suddenly the math got harder.

I think they were performing a version of success they couldn't quite afford. Refinancing, financial aid loopholes, pulling rabbits out of hats. That was your grandpa's phrase for it, and he was good at it. We were quintessential American middle class. Not poor, not wealthy. Dodging struggle with just enough privilege to make the dodging feel normal, even intoxicating sometimes.

When the opportunity to put me in front of a camera came along, I don't think either of them fully understood what they were allowing into their lives. Perhaps it was proof that all the striving had produced something extraordinary. Gifted children can unintentionally become living evidence of their parents' worth, which is why their success means so much to them.

They were both trying to rise above how they'd been raised. To honor what their own parents had sacrificed. I understand that now in a way I couldn't as a kid sitting on those stairs listening to them fight.

But here's what I want you to know, my loves. Worthiness built on what you own can always be taken away. I learned that the hard way. Material success is not an essential family value.

Your dad and I are determined to break this cycle. You are not our escape routes from our deepest insecurities. You're mirrors that reflect them back to us. The only way to raise secure children is to do the work on ourselves first.

I can't wait to see who you choose to become when no one else is watching.

3

Fly Away Home

1992–1993

Ages 8 to 9

We spend almost eight whole weeks in Atlanta over the winter. Mommy and I live in a fancy hotel and eat a lot of Wendy's.

Leaving Atlanta and my *Annie* family is sad, but going back home means I get to audition for new parts and new shows and be back with my pets. Shirley tells Mom she needs an expensive pager, so now Mom clips one to her belt on her jeans and wears it everywhere, all the time, "just in case." When it beeps, it's like Christmas and my birthday all at once. My body feels tingly all over, not knowing what the news could be or what our next adventure will look like. When it doesn't beep, we wait for the sound and spend time with the rest of my family, eating dinner or watching TV. It worries me when it doesn't beep for a few days, because what if I never get an audition or a job again?

In Atlanta, I had a tutor like all the other girls, but now I'm starting school at Trinity Hall, and the kids aren't as nice as my *Annie* family. At recess, some kids tell me we're playing pretend, and then they tell me I have to hold my hands around a pole near the air conditioners behind the playground. I get confused when they tell me I'm their slave and can't move. I do what they direct me to do, but I start to cry when they run off, knowing they don't like me. I wait by the pole for the rest of recess, scared and alone. I just want to be their friend. It's not easy to make friends since I'm new, plus I'm always leaving school early or going late so I can go to auditions in New York. Mommy says the other kids are jealous that I'm talented, and they are ugly and mean. I probably sing too loud in music class, but I can't help it. Onstage you have to project, Bob Marks tells me. I try so hard to make them like me, but nothing really works. I don't like school at all. I just want to be onstage with a theater family.

When we take the train from Milford into the city, the doors of the train burst open, and Mom grabs my hand. We rush through Grand Central, dodge taxis, jump over potholes. Every audition feels like a video game we're trying to win. Mom is always saying we're a team, we're in this together, and if it stops being fun, I can just stop. I know she's trying to make me feel better, but the idea of stopping feels like it would be GAME OVER.

My last callback was for the Broadway musical *Carousel* a few days ago, and we wait to hear if I got the role. Mom says *Carousel* on Broadway will be a great part for me, a huge break, a "game changer." At night, I look at Jesus nailed on the cross, hanging above my bed, and pray for good news.

We're at a small bodega across from what Mom calls the "peekaboo places" with bright, glowing signs that show ladies dancing on Forty-Second Street. Mommy buys a *Backstage* magazine, a Payday candy bar for her, and a Snickers for me. Her pager beeps finally! She pulls it off her hip.

"It's Shirley! Look for a phone, Christy. Come on!"

She pulls me by the arm, holding so tight, it feels like I might get a bruise. She spots a dirty pay phone in a corner and dials Shirley's number. Mom knows it by heart now. She pulls me in tighter as a homeless man, speaking to himself, walks by. I can smell her sweat and Lancôme perfume mixed with the city smells of cigarette smoke and urine.

"Hi, Shirley? It's Sharon Romano calling you back."

I stare at her face while she listens to Shirley. Her mouth crinkles up, and her head hangs down a little, so I hang my head a little too. Mom's nose crinkles funny, and sometimes I make the same face. She told me that my grandpa used to call her "baby bunny" since she could squish her nose up and move it around like a bunny's nose. Now the look is more upset than cute, though.

"Okay, I get it. Thanks for letting us know. Bye."

Mom hangs up, and we get out of the booth. "Well. You didn't book the part in *Carousel*," she says, sounding a little angry. "They wanted to cast someone with rickets, I guess." She shrugs, and somehow she gets two gold subway coins out of a yellow holder on a key ring while still holding on to me tightly.

"What's rickets?" I've never heard that word before, and I'm not sure if it's some kind of talent or skill that I'll have to learn for my résumé. Lately I've added bike riding as a skill after a commercial required me to learn it for a callback, but rickets just seems weird.

"It's when someone is so skinny, you can see their bones," she says, which frightens me. She does this sometimes, says things in a way that scares me so much, I just don't want to ask any more questions at all. So I just nod, imagining a girl my age with beautiful blond hair, big blue eyes, and bones sticking out of her body. "Come on," she says, grabbing my arm tighter and dragging me down the crowded street. The muttering homeless man now walks back in our direction as we turn the corner. "Be careful, Christy. This city is dangerous. Stay close. We have to get to the Palace for another audition."

The Palace Theatre is on Forty-Seventh Street, just a few blocks from Rockefeller Center. Mom leads me inside and backstage, and I hand the casting director my black-and-white headshot and résumé while she signs us in. This audition is another "big one," Shirley told us. It's the first national tour of *The Will Rogers Follies*, a huge musical that is on Broadway right now and won Tony Awards. I'm auditioning for one of the four kids, and superstar Keith Carradine is playing Will Rogers, just like he did on Broadway.

When my name is finally called, I walk onto the stage and stare out at a dark theater. It looks like a scary cave out in the seats, and I can barely see who's there. I know the tall one must be Tommy Tune, the director and choreographer. I squint my eyes to try to see his face, but he looks like a big shadow.

When we finish and they start to call out names, time slows down, and I feel like I'm inside a tornado, spinning and waiting, spinning and waiting.

"Caroline Blunt! Timmy Weiss! Lisa Page!"

My face gets hot, and I feel like I might throw up, right there in the hallway. At least I don't have to pee.

"Stanley Ross! Christy Romano!"

I pop up off the floor. I made the callbacks! I try to stand still instead of jumping up and down like I want to do.

When the casting director finishes calling the names, the kids who weren't called seem sad; some cry, and their parents hush them as they grab their backpacks and head out of the theater to go back home. I feel bad for them, but I'm also excited. I know it's not over, though. I'm still playing the game. I need to get back out there and sing and dance again. I need to make sure they don't give the part to somebody else, somebody with rickets.

I'm trying to control my breathing even though I'm tired from dancing. It's just me onstage now. When I finish, Tommy Tune stands up from his seat in the dark theater. He looks even taller when he uses his hands to jump onto the stage in one quick movement like an athlete. I smile big as he walks over. My heart is beating fast, and I feel a little sick. He puts his large hand on the top of my head. As I look up, the stage lights give him a glowing ring around his head, and he looks like the priest from my First Communion, only in an artsy turtleneck.

"You got the part, kid. See ya in San Fran," he says. I can't wait to tell Mommy, and as soon as I'm allowed to go, I sprint to the hallway and find her.

"Mommy, I got the part!" I say, jumping up and down.

Mommy's eyes bug out of her head, and her mouth drops open.

"Get outta here! Hot damn!" she says, grinning from ear to ear.

My mom has a beautiful smile that I wish I saw more often. She says she has Swedish cheekbones and a large German smile, something I got from her instead of my dark eyes and hair. She says I'm just like *her* mom, Ginny, who died before I was born. She was her mom's best friend, and I'm *her* best friend. As we hurry out of the theater, Mom says we need to call Shirley to tell her and then go talk to Dad downtown, since this means Mom and I will leave home for a year or maybe even more. It's all happening so fast! We celebrate by taking a cab instead of the subway. Now that I think of it, I'm not sure if Dad will be happy like Mom or if he'll be mad that we're leaving the family.

We pull up to the building, and Mom pays the driver. Dad will probably be busy when we get upstairs, and I just say a little prayer that it all goes well, that Mom and Dad don't fight, and that he doesn't stop us from going. In my mind, I'm already packing my bags for our next Mommy-and-me adventure.

We get to the building and head up a small elevator, and a pretty woman shows us into Dad's office. Mom gives the woman that up-and-down look she gives every woman who is around Dad. I can tell she doesn't like her because she barely even says hello or thank you. We go inside, and the woman shuts the door so we can be alone with Dad.

He's wearing his stiff white-collared shirt and sitting in a big brown leather rolling chair, looking important. I smell his sweet-scented aftershave as he gives me a big hug with his scratchy beard like he always does. I love hugging him. It makes me feel safe, even though sometimes, when he fights with Mom, things feel the opposite of safe. I know Daddy will always protect me, though. He says, "Family is the most important thing in the world."

"Okay, so, tell me, what's the big news that you came all this way to see me?" He looks at Mommy, and he's not smiling.

"Christy booked the tour I told you about," Mom says. She doesn't sound happy like she did at the theater and in the taxi. She sounds serious, and I can see that she is uncomfortable by the way she crosses and uncrosses her legs. "It's a big deal if Christy's going to be a real actress."

"Wow! Congratulations, kiddo," Dad calls out. His voice is loud and excited, but I can see that he's sitting back in his chair, looking at Mommy, not me. He puts his hands through his thick black hair.

I begin to kick my feet, since *maybe* he seems happy for me? They're both quiet for a second, so I tune out and focus on the walls in my daddy's office. The room smells like paper and ink.

"Well, we're leaving soon, then," Mom says. I feel like I shouldn't be in the room, but I stay in my chair because that seems like the smart thing to do. We're not leaving *forever*, but it sure sounds like we are. Dad usually always has something to say or some joke to make, but he's very quiet for a minute. He takes a deep breath.

"For how long? We have a family here, you know. And Christy is only eight."

"At least twelve months," Mom says. Neither of them is looking at me or asking me any questions.

I continue to look at Dad's blank white office walls. I stay quiet, hoping this'll all be over soon and we can go buy a big crystal near Grand Central. Dad sighs again and shakes his head.

"You'll be fine. It's your turn, Anthony," Mom says. "I've balanced work and kids for years."

"Excuse me?" Dad's eyebrows raise.

"It's your turn to be the parent." After she says this, they seem to be having a staring contest, and I'm not sure who's winning.

I listen to machines buzzing outside the door, people talking, and phones ringing. I *really* don't want them to fight. I hate arguments, especially when they're because of me. I want to fix this, to perform so well that it makes it all worth it. I make that my goal. To do so well, they come together at the end and say, "That WAS worth it, Christy!"

Instead of yelling, Dad stands up, and then so does Mom. He walks around the big wood desk piled with paper and gives me another bear hug. He tells me he's proud, and we'll figure it out.

"I'll make you proud, Daddy," I say as we leave his office. "I promise."

We've been rehearsing in San Francisco before our first big show, and everyone is so nice, except for Odette. She has strawberry-blond hair that goes all the way to her butt. She's playing Will Rogers's daughter, Mary, so I had to learn all her lines and dances in case she gets sick. All the adults and kids and chorus girls are so nice, especially the dancers, like Sutton Foster, and the stars, like Keith Carradine, but *not* Odette. I don't know why she hates me, but she reminds me of the kids from school back home. I hate that she gives me dirty looks and messes with me while we wait backstage. The worst is, we share a dressing room table. Her mom sometimes talks to Mom, but when we're back at the hotel Grosvenor House, Mom tells me she thinks that Odette and her mom are jealous and to just keep my head down and do my work, so I do. I miss home a little bit, but San Francisco has cable cars, which are way better than the subway!

It's three days before our big premiere in San Francisco, and a stage manager named Bill says he needs to talk to me and Mom. "What did you do?" Mom asks, and I shrug. I've been working so hard, nonstop. I've done everything right, or at least I've tried to. I pray it's nothing bad when we meet him in the dressing room before our last rehearsal.

"So, Christy," he says. Bill is extremely tall, but not as tall as Tommy Tune. He smells like sweet pipe smoke, since he's always smoking one at the stage door. I can't tell yet if Bill is nice, since he never really smiles, and he's always saying things that are supposed to be jokes but that sound pretty mean. Like, when I told him I finished a whole thousand-piece puzzle, he pulled a quarter out of his pocket, handed it to me, and I swear he said, "Here's a quarter, kid. Go call someone who cares." It hurt my feelings, but Mom said that's just his sense of humor. If that's a sense of humor, it's not very good, if you ask me.

"Yes, sir?" I try to sit still and not squirm in my seat from nerves.

"How would you feel about cutting your hair short?"

"Um, how short?"

"Like-a-boy short? Since you're playing Jimmy, Yves will have to put your hair in the wig net before every show, and he says it's taking an extra fifteen minutes."

I'm what they call a working swing, so I'm the understudy for three kid characters, plus my own. I had to learn all their lines and choreography. I don't mind playing a boy, but I definitely don't want to cut all my hair off like one. Odette is allowed to have hair to her butt! I know she's playing a girl, but still. I look over to Mom, hoping maybe she'll make this all go away. I do NOT want to cut my hair. No way. What will the kids at school say when I go back? They'll call me a boy, make fun of me every day. It's *my* hair on *my* head, and now someone I don't know is making me chop it all off. I have the same pain in my stomach that I felt when that casting director asked if I'd be okay being almost naked in the Zest soap commercial. I wish I could just say NO, but I have to make the adults happy and not cause any trouble. I look over at Mom and stay silent.

"Bill, is it mandatory?" Mommy asks. "I mean, it's just fifteen minutes, and what if Odette gets sick and Christy has to play Mary? Then you'll need another wig."

"Why don't you think about it, Christy?" Bill says to me, ignoring Mom. "Let me know by tomorrow."

He leaves us there, and Mom closes the dressing room door after he's gone. She sits back down and looks at me with her serious face. As soon as he's gone, I start crying hot tears.

"Mommy, I don't want to cut all my hair off." I hug her close.

"Well, are you ready to give up the job if we refuse to do it and they fire you? We would have to go home."

I have to think about this, because that would mean we'd pack our suitcases and leave San Francisco and the whole tour forever. It would mean all the work I'd done was for nothing, and I may never get a part like this again in such a fun show. Yves, the hairdresser who doesn't want to do the wig net, isn't that nice, but besides him and Odette, I like everyone in the play. The chorus girls are so fun; Sutton is sweet to me. I'm trying to make friends, even though I know we have to leave eventually.

I wipe away my tears and cross my arms.

"Yes," I say. "It's *my* hair, Mommy. I don't want to get fired, but I can't cut it. I can't." I am crying harder and feeling betrayed by the people who told me I was worth hiring.

"Okay. I'll have to go to bat for you, but I'll tell Bill and see what he says. You might lose the job, but let's hope not."

She goes to tell Bill, and I sit there, feeling like I'm floating outside my body like a ghost, while the room beneath me spins around like a carousel. Should I run out and tell her, "Never mind, I'll do it"? It makes me feel squirmy, though, letting them cut all my hair off. It doesn't seem fair. There's a knock on the door as someone calls a half hour to a full run-through. Odette walks in and puts her backpack down. Our spots at the mirror are right next to each other, and I say hi to her and try to pretend everything is fine and I'm not about to throw up all over the vanity table. She ignores me. I start to get ready, or I pretend to, at least. Odette brushes her long, shiny hair. While she brushes, she scoots some of my crystals and teddy bears over with the back of her free hand.

"Keep your *stuff* on your side. It's annoying," she says. I know she's a year older than I am, but why is she so mean?

I never know what to say at times like this, so I just apologize. If I talk back or say something rude, things might get even worse.

It's our last day of rehearsal, and when I go into the dressing room, Odette is already there, putting her costume on. There's a line of white tape between her space and mine. She looks up at me in the mirror.

"That's your side. This is mine," she says, motioning to the tape. I sit down and make sure my makeup and my wig net stay on my side of the table. Why is Odette so mean to me? What did I do to her, besides maybe have my Golden Gate Bridge snow globe too close to her hairbrush? These little treasures are *mine*, and they make me feel less homesick while we travel. I didn't even tell Bill that I saw her squatting her legs down when he was measuring us to make herself seem smaller so she wouldn't outgrow her part! We all know that once you're too tall, you're fired. I knew what she was doing. Maybe next time, I *will* tell him.

Mom comes in and says hi to Odette and her mom while I'm scooting my things away from Odette and into a pile. Mom leans down and whispers in my ear. "You don't have to cut it," she says. "I talked to Bill and told him you weren't doing it, and he said it was fine. Yves will just have to deal with it."

So I'm keeping the job! I don't even care about Odette's stupid line anymore. I hate being Odette's understudy. She messes up sometimes, and they don't even yell at her or give her notes. I do love everyone else and am having fun onstage, though.

We've been on the road for three months and four days now, and at night Mom drinks her nightcap, and I listen to her begin to snore while we watch reruns of Mary Tyler Moore until we both fall asleep. It's lonely for me, so I know it's probably lonely for Mom too.

"Sit still," Yves says while he pulls a piece of my hair back, hard. "Stop moving." I'm playing with my new collector's edition Barbie and I'm barely moving, but Yves is always so mad about having to pull my hair tight and put this stupid wig cap on. He makes me keep the net on *all day* at the theater, so when we have lunch or dinner breaks, I wear a hat so I don't look like a weirdo. It's December, and my family is coming to visit us while we're doing shows in Miami in a few days. I work Thanksgiving, Christmas, New Year's Eve, and even my birthday in March. We don't get holiday breaks like kids in regular school do.

Bill walks past me out of the local green room at half hour. He passes cowboys stretching their legs, wearing chaps with no covering on the butts, and chorus girls changing into tiny shiny costumes. There are always naked people everywhere in the theater, and no one even cares. I'm used to it now, even though at the beginning, it made me feel embarrassed and uncomfortable. Now it's just "the life," as Mom says. Not everyone has their own dressing room, and there are a million costume changes in the show, so people have to change together in one room. The stars get their own dressing rooms on a different floor with beautiful couches and private bathrooms. If my family back home saw how many naked people were around, they would freak out. I feel like I live in another world from them now. It's fun being a part of this other family, a theater family.

We travel to Southern California and start living in the Oakwood Apartments, which are famous because so many other kid actors live here while they're auditioning or making movies or shows. I meet one kid who's making a movie about a whale called *Free Willy*, and really nice twins who were in a famous chewing-gum commercial down by the pool.

Mom stays with me pretty much all the time, unless I'm onstage or with the tutor. She's always telling me, "Don't trust anybody," and even though Southern California is not as crazy as New York, she still holds my arm tight and makes sure I'm safe wherever we go, since I'm only eight. I still haven't gotten to play Mary Rogers, and I still *hate* being Odette's understudy, but I'm used to playing a boy now, even though sometimes when we do post-show AIDS fundraising, there are little girls who actually think I'm a boy, and they giggle at me like they have a crush on me. It makes me feel weird, but I stay in character since that's what we're supposed to do. I just smile and shake my empty water jug like a boy would do, since I'm still wearing the short wig. We do a lot of charity events and performances in different cities for AIDS, a terrible disease that's killing people, but I don't understand how.

There's a man named Ted who lives down the hall from us at the Oakwood with his wife, and they just got a puppy. Mom *loves* animals, so she says it's fine if I go by there because Ted and his wife are nice to her, and it's just a few doors down. Mom even said once that she likes animals better than she likes people, which is why we have six cats and two dogs back home. Mom is napping this afternoon, so I head down the hallway to Ted's apartment, since she already said I could go whenever. I miss our animals at home and I can't have a pet on the road, so this will be the next best thing. As soon as I knock on the door, the adorable little pug puppy starts barking.

"Who is it?" Ted asks from inside.

"It's Christy, from down the hall? I came to see your puppy."

The door opens, and Ted stands there, holding the cutest snorting, big-eyed sandy-brown puppy I've ever seen.

"Hi, Christy," he says. "Here's Waffle." I've played with Waffle a few times while they walked her around the property.

He puts Waffle on the floor, and I pick her right up.

"Come on in," says Ted. I put Waffle down and step inside, and he closes the door behind me. There are movie posters on the walls and puppy toys all over the floor.

"She's so cute," I say. Waffle tries to bite my shoes, and she runs in circles, jumping and stumbling around. I scoop her up again and kiss her mouth like I would my own dogs back home. I miss playing with my animals in Milford, and all of a sudden, I feel so homesick, I might actually cry. Ted is younger than Dad and doesn't have any kids. He almost seems like a fun uncle, except I'm not sure why he lives at the Oakwood. Ted isn't wearing a suit or aftershave like my dad. He's in baggy shorts and an old, wrinkled T-shirt. Ted sits down and crisscrosses his legs on the floor like they tell us to do in school. That's when I see his privates hanging out of his pants. He doesn't seem bothered and continues to play with the puppy, and our hands touch while I pet Waffle.

I only ever saw Dad's privates when I accidentally walked into his bathroom as he was leaving the shower. I didn't care that much, but he sure did since he got so upset, so I know that seeing Ted's privates isn't a good thing. It's wrong, and I know I should be scared and get home. Well, not *home* home, but get back to my apartment. Time slows down, and I feel like I'm floating out of my body, like before.

Somehow I jump up, thank Ted for letting me see Waffle, and run out the door and back to our apartment, because I don't know what to do or say. I hear his door slam shut and Waffle barking from inside his apartment. I hurry inside to my mom, who is writing in her planner while the news plays on our TV. My heart is beating fast.

"Mom!" She perks up and looks scared when she sees me so upset.

"What happened? What's wrong, Christy?"

I don't even know what to say. I've seen other actors naked backstage a million times, but nothing like this. "I . . . it's . . ."

Mom stands up out of bed and checks me, like she's looking for cuts or scrapes. "Tell me!"

"Mommy?"

"Spit it out, Christy, you're scaring me!"

"I went to Ted's to meet the puppy, like you said I could, and . . ."

"What happened?"

"I was sitting, playing with Waffle, and when I looked up, I saw his privates. So I ran here."

I'm so scared that I'm about to get in huge trouble, that I've just done something so wrong, we'll have to leave the show and go home. Mom asks me a bunch of questions to find out exactly what happened: Did he do it on purpose? Was it maybe an accident? What did he say? When I explain everything, she tells me it's probably just an accident and "that man needs to wear underwear!" She seems angrier that Ted doesn't have good hygiene than she is about me seeing his privates.

I'm so happy to leave the Oakwood and ride the bus to Palm Springs. I never see Ted or Waffle after that day, and Mom tells me to never *ever* even walk down the hall alone again for the rest of the days we're there. "Just keep your head down, and we'll be off in a few days," she says. So that's what I do. I just block it out and try to forget it. Whenever Ted comes into my mind, I close my eyes and concentrate and think about an audience applauding or me finally walking onstage as Mary Rogers, and it helps a little.

After the Palm Springs show, the whole cast and crew are invited to a party at Donald Trump's house, and it is the fanciest house I have ever been in. I even get a picture with him! His wife Marla Maples isn't touring with us, but she was in the Broadway production after it won all the Tonys, so that's why Trump has a party for us, I guess. He spends almost the whole night socializing with our excited chorus girls. Mom seems tense at the party, and she tells me that she's tired of Dad making her feel bad for being away and calling himself "Mr. Mom." I know that when they talk later after the party, they'll probably fight.

It's been four months away, and we're doing shows in Connecticut in March! We've been all over the US and even Canada. When we're not rehearsing or doing a show, our tutor takes us to museums in different towns, aquariums, rodeos, everything. The most magical place is Banff, a Canadian national park. We go sledding and I feel like I'm in a fairy tale. One day, I want to get married in that place. *That's* how magical it is! There are mountains and snow, like someone just dropped you into *The Sound of Music* when Maria is twirling and singing, "The hills are alive."

We're doing shows at the Shubert Theatre in New Haven, so Mom and I get to live at home for two whole weeks. I'm so happy to be back home and have family dinners when we can, and I'm especially happy to be with the cats. It's a little weird not being with just Mom, but at least we don't have to live out of two overstuffed suitcases that Mom has to sit on to zip. Mom and Dad are still fighting a little when he's not working, and I heard Dad ask her when we were coming home for good the other night, and she just said, "When we're ready or when the show ends." I don't think he was very happy when she said that, because I heard a door slam, and then the house got quiet.

Since we're home during my ninth birthday, March 20, Mom and Dad decide to host a big cast-and-crew birthday party just for me! Mom tells me in secret that she's worried about Dad and all the chorus girls, but we're doing it anyway, I guess. She's always worried about Dad and other women, especially now that we're away. When she accuses Dad, he always shrugs it off and says she's "being crazy." Grandpa is bringing an Italian sheet cake from the bakery, and Mom has been planning and getting ready for the party like it's a wedding or like the president is coming to visit. There are streamers and flowers, and I'm wearing my favorite red dress with black tights.

"Christy, fix your tights," Mom says. I look down and see they're all bunched up, so I pull them straight and stare out the window, waiting for my theater family to come. Suddenly a bus that Mom and Dad rented pulls up and parks, and everyone starts coming inside. It makes me feel a little weird having all these people who I've been traveling with on the road walk into my actual home, with my family and pets. It feels like two different worlds crashing together, but I'm happy. They all drove out here for *me.* I feel like a part of another family, like I have my real, actual family, but then I have another family that loves me too.

"Happy birthday, kiddo," they all say as they walk in and tell Mom how much they love the house. Dad gives me a squeeze. I can tell he's happy for me, even though he's always asking Mom how much longer we'll be away from home.

The party was the *best ever.* Everyone was in a good mood. Mom and Dad didn't fight at all. People even told us that it was better than the party at Trump's mansion. Everyone played football in the yard and ate the Romano cake, and some said it was the best cake they'd ever had, which made Dad proud. Odette didn't come, but that was just fine with me.

We've been on the road for a little over a year, and now I'm used to living in hotels and rooming houses. Mom has collected about eight million Playbills, state pushpins, postcards, snow globes, and patches from every city we've visited, and she lugs them all around with her in her overstuffed suitcase. On the nights that she drinks her little brown bottles and we watch Nick at Night, I wonder if she drinks those because she misses our family at home. She doesn't really talk about it, except when she says things like she bets Dad is "living it up" without her around. Sometimes she tells me too much, I think, since they feel like things she should be telling another adult and not a kid like me. But I'm all she's got on the road, so I just listen and pretend to understand.

Yesterday's rehearsal was a little scary. We'd just finished singing "The Big Time," when all of Will Rogers's kids come out in our cowboy outfits, introducing ourselves. Backstage there was a big commotion. We tried to peek out, but I just saw a bunch of people and Bill running into a circle and huddling over one of the girls.

"Call an ambulance!" Bill yelled. Our tutor gathered us up and took us to the dressing room, and we were all frightened. Mom came into the dressing room and told me not to worry, but how could I not? I could hear an ambulance siren outside, and the voices in the hallway sounded like they were definitely worried. The door wasn't shut all the way, and I saw people taking whoever it was out on a stretcher.

"What's happening?" I asked. "Who is it?"

"It's fine," Mom said. "It's one of the chorus girls, Nancy. She's too overworked. Maybe she doesn't have what it takes to hack it on the road." I hate that Mom says this about Nancy, because I don't think it's true at all. On the road, all the chorus girls are so nice to me they feel like family.

We told Dad we'd tour about a year, and we're past that now. I know everything by heart, and I can probably do any role in the entire play by now. I'm getting ready at my spot in the dressing room, and Bill pops his head in the room.

"Christy, come with me. I want to talk to you and your mom." The last time Bill asked us to talk, it was about my hair, so my stomach gets tight right away. Mom gives me a look like *What now?*, but we stay quiet and follow Bill into the office.

"Sit, sit," he says. And then he laughs. "Christy, you look terrified. You can relax. It's nothing bad."

My whole body relaxes, and I can see Mom relax too. Maybe Bill wants to say I did a good job last night, or maybe Odette is sick and I get to be Mary for a night!

"So, Odette is leaving the show in a few weeks," Bill says. "She's getting a little old to be playing Mary, and her mom wants her to start auditioning for more movie roles."

All I can think is *Yes yes yes yes yes!!!!* This is what I've been dreaming about forever, and it's here!

"We want you to play Mary, but that'll mean extending your contract at least another six months, maybe even a year."

"Thank you, Bill!" I blurt out before Mom can even say anything. "You won't be disappointed, I promise! I know all the lines and songs and dances, and I can start any second." No more wig and wig net! No more boy clothes or Yves tugging at my hair because he's angry about the wig. I'm so excited, I could tap-dance right there in the office.

"That's great news, Bill," Mom says, "but I'll have to talk to Christy's dad, of course. I'm sure it'll be fine."

"Of course. Just let me know by Friday. Congratulations, kid."

I give Bill a huge hug. He's not always the nicest, but he always has my back. He even had a serious talk with Yves about his mean comments a few months back, and Yves has been nicer ever since. Mom says to be careful who I trust, but I do trust Bill.

That night in our room, Mom calls Dad to tell him about the promotion. A PROMOTION! Plus, Odette is leaving forever.

"I know it's a long time, but it's a big role for her." Mom sits on the bed with her back to me, but I can tell she's mad, and I can hear Dad yelling through the phone. "You've been parenting for fourteen months, and I basically single-parented for fifteen *years*, so don't even get me started. I know, it's a long time. No, we aren't staying on the road forever."

Mom gets quiet for a while, and I pretend to do my history homework while they talk, but I am concentrating hard on trying to hear what Dad is saying.

"Okay. I understand. I know family is the most important thing. I'll tell Christy and talk to Bill tomorrow."

Mom hangs up and sighs before turning to face me. I'm sure she can see how scared I look, but she doesn't come over to me. She just sits there.

"Christy, we're going home."

"What?! I'm about to play Mary! This is what I've wanted this whole entire time!"

"I know, but it's been fourteen months and your dad misses you. You'll get to see your friends back home . . ."

"What friends? My friends are here!"

"You'll make new friends, and we'll keep going on auditions. You're not quitting acting; we're just moving on to other things. Better things. We'll finish out the next two weeks, and then it's a new chapter. Think of it that way. No more living out of suitcases, right?"

I'm trying not to cry, but I can feel it starting to happen. Mom always tells me to act professional, and I want to believe her that maybe better things will come if we go back home, but all I can think is *Who will play Mary?* Because I know it's not going to be me.

The stage lights are on before my last show. I'm wearing no wig and a dress. The whole cast stands around the giant glitter staircase that's always out for chorus girl numbers. They're all looking at me, singing to me in beautiful harmonies.

"Happy trails to you, until we meet again."

Even Bill is singing, and the tutor, and all the crew. Gina, my replacement, is there too. She's super nice.

"Happy trails to you. Keep smiling on, my friend . . ."

I've sung this song a few times when people leave the show, and now I'm the one leaving. It's a tradition, and it's so sad, but I also feel like part of a family, and I wonder if I will ever see any of these people again. As they sing, I think of a poem Mom gave me on my last birthday. It's about always having a good attitude, no matter what.

I don't know if it's good or bad that we're leaving. I'm having so much fun, but I do miss my actual family. It would be nice to unpack a suitcase and put it away in a closet for a while. I do know one thing as they all stand there under the stage lights singing, though: I am so glad I didn't cut my hair.

Dear Girls,

When you were very little, I hung an excerpt from a Billy Dean country song in a frame in your playroom. The song "Let Them Be Little" is about allowing children to be free and silly and innocent for as long as possible. It's about appreciating the years when your kids are still kids.

This was a reminder for me to acknowledge that, even when I felt exhausted balancing work struggles with sleepless nights of breastfeeding and comforting your nightmares, childhood is finite. You would not be little forever, and I needed to remember that frequently.

I hold these words close because letting a child be little is something I've had the hardest time relating to. My childhood was a contradiction. To her credit, your grandmother was desperate to give me some version of normal childhood experiences through elaborate holiday decorations in hotel rooms, specialized summer camps, and countless souvenirs. But at the same time, I was hearing crew members joke about hookers and watching grown adults walk around naked backstage, working night hours and through fevers and strep throat. These adult environments shaped my worldview and separated me from other children permanently.

The casual graphic content that was normalized in my work environments taught me to make sexual jokes with crew members just to fit in. This is why I believe so deeply that children don't belong in adult working environments without strict regulations and why, years from now, I hope you'll protect your own children the same way in their chosen fields.

My opposition to child labor in Hollywood—and high-functioning kids training and working in any elite field—isn't about money. It's about the pricelessness of childhood itself. There's a fine line between supporting a child's dreams and setting them up for failure. When stats show that only a small percentage of SAG members can make a good living solely from acting, asking a family to blow up their kid's childhood, uproot their whole lives, and destroy their marriage for those odds is insane. You're also displacing the siblings. If someone told me to risk your childhood experience for the small chance that you could make a living as an adult, I would tell them you'd have better odds in Vegas—before telling them to go to hell. If I sound bitter, a label I find conveniently used for women who speak their truth, it's because the system failed little me over time, and I don't think that it's going to change without a larger effort from the union to represent its minor members properly with mental health and social work policies at every level of intervention.

Here's what nobody told me and what I want you to understand deeply: When you spend your childhood being rewarded for compliance, for never complaining, for being professional and easy and grateful, you lose the ability to recognize when someone is taking advantage of you. That muscle never develops. And the world is full of people who can spot that from a mile away. The little girl who learned to hold it rather than ask to use the bathroom grows into the woman who stays too long, forgives too quickly, and apologizes for things that were never her fault. I know that girl. I was that girl for a very long time.

What I can do for you, my darlings, is protect your right to be little, to process the world at an age-appropriate pace, and to meet you where you are developmentally. I want to be the steward of your growing independence, not the architect of premature adulthood.

The lesson I've learned through all of this is as a mom, it's the adult's responsibility to manage their expectations of their child, not the child's responsibility to fulfill the adult's unmet needs or dreams. And my greatest dream for you is simply that you'll get to be children first and everything else second.

4

Othered

1994–1997

Ages 10 to 13

I write the angry letter as fast as I can.

> *Dear Family,*
>
> *I can't live in a house that's so angry and mean. I'm leaving forever and never coming back. I'll find work and live on the road, and you can all miss me . . . or not!*

I throw it down on my squeaky old brass bed that's covered in an itchy baby-pink blanket. I go into the bathroom down the hall to pack some more things.

Mom has been snapping at all of us more, me especially. She's been angry at everything I do, and this morning when I back-talked to her about not wanting to do my chores, Mom smacked me right in the face. It's been hard living back at home and not being on the road anymore. I went from having a family that sang beautiful songs in perfect harmony to a family that shouts all the time for no reason at all. It's like there is always a problem in our house and I'm never sure if it's my fault. I wish we could be normal and have game nights, like the ones I acted out with fake families in audition rooms.

Dad sometimes travels for work. Whenever he comes back from one of his trips, he hands me a bunch of coins and tells me to save his pocket change with a hug and a smile. It makes me feel protected. Sometimes he'll get angry if someone isn't minding him, and he'll lose his temper and yell like Mom. For some reason, maybe because I'm the youngest, I'm mostly off-limits to Dad's strictness. It feels like it is just me, my grumpy mom, the four cats (two died while we were on the road, and Mom thinks Dad threw them out of the car into the woods), and our two messy dogs. How can I stay in a smelly, sad house like this? I'm only in fifth grade, but I have to leave and never ever come back. The road is calling me back. I'll figure out how to live and where to go, and then she'll regret ever hitting me or yelling at me. Or making me feel small. She'll miss me! They all will, and then they'll *wish* they actually had played board games with me.

"Christy, get down here right now!" Mom sounds angry, so I leave the bathroom and run back to my room to grab my bag so I can escape out the back door. When I go to grab my bag, that's when I realize what's missing. My angry goodbye note is gone.

"Christy! *Now!*" she growls. I can tell she's making that toothy dog face she makes to seem powerful and to scare me. She's been making it for as long as I can remember, and it's the ugliest face I've ever seen on a woman. I am frozen in place. I feel tingly and might pee my pants.

I take a deep breath because my stomach is in knots, and I walk downstairs to find Mom standing in the kitchen, holding the note. The note that says I'm running away and never coming back.

"Get in the car."

I do as she says and follow her out to the gravel driveway and climb into the cold blue Cadillac. I'm shaking and too scared to ask any questions, so I stay silent as she drives down the Boston Post Road. A few blocks away, she begins to pull off the street and into a driveway I have seen but never entered. It's a large brick building with the words "Milford Police Station" at the top. The Cadillac is idly running when she jerks it into park.

"Get out," she says. I'm frozen in fear.

"Why?" I ask, beginning to sob. My tears feel hot as I lean into the metal of the side door.

"If life at home is so bad that you want to run away, go tell the police," she says. "Go find another family to live with or go into foster care and see how you like that. People who use you for a government check and molest you. You'll wish you never wrote that note. Go on. Go inside!" She throws her head back to signal I leave the car immediately. Her hazel eyes are cold. I feel like I don't know her at all.

Now I'm really shaking. My own mom wants me to go to the police and go live with some scary family somewhere? Is she happy to give me up? Am I a burden? I need to crawl my way back so she'll see I love her. Hot tears are gushing out of my eyes. I'm so scared; all I want to do is go home.

"Please, Mommy! I—I'm sorry! I wish I never wrote that note. Please don't make me go in there! I promise I'll do whatever you say!" My voice is desperate and hoarse. I want to paw at her for a hug but think better of it. I don't want to get sent away.

She stares at me blankly from the driver's side of the car, and for a minute, I'm afraid she'll push me out. I know it's not possible that hours go by with her sitting there, but it feels like it. It feels like forever.

"Don't do it again," she says finally. I shudder and let out a sigh while I try to collect myself. My heart is pounding out of my chest. My ears are ringing.

"I'm sorry, Mom," I say.

Mom drives us back home, and we don't say another word. I make a silent promise to myself to never talk back to her again. I'll go to school on Monday like nothing happened. I'll do what I have to do to be a part of this family, even the things that I don't like. Even if they don't want me or feel like my family anymore. I won't give her a reason to throw me away ever again.

Ever since Mom and I got back from touring, I've been trying to get used to having a "normal" life at a "normal" school. No one at my new school, the local Meadow Wood Elementary, cares that I act or that I won the Miss Southern New England Pre-Teen or that I got to sing onstage with Marie Osmond in *The Sound of Music* last summer. I wonder if Mom and Dad put us into a public school because of money problems, but Mom says it's so I can experience what it's like to be "normal," even though she's always saying I'm "special." She also says private schools are too strict about me missing so much school since I'm leaving for auditions all the time.

I was so nervous taking the bus on the first day, but I did it. The teachers at Meadow Wood are nice, but the kids are always calling me "Bucky Beaver" because of my large front teeth or "the Ethiopian" because I'm tall and skinny for my age. A few even call me "Triple A" since I don't need to wear a bra yet. It's so rude and gross, and I try to just pretend it doesn't hurt my feelings, even though *of course* it does. The other week, Lana Amato slapped me in the locker room after PE because she said I was flirting with David Gonzalez, like he's her boyfriend or something. David is a tall, cute Puerto Rican boy, but I'm too young to even know how to flirt. We held hands in the meadow behind my house one afternoon, but the very next week, David and his friends woofed me off the bus like I was a dog. Why does everybody hate me so much?

I'm getting taller fast, so my pants are too short, which is yet another thing that is completely embarrassing. I don't want crystals to celebrate booking parts anymore; I want clothes that fit. I want to look like a girl in a dELiA*s catalogue. If I say that to Mom, though, she probably won't like it, or she'll say something about money not growing on trees. Sometimes she makes me so mad, but other times, it feels like it's me and Mom against the world. Like we're in it together, going to auditions, trying to build a career. She's less mean when I'm successful, when I book things or get praise from a casting director. I know she wants the best for me, so I just try to do my best.

I'm always leaving Meadow Wood to go to auditions in New York, and some of my teachers are starting to get a little mad about it. The other day, Mom was waiting outside to pick me up, and Mr. Lombardo told me I couldn't leave music class, even if I had permission. He's a music teacher, so you'd think he would understand about being an *artist.* I reminded him that I had a commercial audition and that Mom already cleared it with the front desk, but he didn't care at all.

"Time is money, Mr. Lombardo," I said when he told me I had to finish out the last fifteen minutes of class before I could leave. I'd heard "Time is money" a million times during the *Follies* tour, but I guess it's not something a kid says to a teacher, because Mr. Lombardo got pretty angry.

"Excuse me, Miss Romano?"

His question caught me off guard, so I just repeated myself, because I was confused and didn't know what else to say. "Time is . . . money?"

He crossed his arms and stared at me, and a few of the kids giggled. He didn't giggle, though. The air in the room was uncomfortable. Was this a standoff?

"Go on, then," he said. "Go to your *audition*, Romano."

I thought I would love Meadow Wood, but it's not easy dealing with bullies and mean teachers and rude boys. All I wanted was to go to a normal public school and find friends to hang with, but when you're the tall, skinny kid with too-short pants and big teeth who's always leaving class to go audition for movies and plays and commercials, it's like there's a target on your back.

It's my new manager, Ann Lauren, who tells Mom about PCS. Professional Children's School is on West Sixtieth, and it's for "high-achieving" kids who are working in entertainment and the arts. There are some athletes and inventors too. As much as I want to go to public school, it was too hard to keep asking teachers if I could leave early the previous year, and the principal started getting annoyed. I really was a burden. Plus the kids were pretty mean, so when I went for the interview at PCS and Mom told me I could start sixth grade there, I was so relieved. A new school year means I can get new back-to-school clothes that fit.

A few days before school starts, Mom takes me to the Gap in Midtown, and I pick out my first-day-of-school outfit: a pink beret, a pink shirt with a white shirt underneath it, a pink plaid skirt, and gray argyle stockings. I'll wear them with my black Steve Maddens. I think that I look just like Cher from *Clueless*. I'll be unstoppable. I know I can reinvent myself at PCS. That I can be around other "special" kids while also just being normal. Is that even possible? I have to believe that it is.

While we're shopping, Mom tells me about some of the people who've gone to this elite private school: Carrie Fisher (aka Princess Leia), Uma Thurman, Christina Ricci, Sarah Michelle Gellar, and a whole lot more. The list is a Who's Who of some of the most famous people out there. When I start in the fall, Macaulay Culkin will still be there, and he's about the most famous kid actor who ever lived because of *Home Alone*. Even though he's a teenager now, everyone still knows exactly who he is. Every single person on this planet probably knows his famous surprised face. I wonder what he'll look like in person.

"This will be so much better for you, Christy," Mom says while we shop. "You can leave for auditions or shows or shoots anytime, and they completely understand. In fact, they encourage it. If you're not leaving *this* school, you're probably not working hard enough on your career. You're too special for a public school. You need to be with other high-achieving kids, other working artists who understand what you're doing."

The night before school starts, I lay my new pink Gap outfit out on my pink fabric sitting chair. I smile because I won't be bullied anymore. I've finally found my place.

The next morning, Mom flicks my bedroom light on at five a.m. to wake me up so we can make the train on time.

"Get up. We gotta catch the train."

Even before PCS, she's always gotten me up this way, by flicking on the bright lights. It burns my eyes and startles me, but I never complain.

We usually get to the city later in the day, so this early morning is new for me. I put on my pink outfit and walk downstairs. I can smell my parents' coffee brewing in the kitchen. The space heaters are on because it's already getting cold. I put my jacket on and stuff my Trapper Keeper binder and my Game Boy into my new JanSport backpack so I'll have something to do on the train besides sleep.

I also stuff my sticker book inside, because I'm obsessed with going to Lee's Art Shop on Fifty-Seventh. Maybe Mom will bring me there after school as a start-of-school celebration. I now collect scratch-and-sniff stickers that smell like pineapples or bananas. I have all sorts of rare ones, like stickers of the Garbage Pail Kids characters and an oversized brown bear holding hearts. I have strips of every kind of animal, flower, and food item, from puffy hot dogs to cupcakes. Looking through my stickers gives me something to do; plus flipping through the book makes me happy. It's sort of like collecting pins and patches when I was in the *Follies* or crystals when I would book jobs as a little kid. My sticker book is like a little treasure but just for me. And it has nothing to do with work. It's worth the extra weight in my backpack.

Two weeks into PCS and I already have two best friends, Linda and Harper. Our classes are tiny, with maybe ten kids in each one, so it's easier to get to know people. Our teachers are all zany and have big personalities, which makes me feel comfortable. Everyone seems to really like school. Linda is a ballet dancer, so she also goes to classes at the School of American Ballet every day like I do, a couple blocks away from PCS. She takes it way more seriously than I do. Mom says I'm going there for "cross-training." Linda has shiny, long black hair and is beautiful, but she's not at all a mean girl like Odette from the *Follies*. She has that dancer walk where her feet turn out like a duck, and she's always stretching and talking about becoming a principal one day. Her parents are divorced. Her dad is a diplomat to China and lives in Canada, and her mom is a former opera teacher who is older than my mom. Linda says she's super strict. She asks about Mom, and I just smile and tell her she's really protective but not that strict. I don't say anything about the time she took me to the police station, or the way she still grabs my arm when we're running around the city.

Harper is—get this—related to Macaulay Culkin, who also goes to the school. Macaulay's brother Kieran is here too, a few years ahead of me. The minute I met Linda and Harper, we were instant best friends, and that kind of thing never happened to me at Meadow Wood or any other school I'd been to. PCS is in a tall building that looks like an office. You walk up and down old, thick gray cement stairs to go from your classes to the cafeteria (which, coincidentally, is also our gym and auditorium with wall dividers). The walls are like cement blocks, so it feels a little bit like we're factory workers going up and down the stairs all day.

All the popular guys dress like messy skater kids with weird-colored hair. Macaulay and Kieran and a few other guys think they're so tough, wearing Black Flag and NOFX pins on their black trench coats or those stupid pins that say "Life Sucks, and Then You Die" on their silver-graffitied black bike messenger bags. Like, what does that even mean? Mac is a huge movie star, so how much can his life suck? I feel like he's not really acting anymore because he maybe smokes pot? I have no idea if that's true because there are a million rumors around school. He started mooing at me on the stairwell like a cow and seemed super out of it one day, at least to me. In my head, I can only think that he's such a waste of talent, and I feel embarrassed that he goes to our school looking like that. I feel bad for Harper, since she's so nice and I want to be her friend because I don't have many. But Mac and his gang are basically the "popular kids," since popular in this school means famous—or at least, used-to-be famous.

While there are a few kids who commute like me, most everyone at school lives in the city. The School of American Ballet dancers and foreign musicians going to pre-college Juilliard classes live in dorms because most of them are from other states and countries. You'd think Harper would be full of herself since her family member is so famous, but she's the sweetest, and she belly-laughs at all my jokes, even when they're dumb. I love to see her smile through her messy blond hair. The younger kids make eye contact with the older ones awkwardly, hoping to see famous students like goth girl Christina Ricci, glossy and perfect Jordana Brewster, or indie-cool Gaby Hoffmann. I know I get excited when I see them.

There's no playground or outside space at PCS except for some chairs out in the back alleyway. The old elevators in the school have gates on them, and they creak like they're about to break. When you walk inside, there's a lobby with low ceilings, and Angela the receptionist always says hello with a huge smile on her face. She's from Haiti, and she knows every single kid at the school. On the first floor, right by the water fountain, is the bulletin board. In a normal school, the bulletin board would have articles and newspaper clippings about who made the basketball team or who got into the marching band, but the PCS board is full of notices about students who are doing something outstanding, like winning an Oscar, dancing in *The Nutcracker* at Lincoln Center, or getting a record deal. There are tiny holes all over the board from all the notices they've pinned there before. Every time I look up and see it, I close my eyes and pray that one of those clippings will be about me. I want to be on that board more than anything. More than I even want to make real friends.

I'm always leaving class and signing in and out at Angela's desk before meeting my mom by the school's front door to audition for commercials or voice-over work or movies or plays. PCS is not like Meadow Wood at all, since the teachers *want* you to leave for auditions. It's on you to finish your work. If I'm not studying or going to class or taking voice or dance lessons at Broadway Dance, I'm going to auditions and jobs or singing at malls in New Jersey and Connecticut with our singing troupe, the Broadway Kids. Lacey is in it, and this small girl with big curly hair. Tina just joined. Mom really likes Tina's mom, so I'm getting to know her, and she seems really sweet so far. I have a secret crush on this guy who's in the troupe, Jesse Eisenberg, but I haven't even told Tina about it yet. I think that the troupe is fun, but the "cool" indie-movie kids always think that it's lame, and other, regular kids think so too. Once, at the Paramus mall, we were getting ready to sing, and some regular kids started spitting on us from the second-floor balcony while we were singing something from *Annie*. It was disgusting and made me feel like a dweeb, but the show must go on. Even when other kids spit on your head, I guess.

After two weeks of school, I'm already so tired from the commute. Wake up at five to lights flicking on, rush to the train, run to the subway, hurry down the long avenues from the number 9 Lincoln Center stop and into school before the bell rings. My backpack feels like it weighs fifty pounds because of all the books I have to carry back and forth to Connecticut, plus my dance gear, plus any scripts I'm learning. Even looking at the school staircase in the building stresses me out, thinking of lugging my bag up.

Besides homework, I'm always working on learning my lines for an audition or a commercial I booked. Some jobs I get, and some I don't, because a kid who has my same "look," like Emmy Rossum, winds up booking it. When that happens, I feel deeply embarrassed, even though I try not to show it. I just try to prepare more for the next potential job. It's bad enough when I lose out to someone with light eyes and hair who looks nothing like me, but to lose out to my own "type" really stings. I'm so confused, because one thing Mom says is that, even if I get rejected for the millionth time, the key is to keep going and never quit, but she also says we can quit if it "stops being fun." Acting is "fun," I guess. I'm good at it, after all, but I'm also so tired all the time. I don't know if a twelve-year-old is supposed to be so tired. But when I book something or when I sing perfectly in an audition, that feeling makes these years all worth it for me and—I hope—for Mom. So I'm going to keep trying my hardest, even if I'm tired.

"Christy, hurry up," Mom says. I'm changing out of my dance class clothes and back into street clothes as fast as I can. "Dad called, and he wants us to meet him in Little Italy for dinner. He's already at the restaurant. Let's go!"

Mom brought the car into Manhattan this morning instead of taking the train, so now we'll have to drive all the way down to Little Italy during rush hour. Mom always gets tense and yells at me when she's driving in traffic, so while I put my ballet slippers and tights back in my bag, I prepare myself for a stressful ride. Mom has been in a bad mood since this morning.

"Ready, Christy? What's taking so long?" I hurry into the hallway and follow Mom outside and to the parking lot. I know better than to question her on a day like today, so I just keep quiet and try to walk as fast as she walks.

Mom snaps at me all the way down to Little Italy, like the traffic and the lack of parking are all my fault. I just ignore it and try to focus on my math homework, but I'm too distracted to get much done, so I look out the window. We head into a tiny, dark restaurant with brick walls and red-and-white-checkered tablecloths. We find Dad sitting at a table in the back with a man I've never met before. He looks like a gangster in a mob movie with his white hair slicked back and his dark gray suit and sharp white button-up. Mom says that Dad is "loyal to a fault," and that he's stayed friends with people he grew up with, which is why he hangs out with guys like this even though he moved on and "moved up," as Mom says. I love Dad, but sometimes it feels like my parents have another life that I know nothing about.

"My baby," Dad says warmly as he stands up from the small café table to give me a hug with his big hands. He smells of Aramis cologne and red wine, but his embrace still makes me smile. "Hi, Shar." He kisses my mom on the cheek as she pulls her chair out to sit down. "Leo and I were just talking about how you're my little superstar," Dad says. "How was school? Let's get you girls some pasta."

I look over at Leo, and his eyes look like two black holes with a broken yellow smile beneath them. His eyes freak me out. He seems dangerous, like a bad guy from a movie. He has a few dark moles on his face, and he's flushed and sweaty, so he's probably drunk. The smell of his cologne mixes with Dad's and it makes me a little sick, since all I've eaten since lunch is a banana protein bar, so I grab some Italian bread and dip it in some olive oil to settle my stomach. Dad pours Mom some red wine and orders me a Shirley Temple. He's extra loud, maybe because of the wine, and he seems like he knows everyone who works here. "We'll have Pauli's secret ziti, that pizza he makes with the extra-spicy pepperoni, and antipasti Nico." Dad loves ordering off the menu when we eat Italian food. "Angel hair for my baby."

"Thanks, Daddy." He makes me smile with how proud he seems of me. I didn't even do anything. Mom sits there, quiet as a mouse, and takes a heavy drink from her wineglass.

"You got it, Mr. Romano," says the server.

I try not to make eye contact with Leo, but he's right across from me, so it's awkward. He gulps his wine while we talk, and Dad asks me to tell Leo about my career. Every once in a while, Leo says something like "Wow! You're a great kid!" in a booming voice as he slaps the table with his large hand, covered in gold jewelry. It's starting to make me nervous, and I can tell Mom doesn't like this guy by how quiet she is.

"I love the Romano family!" Leo shouts. "Just like my own! You know your dad was the greatest when we were kids! He was one of the smart ones."

And then, just like in a movie, Leo pulls a gun out of his jacket and slams it down so hard, it makes the table shake. I've never seen a real gun, only prop guns, so I freeze in my seat. Is he going to shoot us, even though he said he loves us? Are there bullets inside? I look at Mom, who looks scared but also angry, and then at Dad, who is furious.

"I would kill anybody who tried to hurt a Romano!" Then Leo starts to cry. I realize he might be a little (or a lot) unstable, like people on the street in NYC who I'm supposed to stay away from. Is he crying because he loves my dad so much? Is it the wine? I've seen Mom cry after too much wine, so maybe this is just one of the side effects.

"It's okay, Leo. Let's put that away," Dad says. "We don't wanna scare anybody."

Leo seems like a confused child, but he takes the gun and puts it back in his jacket like Dad said. Like nothing happened, Leo just dunks some bread in olive oil and takes a huge bite.

"I just want you guys to know how much I love you!" He moves the bread around in his hand before chomping down on it with a killer smile.

"I appreciate that, Leo," says Dad. "But cool it with the gun."

Mom is silent and staring at Dad like she wants to shoot *him* with the gun.

"Angel hair for the little girl," the waiter says, placing the steaming plate in front of me. I want to say, "I'm not a little girl. I'm in sixth grade," but I'm too nervous to talk or eat at all. I force myself to have some pasta, but I can barely taste anything.

Driving home that night, Mom is angrier than I've seen her in a long time. She's ranting about Dad thinking he's a "big shot" and staying in touch with guys like Leo. I'm not sure why they think I can't hear them. Dad always tries to keep a cheerful tone, but he tells her, "Would you just shut up, Shar? Jesus." I pretend to sleep so I don't get pulled into their fight. I stay slumped over my fifty-pound backpack for support as the sporadic lights from the I-95 flash through the windows of the car.

Even a couple weeks after the incident, I'm still having nightmares about Leo coming to our house and killing our whole family. Mom says that Dad promises that he won't bring Leo around anymore. But then, one morning, the house phone rings.

"Hello? Romano residence," I answer as politely as I can.

"Is your dad there?" I recognize the gruff voice immediately as Leo's. His voice sounds like metal being crushed in a machine. My whole body tenses up, and my heart races. "Um, who is this?"

"It's the Easter Bunny," he says. "Put your dad on."

When Dad gets on with Leo, he motions for me to leave his office.

Leo has never called before, and I can tell by Dad's voice that he'll make sure he never calls again. A little spooked, I rush back upstairs to finish my social studies homework. Dad has so many people coming in and out of his life, I just hope Leo is now *out*. I can't let creepy Leo distract me, because I have a costume fitting for a movie I booked with one of the biggest directors in the world later today, so I'm praying it goes well. It's not a huge part, but it's a Woody Allen film, so Mom said that no part is too small in his movies. Maybe this part will get me on the bulletin board at PCS finally.

On the Woody Allen set, two boys in brownface makeup and islander outfits with straw hats meet with the choreographer one last time to rehearse our big musical number. I've met Greg Raposo, one of the kids in the scene, before because he's in Broadway Kids. When I find out that all the stars of the movie (Julia Roberts, Goldie Hawn, Alan Alda, Edward Norton, Drew Barrymore, Natasha Lyonne, and Gaby Hoffmann!) will be in the scene, watching me perform, I freak out a little. Woody Allen will be watching too, so I work hard to make sure I know every step, every note. I can't wait to tell Linda and Harper and everyone at PCS about this. I know they'll be happy for me.

The first time I meet Woody, or Mr. Allen, I'm wearing this dorky banana costume. Mom was nervous that morning on the ride into the city for the shoot because of all the stars and everything. She has her camera and fully plans on getting pictures of me with them if she can. I have to be professional, though, so I can't freak out and act like some crazy fan in the streets. I'm an actress. I'm here to do a job.

"Christy, go up to Goldie and Drew and ask for a picture," Mom says from the corner of the set, holding her disposable Kodak camera. "You should always be friendly to people, because you just never know how they can help you down the road." Ever since the *Follies*, Mom has been telling me to "get to know" the big actors or producers or directors because they could push my career forward and get me that big break. I'm always so nervous approaching people I don't know, but it makes Mom happy, so I do it. When I get through hair and makeup, I have a slick bun and a bright yellow banana face. I have time to wait around in my suit, so I do get to talk to some of the actors a little bit. Mom flashes her camera a bunch. First with Goldie and then with Alan Alda. Mom and I watch Drew after we film my scene. She is so sweet to me, with a big smile. Maybe because she was a kid actor too. Out of nowhere, a short man with reddish hair and thick black glasses comes up to me and Mom. He shakes my hand and begins to tell my mom that he thinks I am very talented. It takes me a second to realize that it's Woody Allen. I'm a bit starstruck since Mom has built him up to be God's gift to film. Mom musters the courage to ask for a picture, and he puts his arm around my banana suit. I may be dressed like a large dancing yellow fruit, but on this set, surrounded by all these people, I feel like a star.

With what's been going on lately and all the work that I've been booking, I barely think about Leo anymore, which is a relief, because I need all the sleep I can get, and thinking about him murdering my entire family, plus all our pets, wasn't helping.

I haven't brought Leo up to Dad again. He tries his best to support me with my acting, but I don't think he gets it like Mom does. He doesn't fully understand my dream to be the best actress and singer onstage and on-screen. Mom says we use the money I make on jobs to pay for everything we do: my tuition, our train passes, subway tokens, my schoolbooks, my stickers. I'm "investing in myself," Mom says. That way, if I keep succeeding, Dad can never say no to us. I'm not exactly sure where all the rest of my money goes.

Dad always seems proud of me when I book something, but he's not *interested* the way Mom is. My brother couldn't care less since he's always with his girlfriend now, and my sisters are busy with college. It's like we're all roommates, but we never really tell one another things, except me and Mom, of course. We tell each other everything. Well, almost everything.

She also keeps saying that for me to be a "real actress," I need to do more independent films. It's tricky, because Dad won't let me audition for the kinds of parts that are out there. For *The Devil's Advocate* audition, I'm going to read for the part of a girl who's going on the stand in court and talking about a pedophile touching her, and Dad demands that I don't audition. Mom is really upset and tells me that it's his fault I missed out on the opportunity. He says that he's just trying to be protective. Truth is, I'm in seventh grade! I'm in New York *all the time*, so I see and hear everything. It's not like he can shelter me forever. After that, Mom just says to keep certain things between us because it's easier that way. Sometimes I feel like I'm acting when I'm at home with my family, and I'm myself when I'm on the train or auditioning or on set. It's like there's the world of me and Mom and then the world of Dad and my siblings, and the only time they feel like the same place is maybe Christmas, when we're all at home, on our best behavior. Besides that, they feel a little bit like strangers, and I'm the Good Little Girl who is burning herself out trying to make everyone happy. If there were an Oscar for this role, I might just get it.

"We're working hard," Mom tells me whenever I bring up anything about feeling distant from Dad or the rest of the family. "We've just got to do what we need to do, whether Dad understands or not."

I'm always scared about Mom and Dad splitting up. She recently told me that she thinks he's "entertaining other women," but I don't think that's true because he always says family is the most important thing. Divorce is on my mind all the time, but I don't want to make things worse, so I never ask. I never tell them how I feel. But I stay awake at night worrying about it, and my entire body gets tense every time I hear them fighting. I just push it all away and try to channel it into acting or singing. I just want to pretend the tension doesn't exist, but some days I feel like I'm coiling into a ball so tight, it might explode.

"Christy, you seem haunted."

Hal looks straight into my eyes when he says this. "It's like you've seen things, which is why I cast you."

I'm a little uncomfortable, since I don't know what he thinks I've seen, but he's Hal Hartley, and Mom said his movies win awards at Sundance, so I trust him. He's sweet to me, even though the haunting thing is weird. What have I seen? I'm not sure, but I got the part, so I'm just going with it.

I wonder if he knows how stressed I am about my family, and Mom and Dad's fighting. I hate it. I also hate thinking of the times Mom has been rough with me, like the time she was dragging me down the street to PCS and yelling at me because I was too slow. I feel like some teachers saw her being rough with me, and I was so embarrassed and ashamed, even though I tried to blow it off. The vice principal called me in after that to make sure everything was fine at home.

Life at home is really crazy. Dad is always coming or going to a new consultant job, which makes him on edge, since he's worried about our finances. Mom has been venting to me on our commutes that they might go bankrupt again or lose the house if Dad doesn't find another high-paying job soon. Our house. And while the house isn't my favorite place, it's where I grew up, and I have as much pride as she does about where we live.

During rehearsals for *Henry Fool*, Hal never wants me to say *the line* because he wants it to be spontaneous and raw when we shoot the scene. I know Dad would kill me for saying this line, but I follow Mom's lead and just never mention anything to him. Mom says the producers "tricked" her and cast me without telling us the whole truth about what exactly I'd be saying on camera. She felt "blindsided," but she also knows that sometimes true art isn't always wholesome and sanitized. "I'm not happy about it, but sometimes you do things that might seem wild, but really, you're making something artistic," Mom says. I'm not sure they tricked us because they're not bad people and they've always been so nice to me. That's how she feels, I guess.

"He doesn't need to know, and he would fly off the handle and make us drop out. We've been working so hard, Christy. We just have to do what we have to do for your career." The only way Dad will see the movie is if he comes to the premiere, sees it in a theater in New York, or gets it on VHS. How else would he possibly watch it? He probably isn't going to do any of those things, so Mom just tells him we're doing a little indie movie in New York and leaves it at that. He doesn't ask follow-up questions.

I'm only in one scene of *Henry Fool*, but it's an important moment because it shifts the whole plot. Hal says the scene is "pivotal," so we have to get the tone right. The movie is a dark comedy, but my part isn't laugh-out-loud funny at all. I feel nervous about the lines but also a little bit excited because it's a challenge and it's edgy, which is what the PCS kids are all about. We've signed the contract, so there's no turning back unless I want to ruin my whole career and get a reputation as "difficult."

On the day we shoot, I'm sitting in a cold holding room in a church in Queens, waiting to be called to set.

Parker Posey walks in, which makes me even more nervous. She's, like, *the* indie-movie queen, since she's made all these cool films like *Party Girl* and *Dazed and Confused* and *Waiting for Guffman*. Parker is super sweet and bubbly and has tons of energy behind her eyes.

"Hey, Christy!" Parker says, sitting next to me in her own plastic church chair, shivering away the cold draft in the basement. "Are you doing okay?"

"I'm great!" I lie, sounding a little too excited for a girl playing a character who's being abused by her stepfather. "A little nervous but good." I look to my mom, who nods with a quiet smile. She has a "make friends with Parker, she's a big deal" look on her face.

"Hal is the best," says Parker. "You'll do great. Just be yourself."

My character Pearl, at fourteen, is a neighborhood girl. She asks a mysterious drifter guy to commit a crime for her, and in return, she'll do something unspeakable. I'm stressing out, sitting there with Parker, waiting to be called. I just have to think about Pearl and being haunted.

The assistant director pops in and yells, "Christy! You're up!"

Parker smiles and says, "You'll do great," which eases my nerves just a little. I walk onto set in a cramped, dingy basement that's more like a crawl space, since it's so tight and dimly lit. Thomas Jay Ryan, who plays Henry, and Hal are there, along with the whole crew. There's a red glow from a radiator, and Hal shows me my marks so I know where to sit, like in rehearsal.

"You doing okay?" Hal asks, which I appreciate. He always goes out of his way to make me feel like I belong, which not every director does. Some of them just treat you like a prop moving around the room, but the good ones really talk to you. They seem like they actually care. "Do you have any questions before we roll?"

"Nope, I'm good!" I smile big, but then I quickly lose the smile, remembering that I'm not playing Molly in *Annie*; I'm playing a girl who is tortured inside.

Thomas comes over with his hair long and shaggy.

"Heya," says Thomas. "You good?"

"I'm feeling ready," I say, remembering not to smile like I'm a kid at Disneyland. Now I'm self-conscious about my big, crooked teeth. A voice in my mind pipes up, telling me I'm ugly and I don't belong here. I try to ignore it.

Hal gives us some direction and talks us through the scene again before we shoot. Movies are so different from theater, where it's wild and chaotic and crazy. The *Follies* tour was like one long party, but on movie sets, you must get serious, even when it's a comedy.

I'm too focused to care where Mom is. I'm sure she's close by, unless Hal made this a closed set. The script described Pearl as "hardened and disturbed but frequently vulnerable and scared; a troubled kid." So I channel that. I surprise Henry as he comes into the dark, creepy room to sleep, and I hand him the bottle of wine Pearl has been drinking. At just the right moment, the tears come, the tears I've been rehearsing for weeks. They flow right out. And then, for the first time, I say it. Or Pearl says it.

"I'll suck your cock if you kill him for me."

Thomas/Henry jumps away, and I throw myself down and cry even harder.

"Cut!" Hal says. "That was great, guys. Perfect, Christy."

After we do the scene a few more times, I collect myself, a bit disgusted but also feeling deeply connected to the art of moviemaking. I somehow feel broken and confident at the same time. This is what it takes to be a serious actress. I'll never be the same. I see now that this is what Mom and I have been working so hard for. Hal and Thomas both give me parental hugs before I leave. I feel vulnerable because of what I've just said and done, even though Hal and Thomas and the crew are kind to me. On the ride home from the shoot, I tell Mom how guilty I feel. Not just about keeping this a secret from Dad but because we're Catholic and . . . maybe this was wrong? It's all so confusing.

"Don't feel guilty. Your dad doesn't understand art, Christy," she says. "And it's not like he tells us everything about his life either."

Even during the summers, I'm working. Plays and commercials are slow, but Mom usually puts me in some sort of class or activity, whether it's dance or voice, anything to "keep my résumé fresh," as she says. This time, though, I'm touring around New England, doing summer stock. Mom is always happier when we're on the road. Lonely, maybe, but happier than when we're at home or commuting into the city all the time. Maine is beautiful in the summer, and I'm in an Agatha Christie play called *Spider's Web*, which is pretty fun. I play the spunky character Pippa Hailsham-Brown, and I speak with a fun British accent. It's a cute murder mystery, and it's a lot less stressful and heavy than playing Pearl in *Henry Fool*. We didn't even go to the premiere of that movie, which was kind of a letdown, but they did send me a cast jacket in the mail, which made Dad ask what the gift was all about. Mom just told him it was the indie movie I did and left it at that.

"Remember when you met the presidents, Christy?" Mom asks out of the blue as we drive to the theater the next day. We've been staying in a lake cottage across from the Cape Playhouse in Dennis.

"Yeah, of course. Why?"

I'd met a few US presidents after performing in Washington, DC, when I was in Broadway Kids and another group called City Kids. I met Bill Clinton, Gerald Ford, and George H. W. Bush, but it's not like we became pen pals. Right?

"Oh, just reminiscing, is all. Not every kid gets to meet presidents. You're special."

A few days later, I have a matinee of *Spider's Web* at the Ogunquit Playhouse. Mom is acting so casual that it's almost fishy. She's been more relaxed than normal this summer, but this is plain weird.

"Mom, are you okay?" I ask while we walk to the theater. "Is something going on?"

"I'm good," she says. "I do have a surprise for you, though."

She points to a line of shiny black SUVs outside. There are a bunch of burly men in black suits and dark glasses by the cars, some chattering into walkie-talkies.

"Mom, what's happening?" I ask. She has a mischievous smile, and I'm almost worried that she's having me kidnapped by the Mafia or something.

"Remember when you met President Bush and his wife, Barbara, at the City Kids event? Well, I wrote to his office and let him know you would be here performing. I invited him here! I can't believe it, but he's here with his son George and George's wife and kids! They're staying nearby. Can you believe it?"

Whose mom writes to a PRESIDENT and invites them to their kid's summer stock play? I'm mortified but also excited. It's like a *Forrest Gump* moment, where I wind up in crazy situations with famous people. And even if it's a little embarrassing, it also means Mom really loves me. This is how she shows it sometimes.

During intermission Mom and the stage manager bring me up to the high balcony box where the Bushes are sitting. Mom has already wound her Kodak camera.

"Be polite! And say, 'Thank you so much for coming,'" Mom says as we rush up the stairs. "Make sure we get a photo with him. And call him Mr. President!"

We get to the box and say hello to everyone. President Bush; George and his wife, Laura; and their kids, twin girls who are almost exactly my age. The girls look bored and hot, since there is no AC in this balcony. The guys in black suits are standing in every corner, watching.

"Hello, Christy. Wonderful performance," President Bush says.

"Thank you so much, Mr. President," I say, just like I was told. "Thanks for coming!" I'm as smiley and upbeat as I can be, far away from playing Pearl and back to the cheery Christy that I put on for cereal commercials and toy ads. The Bush twins giggle together, and the president hands me a pin, which I can add to my collection of *other* presidential pins I've gotten in the past.

"Can we take a photo?" Mom asks, pulling the disposable camera out.

"Of course."

I stand with them all, smiling as big as I can. Mom clicks the camera. I wonder if she made all this happen for me or for her. Either way, it's pretty amazing. Not many twelve-year-olds are meeting presidents during their summer breaks. They're swimming or biking, walking around malls. They're doing normal things. Some days I feel like normal is what I really want, but not on this day.

Dear Girls,

I was occasionally hit as a kid. From what I gathered, my siblings were also hit and spanked, and this made us afraid of our parents until we got older. I will not speak for my siblings in detail, but I have every right to talk about myself. After a smack, I was always reminded that their generation "got it worse," and no doubt they did. I believe the lore that my dad got hit with a lead pipe by my grandfather to keep him and his brothers in line. The medieval practice of "spare the rod, spoil the child" was ingrained in my parents by their parents. But as a kid, I didn't understand generational trauma. I just knew I was scared.

My generation likes to joke about getting "the shoe" or getting "whooped," because dark humor helps us cope when recalling these traumatic episodes. But honestly, a lot of us still carry scars from childhoods lived in fear of the people who claimed to love us most. I know I do.

I believe the bullying and exclusion I experienced were partly because I was already conditioned to accept fighting and conflict. Kids can be cruel. My talent made me exploitable, but my inability to relate to other kids because of what I was dealing with at home made me a social outsider. And with my crazy teeth and too-short pants, I was basically a walking target with jazz hands.

The truth is, kids can be mean, even when they're taught better. We haven't evolved much beyond tribalism, even as adults. But being the perpetual outsider gave me a superpower: I can spot elitism and manipulation from miles away. I can read a room instantly and help protect you both from the people who would try to make you feel less than. I can teach you when to blend in and when to stand out, depending on what feels right and what keeps you safe.

Here's what I learned from all those years of not fitting in, of being a dork; a weirdo; a skinny, bucktoothed theater kid: Being different isn't the problem. Being ashamed of being different is. The casting process that would later define my career was just middle school bullying with a crappy waiting room and awkward pleasantries. The same people who decide you're not enough based on your looks, your teeth, your height, your personality—they're everywhere. But when you've already survived being the weird kid, when you've learned that your worth isn't determined by other people's approval, you become unbreakable.

Sometimes our limitations are our superpowers. Your differences aren't flaws to be fixed, girls. They're your competitive advantages, waiting to be discovered. I spent years trying to sand down my edges to fit in, but my edges were exactly what made me memorable. The same will be true for both of you.

5

Who's That Girl?

1997–1999

Ages 13 to 16

She walks into our eighth-grade homeroom class at PCS on a gray New York morning, wearing baggy jeans and a baby tee that shows her belly. She looks permanently bored. Even though she's pretty short, she's got big boobs, swollen lips, and grown-up curves, plus dirty-blond hair and squinty green eyes that look like they couldn't care less what anyone thinks of her. She's the exact opposite of me. I'm still flat-chested, tall, and skinny, with bad teeth, even in eighth grade. We all knew she was starting school today, because when someone has starred in a big movie with Robert Redford, the kids at PCS talk. It's still kind of shocking when she walks in, though. I mean, she's practically a movie star.

Our vice principal brings her in and introduces her.

"Class, this is Scarlett."

We all know her last name is Johansson.

"Hey," she says in a raspy, deep voice that makes her seem much older than the rest of us. This girl definitely smokes cigarettes.

We all say hello, trying to be as cool as she is as she finds a seat at one of the empty desks near Linda. We only have thirteen kids in our eighth grade, which means that everyone is already getting a lot of attention from the teachers and from one another. I watch as Scarlett takes her messenger bag off. I flinch inside. I met her once, but I doubt she remembers. We did a table read for a play together, and I was playing her little sister, which was really weird, since we're the same age. How is she always so confident? Maybe it's for show. Maybe she's pretending, like me. I care too much but pretend not to. It never works, though. The harder I try *not* to try, the more it looks and feels like I'm trying.

In my head, the cool kids are doing things that I've seen in movies like *She's All That*. They're going to crazy parties at other rich kids' penthouses in Trump Tower, which is down the street. I imagine bowls of drugs and people having sex all over the place at those parties. As much as I want to be part of things, I *hate* drugs. They're disgusting. My mom recently had a big talk with my brother about it, telling him to never try drugs, especially because he's an athlete. I also recently watched *The Basketball Diaries* on VHS from Blockbuster. Drugs are the scariest thing in the world, and I hope my brother never does them.

"Okay, focus up, kids!" The teacher gets back to lecturing us about American history, and I watch Scarlett slouch into her seat with a "puss on her face," as Mom would say. It's like she already belongs, and she's somehow already popular. She catches my gaze, and I quickly look away, because she's so cool and I don't want to seem like I'm trying too hard or like I'm obsessed with her or something.

Sometimes it seems like everyone is hooking up or having sex except me. I've kissed boys and had a few crushes, but I haven't even started my period yet. I'm tired of being the weirdo. My brother is always with his girlfriend now, and my sisters are pretty much out of the house, so there isn't anyone at home to tell me how to be with boys. I'm scared every day that Mom and Dad will split up, since they're constantly angry at each other. It's like we're all playing roles at home—I'm playing the good girl with a clean room, Mom is the dedicated manager and victim of a bad marriage, and Dad is the suave mystery man who would do anything for his family. On the days Mom and I take the train into the city, I transform between point A and point B. When Mom and I exit the train and ascend into the city streets, it's like different versions of us come alive. We're stronger, tougher, just to endure the day. It's a version of us that the rest of our family doesn't even know.

I'm still waiting for my big break, even after working with Woody Allen and Hal Hartley. I'm working all the time, but not like Scarlett, who is doing huge movies and who everybody knows is destined to become a *real* actor. When I told Mom about Scarlett, she said we sounded like "oil and water," two things that don't mix. Somehow, though, over the last few months, I've been hanging out with Scarlett, Linda, and Harper during class time and sitting with them at lunch. I'm not going to city parties with them and the ninth graders, but we're friends. Or close to friends. There's something about Scarlett that makes me feel uneasy and insecure. It's confusing. We're not competing against each other for roles, since I'm a brunette and Scarlett is blond. I can sing, and she can be a tough indie chick.

I say bye to Mom at the door to school, lugging my backpack along. I still keep my sticker collection inside it, even though I know I'm getting too old to collect puffy penguins and scratch-and-sniff pineapples. I still love picking stickers out and looking through them, even if it's a little babyish. It's better than being addicted to drugs or cigarettes, right? They're not hurting anyone, plus they make me happy. I've spent about two years collecting these stickers, and I can flip through them and remember roles I've landed and auditions that went well. I can feel proud of my accomplishments, since I've gotten most of these stickers after booking something and spending that money at Lee's Art Shop on Fifty-Seventh. Mom collects Playbills and casting notices to commemorate big moments. I don't know if Linda, Harper, or Scarlett collect anything. I've never once been to their homes, just like they've never been to mine. But I want that to change. I haven't told them yet, but I want to invite them to Milford for an eighth-grade graduation sleepover.

After homeroom and English class, we walk to the cafeteria for lunch. Scarlett is out on an audition, so I sit with Linda and Harper, bursting to tell them about the sleepover. I'm inviting our friend Bianca too. I want to wait until all five of us are together, but I'm too excited—or too nervous—to hold it in.

"Come to my house for a sleepover next month!"

My voice sounds a little too chirpy, too eager. For a second, I'm terrified they'll burst out laughing or mumble excuses about why they can't make it. Or both.

"Cool!" Harper says. "When?! I've never been to Milford."

"April? Right before graduation," I say, eyeing Linda.

"I'd love to get out of the city for a night," says Bianca.

"Me too," Linda joins in. "My mom has been *so lame.* I could use a break. Is Scarlett coming?"

"Yeah, of course." I shrug, hoping that Linda doesn't just want to come because Scarlett might come. "I'll ask her when she's back. It'll be fun. Or . . . cool? It'll be cool." I stop myself before saying something completely *un*cool, like telling them my dad will make us pasta and sing Frank Sinatra songs. These girls go to city parties. I doubt eating my dad's linguini will sound badass to them.

"I'm there. I'll tell my mom," says Harper. She's still the girl I'm closest to, even though she doesn't laugh as hard at my jokes anymore.

After lunch, I head back to class, feeling like I'm floating up the stairwell. I haven't had a big party at home since the *Follies*, when the whole cast and crew came over for my birthday. Then I was just a little kid, and now I'm almost fourteen. We'll just hang out and do whatever they do at their city parties, except for the drugs and sex, I guess. Mom is excited for me to have PCS kids at the house, and Dad offered to make us all dinner. My brother will probably be hiding out in his room, so we'll be able to do whatever we want, like run around our big drafty house, watch movies, eat pizza. It's going to be so awes—

And then I see it.

All over the backs of chairs in my homeroom are stickers. My sticker book is open on the floor, and puffy penguins, scratch-and-sniff pineapples, beach balls, rainbows, cats, little hamburgers, bumblebees, and more are all torn out of my book and stuck to the furniture. I am alone in this room. Everything feels like slow-motion, and I can't move. All I can do is let out a guttural SCREAM. And everything goes black.

Mom rushes into the principal's office. I have no idea how much time has passed. I just remember screaming with rage, my heart broken. Over a bunch of stickers. But they're *my* stickers. Maybe it sounds dumb or childish, but I picked every single one of them. Each one reminded me of something good that happened, some accomplishment or "win," as Mom says. And now? Now they just mean nothing. They are gone.

"What's going on?" Mom asks, and I'm not sure if she's talking to me or the principal.

"Well, Mrs. Romano—"

"Kids in this school ripped my daughter's sticker collection up and stuck it all over the chairs! You need to find them and punish them." Mom looks pissed. "Christy pays her own tuition and comes here every day from Connecticut. She doesn't deserve this. The kids who did this need to apologize."

"I understand, but . . ."

"No buts," Mom says. "It's bullying, end of story. They need to apologize at the very least. Christy, do you know who did this?"

"Maybe? I think maybe some older kids?"

I try not to cry, but it doesn't work. I'm too hurt. Mom stands up for me, instead of calling my stickers immature or brushing this off. I *know* I can be a dork. I know I can annoy the other kids by being immature or trying too hard to be friendly or make everyone like me. But right now? Right now, I *hate* those ninth graders. I don't feel like being compliant or meek. I feel furious. I want to rip *their* notebooks to shreds, to scream in their faces, to get a role so huge and so prestigious that they are boiling with jealousy.

"You're right, Mrs. Romano," says the principal. "Christy, I am so sorry this happened to you, and we'll make sure the kids who did this apologize and never do anything like this again."

The principal looks worried. Last time I was in her office officially, it was years ago, when she asked if everything was okay at home. Mom could be pretty physical with me, and I think someone around campus saw something; maybe she yelled at me on the sidewalk or tugged at me too hard. She still gets randomly mad at me sometimes, but as I'm getting older, she doesn't fight with me as much.

I bite my lip hard to keep the tears at bay.

"Okay. Thank you." I nod, standing up to leave with Mom. And the minute I stand up, I know my graduation party in Milford will be a goodbye party. I'm done with PCS. Done with the "cool" city kids who watched the movie *Kids* too many times and who think they're so tough, pretending to tag things, pretending to be hard. The rich white kids who smoke pot and play bongos in Union Square Park. The kids who hang out at the deli and smoke without me. The kids who spend hundreds of dollars to look "grunge chic" and who secretly laugh at my preppy, uncool, ill-fitting clothes. The asshole kids who ripped out my stickers as a joke. I'm done with stickers, with cliques, with bullies. I know it wasn't Linda or Harper or Bianca who started Stickergate. I'm pretty sure Scarlett wasn't in on it. So I'll have my party, and then I'll be able to be a "normal" suburban kid again. Whatever that even means. It's got to be better than this.

"Don't you hate when it gets all gloppy and chunky?"

We're sitting in a circle on the floor in my room, and Scarlett is talking about her period. My sisters and mom never talk about this stuff. My stomach gets queasy as she talks. I can't shake this feeling that she is trying to freak me out. I haven't even started my period, so I stay quiet and pretend to understand, nodding vaguely. I still barely have boobs, and I'm *waiting* for my period, but so far, nada. Nothing. Zilch. Another thing she's better at than me, like acting or being cool.

She shifts her weight, and I can see her bare belly exposed. Her bra straps hang out of her spaghetti-strap tee. She gets into details that make me even more nauseous.

"Yeah, it's nasty." Harper snickers. Linda and Bianca laugh and shrug. I don't say what I want to say, which is *Don't tampons break your hymen and make you not a virgin anymore?* At least, that's the rumor my sisters passed down to me from when they were in Catholic school. I figure it's best to keep my mouth shut about that one, though. I don't want to think I'm lame. I want them to keep liking me.

Dad is watching a movie, and Mom told me she just wants us to have fun, so we're pretty much on our own for the night. As strict as Mom can be about me staying safe in the city or not going into casting rooms alone with men, she's lenient at home. We stole some of my siblings' cigarettes and smoked them out back. I'm pretty sure the girls got into the liquor cabinet too while I was getting us snacks, but I don't say anything. I'm trying not to be lame, which is why I just nod along again when they start talking about sex.

We put a VHS from Blockbuster on in the living room and eat pizza. Mom is out of earshot, so we can gossip and talk about anything we want.

"Art is hot, but I wouldn't blow him or anything . . ." Linda says.

"I think Lee had sex with Penelope at Sandra's party last week," Harper adds. "They walked out of one of the rooms together and looked all sweaty."

"Gross," I say, having no clue how to have a conversation about sex. Is it gross? Or is it cool? Or . . .

"Where's your brother?" Scarlett asks, totally out of the blue.

Why she wants to know where my brother is, I have no idea. Or I have an idea, and I don't like it one bit.

"He's probably locked in his room upstairs. He just watches movies all night and never comes out."

Scarlett gets up and heads to his bedroom door.

"What're you doing?" whispers Linda, giggling. My eyes widen in disbelief.

Scarlett walks into the hallway, and everyone laughs, listening as she knocks on his door. I'm not laughing, though. What if he answers? What if she goes in there and has sex with him while our mom is in her room, watching the nightly news?

Knock, knock, knock . . .

"Hey there . . ."

My heart clenches, waiting to hear if my brother answers, and thankfully he does not. As usual. I imagine him in his bed, covers pulled up, ignoring the eighth-grade girl banging on his door. My brother isn't perfect, but he *does* love his girlfriend. She would kill him if she knew he hooked up with another girl. After a few more knocks, Scarlett walks back into the room and collapses on the floor, pretending to feel defeated. I know it's just a game, just drama. I go along with it because I still want this to be the *perfect* sleepover. I want them to talk about it at PCS long after I'm gone. I want to leave that place not as the overly friendly, way-too-eager girl with the stickers, but as the girl who had a pretty cool sleepover. I want to be someone worth remembering.

Around three in the morning, Linda, Harper, Bianca, and Scarlett go to sleep, one by one. They're all here. With me. I finally let my heavy eyelids close. We may not be friends forever, since I don't expect city kids to take the train to Milford just to drink from my parents' liquor cabinet, but in this moment, I'm happy. Right now, I'm part of this elite group of creative kids. I'll never forget this feeling.

Mom is ranting in the car about Dad and how miserable she feels. We're driving to Abercrombie so I can get new back-to-school clothes before the start of ninth grade. Even though I'll be wearing a uniform when I start St. Joseph's in a couple weeks, all I want to wear is head-to-toe Abercrombie everywhere else. It's all anyone my age wears in Connecticut. I'm changing schools because I'm over PCS, and I just want to be in a regular school with normal kids.

"I bet your father cheats on me," says Mom. "I would not be surprised if he had a mistress right in our town. I know that your father doesn't love me anymore. I wouldn't be surprised if he serves me papers."

Mom swerves to avoid hitting a car in the next lane. Whenever she's angry, she drives like a maniac, so I grip the door handle, as if that will save me in case she goes flying off a bridge at seventy-five miles an hour. Mom always tells me too much. It's been this way for years now, when she started to tell me all sorts of things about Dad or their marriage or gossip about other adults when we were on the road. I used to think it was because we're so close or I'm so mature. I used to just listen when Mom ranted about Dad and other women, but not anymore. She's never going to do anything about her pain, so why should I listen or feel bad for her?

"Then leave him, Mom."

"What?"

"Why don't you leave him? People do it all the time. It can't be that hard."

Mom huffs and waves her hand like she's swatting away a fly. "It's not that easy. Your siblings are in college, and he'd stop paying for it. I'd lose the house, and I wouldn't give him that satisfaction."

Mom hits the gas, and the car lurches ahead as we turn into the mall parking lot.

I'm flooded with memories of my parents fighting at night while I'm rearranging my room and listening to rap battles on Hot 97. Most of my home life is defined by their yelling and screaming. I don't ever want to be that miserable in a relationship.

"If it's so bad, then leave! I don't understand why you don't. It's been years! You are so unhappy."

"Life isn't like a movie, Christy. It doesn't work that way all the time." She exhales and puts the car in park.

I spent so much of my childhood terrified that my parents would get divorced, and now I'm begging my mom to leave. I guess I'm just tired of hearing her complain about him after all these years. If you're so unhappy, why stay? She's weak. I can't believe I ever looked up to her. I will never ever let a guy treat me that way. And if he does, I'll walk away.

At the store, one of the cute girls in a bright white hoodie and pink lip gloss gives us a friends-and-family discount. My family loves a discount and can't help but try to work any system they can. I've made enough money doing commercials and voice-overs that I don't feel guilty about doing a little shopping. I also don't have to endure my father's passive-aggressive inquisition: "That looks nice; is that new?" It feels good to be better at providing for myself than he's been.

A new high school means a chance to be someone different. I don't have to be the annoying sticker girl like I was at PCS. I've been hanging out with Blair, a newish friend who's two years older than me and whose dad sometimes works with mine. She takes me everywhere, and I meet her high school friends. The Orange Firemen's Carnival, the movie theater at the mall, and Amity High School house parties, which is basically the coolest high school in southern Connecticut. She's like a big sister. Blair drives me all over town, and she's so cool that it doesn't even bother me that she smokes pot. I pretended to try it once, but I didn't inhale. When Blair smoked cigarettes, I pretended to do that too, and I made a joke about being in an anti-smoking PSA ad I was in where I said, "I don't smoke, because sometimes it's what you don't do that makes you who you are." Pretty lame, but it got a laugh from her and the other Abercrombie-clad high school kids at one of the parties she took me to.

I booked it. My first actual Broadway show. Well, it's not physically *on* Broadway, since it's at Lincoln Center, but it's technically listed as Broadway within the industry and for the Tony Awards. The musical is *Parade*, and Jason Robert Brown wrote the play and the music, and my agent Ann Lauren calls him "the next big thing. The next Sondheim." *Parade* is really a huge deal, though, because of legendary producer and director Hal Prince, who has won a million Tony Awards. I auditioned for Hal a few years ago for a part in *Whistle Down the Wind*, but I'd been "too small and too young." Andrew Lloyd Webber had been in the room and audibly whispered through my audition. I had been equally devastated and pissed. Not this time, though!

I left Spanish class early for the audition, and I nailed it. It was one of those auditions where I just was "on." I sang "Since I Don't Have You" from *Grease*, and I practiced so much with my voice coach, Bob Marks, that Mom says that's why I must have killed it. In fact, the audition room erupted in cheers after I sang. I was so excited and felt so confident. It had to have been the best audition I'd ever given.

In *Parade*, I'm playing a historically accurate Mary Phagan. She was a thirteen-year-old factory worker from Marietta, Georgia, who was raped and murdered in 1913. The main character, Leo Frank, is a Jewish man who is wrongly accused of the crime and then hung by a Southern vigilante lynch mob. It's not a huge part, and I just appear at the beginning and the end of the show, but it's an important part. Without Mary and the convention of humanizing her essence in my songs and small scenes, there's no story to connect to. It was my job to make the audience love me every night.

I don't love missing class, but because my role is small, I have plenty of time to do homework during rehearsals or offstage. Mom found us an apartment in Midtown near the theater so we can sleep there on weekends if we need to. It's a temporary sublet with this out-of-work vegan actress named Hannah, who sleeps on a box spring mattress on the living room floor while Mom and I stay in the tiny bedroom on two twin mattresses. I hate it, since Hannah and her boyfriend stay in the living room and I'm pretty sure I've heard them having sex, but it's a place to sleep, I guess. Commuting is not an option. I'm trying not to complain and to be a good teammate for Mom, especially since this is a huge opportunity. Mom even hired a personal publicist to help "generate buzz" about my performance leading up to the premiere. When she told me, it made me feel like she really, truly does care.

I'm usually pretty confident about my voice, but after that amazing audition, I'm suddenly worried my singing isn't right for the part. I'm not admitting that to anyone in case it puts doubts in *their* heads and they replace me when we're still in rehearsals, but it's making me really anxious.

One extremely cool thing is rushing through Grand Central and seeing big posters for *Parade* on the wall or riding the subway and seeing them there too. I'm not on the posters since Mary isn't a major role, but to be part of it is a huge thrill. Mom loves seeing the posters. She brags to everyone she sees about it. She snags so many Playbills.

"You'll thank me one day when you write your book about your life!" she says when I ask her why she keeps them all.

She's so pushy sometimes, but I've learned to just go with the flow by now. I can tell people think she's a "stage mom," even though she says she's the opposite. She acts like she's a relaxed, uninvolved mom who cares but doesn't go over the top, but I'm not so sure about that. I'm getting older, so I'm way more aware of how other people see the way she treats me. She's not aggressive anymore, because by now, she doesn't have to be. I already do what she wants when she wants me to. We're one brain in this way. We both think this show will open bigger doors for me. Or at least I try to think that way.

"Say that to the journalists when they interview you about the show, Christy," she tells me. "Say it's a 'springboard.'"

"Christy, Hal wants to see you," the stage manager calls to me in my shared dressing room at Lincoln Center.

It's one day before opening night, and this is the first time Hal, the director, has ever asked me to his office. My heart clenches. I'm convinced he's about to fire me because my voice isn't strong enough. My not-technically-on-Broadway Broadway debut is about to get cut short because I can't hit the high notes. Because I'm a belter.

I follow the stage manager back to Hal's office, where he sits buried behind piles of scripts and books. Everyone is nervous before an opening night, especially with this play, which is supposed to be a "hot ticket" of the season. We're opening right before Christmas, so there's a lot of pressure. Hal puts down the papers he's marking up and leans forward on his elbows. He has a copy of an article with my name on it in front of him. My personal publicist was able to get me an interview with *Playbill* magazine, which had Mom freaking out with excitement. I was excited too, but I wasn't telling all our neighbors and the checkers at the grocery store like she was.

"Come in, Christy. Sit."

He motions for me to sit in the wooden chair facing him, so I do. I try to look chipper and ready. Agreeable. Even though my insides are melting from fear.

"Hi, Hal!" I shuffle my feet and take a deep breath. The air in the room is thin. I put on my biggest people-pleasing face in hopes he likes me so much at that instant that I don't get fired. "Are you excited for opening night?" I ask.

"Not sure if 'excited' is the right word, but yes. I think we're ready. You've all been working hard the last few months." He takes off his glasses and rubs his face. I can tell he's stressed because his face is redder than usual. He puts his glasses back on and looks right at me.

Here it comes. The "I hate to tell you this, but we're cutting you and giving the Mary role to your understudy" part. She is from the South and has a pretty, high, operatic voice. Here's the part when my whole career falls apart. When Mom and everyone at St. Joe's and PCS will find out I can't sing. That I'm a fraud.

"Christy, I wanted to talk to you about the *Playbill* interview you did and some of the other publicity."

"Oh. Okay?"

"Don't gild the lily, Christy."

I've heard the phrase before, but I'm so dizzy from fear, I can't remember what it means or understand why Hal is saying it to me here, now. He studies the confused look on my face and adds, "We have our own publicity team, and none of the other cast members have their own personal publicist. So just do the work. Focus on the work and not the fluff. Sound good?"

"Sounds good. I'm so sorry, Hal."

"It's okay, kid. I'm sure it wasn't your idea anyway. See you at tech."

I am mortified, but at least I still have my job. In moments like this, when I'm terrified of losing a job, I realize how much I need and want to succeed in this career. There are five hundred girls who would kill to be in this position, so I better not screw it up.

Balancing rehearsals plus school and homework and commuting has been brutal, but I've been doing this since I was six, so in a way, I guess I'm programmed for it. I love my two solos, "The Picture Show" and "The Trial Song," even though I'm still nervous about my voice. I remember once seeing the actress Carolee Carmello, who plays the female lead, in the wings, about to blow the house down with a solo, and I thought to myself, *I want to be just like her.* When the *Playbill* journalist asked about my "special skills," I read straight from the résumé Mom held in front of me: jazz dancing, tap, ballet, lyrical dance, singing, swimming, gymnastics, bike riding, tennis, basketball, softball, soccer, ice skating, Rollerblading, monologues, interviewer, host. I told her I wanted to study opera at Juilliard. I didn't mention that I had studied for the program but got waitlisted last year. Emmy Rossum made it into one of the spots instead of me. Now I feel ridiculous, like I was out there bragging while the rest of the cast was just doing the work. Sometimes Mom has great ideas, and sometimes I need to listen to my own instincts for a change. But how do I even tell her that when I know she's doing all this for me? She knows best, right? I believed that with all my heart when I was younger, but now sometimes I have doubts. I don't tell that to Mom, though.

The cast and crew worked so hard to prepare for *Parade*. We had amazing producers, and we had Hal and Jason, but even that doesn't guarantee anything in this business. We premiered on December 17, and by February, we were canceled.

Mom tries to reassure me after the play ends. She tells me that there are more opportunities ahead, that it wasn't my fault, that I need to keep the faith.

Two Saturday mornings after the last show, when I walk downstairs for breakfast, she looks more chipper than usual.

"Christy, we're going to LA for spring break. I booked tickets."

I'm not jumping up and down when Mom says this, because I know we're not going for Disneyland or the beach. We're going for pilot season.

"We'll stay at the Oakwood while you audition. We stayed there before, remember?"

The Oakwood. How could I forget those apartments, where the weird neighbor with the cute puppy flashed me? The place all kid actors from out of town stay when they're trying to book THE JOB. The one that'll change their lives, and their parents' lives, forever.

"But I thought I could hang out here, with my friends," I say, already knowing this isn't an option.

"You have to keep your résumé fresh," Mom says as she gets breakfast ready. "What will it look like coming off a canceled show and then having no work for months on end? It's just a few weeks. You won't even miss much school."

Mom and I are using the severance check I got from *Parade* to pay for our LA trip. My agent Ann has already booked ten auditions for pilots. Pilot season is every spring for three months like clockwork, and it's a crazy rush of auditions and callbacks, all crammed into a few weeks in Studio City. If you're lucky, you get cast and the pilot gets picked up. If you're *really* lucky, you'll get cast in something that goes on to be really big, like *Friends* or *Felicity.* Maybe I'm finished with theater anyway. Maybe the grind of New York isn't what I'm meant to do.

"One of the pilots is a new Disney show!" Mom yells from the kitchen. All this time, I thought she wanted me to be a serious actress in indie films, saying lines like "I'll suck your cock." Now it's Disney? Yuck. This is child's play. I just did a play about race and antisemitism on Broadway.

"Whatever," I yell back. I'm bummed about leaving my friends for spring break, but the chances of me getting a pilot that gets picked up are pretty slim. That's just how this stupid business is. No matter how much I want to stay home, I start packing my suitcase for California.

"I despise driving in this city!"

Mom glances over at the huge Thomas Guide between us, trying to figure out where we are on the map as she careens through traffic. *BEEP!* I duck my head a little, embarrassed by her maniac driving on the 405. It's not like she's the only crazy driver in Los Angeles, but she's an East Coast–crazy driver—way more attitude and profanity. She has zero patience and takes her anger out on me.

In every audition here, I feel like the only brown-eyed, brown-haired New York girl in a sea of blue-eyed blonds. Mom says it makes me stand out "in a good way." One of the casting agents told Mom that she loves East Coast actors because they're classically trained and more "disciplined" than LA kids, who "have chips on their shoulders and are too glossy." New York kids learn their lines and understand hard work, and we never whine. I don't know if "never" is true, but it does make me feel confident knowing this while I sit in packed hallways, waiting for auditions. That I'm disciplined. That I do the work. That most of these girls are brats.

Mom keeps yelling at her Thomas Guide as she drives up Barham, a road near Burbank and Universal Studios. We're heading to my last audition, a network test for a show called *Spivey's Kid Brother*, before we fly home. There's nowhere to park. Even though Mom makes sure we are always early to everything, it always feels like we're running late, always in a rush. All her crazy energy doesn't help me feel relaxed when I head into auditions, that's for sure.

"Finally, a parking spot!" Mom barrels into the spot and slams on the breaks. Sometimes I think she'd rather kill us both than be late to an audition.

"Jeez, Mom. Do you have to slam the brakes so hard?" She annoys me so much these days.

"Get out! Let's go!"

I follow her out of the car and into an intimidating white stucco building with green detailing and Mickey Mouse on the logo. We splurged on a navy Ralph Lauren blazer-and-skirt set with the huge gold crest sewn onto the front, plus a red knit turtleneck. It's something Mom and I thought the character, Ren, would wear. She's a debater and the class president, so Mom and I went full preppy. We're from Connecticut—we can dress preppy in our sleep. I'm nervous because Ren makes so many speeches, so I pray I don't forget my lines in front of the network execs. I stayed up half the night memorizing them in my crappy Oakwood bed that a million other kids just like me probably memorized lines in. I recited them as I fell asleep. I feel nervous, even though after *Parade*, I swore I was done with acting, at least for a little bit. But there's that strange thing again, the pull that I need to get the role, nail the audition. The feeling I need to deliver, to impress. To succeed. To please. If I don't, I'm scared I'll be left standing at the edge of a cliff, with nowhere to go but down.

Inside the room, I see a casting agent named Joey Paul Jensen, who is tiny and blond and bubbly. She looks genuinely happy to see me. The creator of the show, Matt Dearborn, is there, plus several Disney execs in suits. One man with dark hair and glasses seems to be in charge. This time, I'm doing a chemistry test with this kid, Shia, who's already been cast as the main character, Louis Stevens, Ren's younger brother. The minute I see Shia, he reminds me a little of the "punk" PCS kids, Macaulay and Kieran. His pants are baggy and his hair is a mess, and I can tell the second I meet him that we're probably not going to get along. The other kid they sent home after he almost got the Louis part was a New York friend, Chris Marquette, who had been in Broadway Kids with me. I like him. I wish he were the one doing the chemistry read. He's a pro.

"Yo, what up?" Shia says as I get ready to do the scene.

"Hi!"

I smile and try to look as upbeat as possible in front of the audience of execs gawking at us in this corporate boardroom overlooking the mountains. This whole situation feels weird. LA is weird in general. Mom reminded me eight thousand times in the car that this was Disney, so I needed to be peppy. Ren talks a mile a minute, so I channel all the crazy energy I have, which, at this moment, with all my nerves, is not tough to tap into.

We do the scene and get laughs exactly when we're supposed to.

"Funny, guys. Go again. This time, have fun with it," Matt says.

Shia seemed to forget his lines so he made up some extra ones, which I had to work around. I hide my frustration like a "pro," and we do the scene *again*. He flubs it *again*, and the producers all laugh and clap at his offbeat antics. I try to make it fresh each time, to keep my energy level up, and to stay focused and on book. They can't know that I'm frustrated or that I think this kid is totally annoying. His hair is literally two clashing colors. We couldn't be more different. Then I get it. The execs seem to think that it's funny that he frustrates me. It's exactly what they're looking for.

Maybe it was the preppy clothing, or maybe it's because I'm like Ren in some ways. Maybe the fact that Shia and I had some tension worked in my favor, since it made the brother-sister bond seem real. Most siblings annoy one another, right? I know I annoy my older siblings, even though I try not to.

My agent calls us to tell us the news as soon as we get home to Milford.

"Matt said he knew the minute you walked into the room wearing that crazy blazer that you were the girl," she tells me and Mom as we listen in on the call. I don't think the blazer was that crazy. I think I looked nice. In Connecticut it wouldn't be so "crazy."

After I book the show, I have a *Law & Order* audition over the summer. While we wait in the hallway, I tell an old friend, Jess DeCicco, about the pilot. She looks worried and says, "Are you sure you really wanna do *Disney*? Once you do Disney, you're . . . a Disney kid."

Maybe she has a point. It's not Hal Hartley or an indie, but the idea of real money, Disney money, makes me *and* my family happy. I don't care what the job is; I'll make the best of it.

Things happen in a whirlwind. Disney picks the show up, which means Mom and I are moving to Los Angeles. Actually moving. Also, *Parade* gets nine Tony nominations. NINE! All for a show that barely lasted three months. I feel proud, but also a little left out. I know I won't be invited to perform at the awards ceremony. I know I was a minor part. It hurts, but Mom reminds me that I am onto "bigger and better things." She also says we have to open a Coogan Account, which is mandatory in California for actors under eighteen. It makes sure that 15 percent of my earnings go into a secure account that I can access on my eighteenth birthday, which sounds good to me, since I have never seen the money I've made.

"You can go, but you're taking the dogs," Dad says when Mom tells him about *Even Stevens*. They changed the original name of the pilot because it "tested better." Dad says he's been "Mr. Mom" enough over the years, and this time he isn't dealing with the animals.

"Fine," Mom says. And that's that.

~

I wish I could have more time with Steve, my boyfriend. He goes to Derby High and is the star quarterback. We met through mutual friends. Of course, just when I meet someone and fall madly in love, I have to leave for Los Angeles.

Mom and I pack up the minivan with piles of suitcases and the two dogs. I tearfully say goodbye to Carrie and Sybil, my friends from the neighborhood, making them promise to visit. They're excited for me, but I can't help but feel like everything is about to change. Like I'll never see them again. Before we say goodbye, I have my sixteenth birthday at the Club Vandome and make out with Steve the whole time. We even drink some vodka and OJ out of water bottles.

"I want to lose my virginity with you," Steve says before I leave. We're parked outside my house after a party. We've been making out, and he decides to take a breathless stand. "I'm going to college in the fall, and I don't want to start college as a virgin." I grimace. It isn't the most romantic thing I've ever heard. He could have at least acted like Freddie Prinze Jr. in *She's All That* or Paul Rudd in *Clueless*. Why are guys in real life so much lamer than the ones in movies? Maybe Steve watched *American Pie* too many times. As much as I think I love Steve, I know I'm not ready. Plus I'm about to star in a Disney show. There's a voice inside me that stands firm: *You are too young.*

"I can't, Steve. Come visit me in California?"

In my mind, he will. He'll come visit, and maybe we'll have sex, even though I'd be scared. I've just barely gotten brave enough to use tampons, so actual sex is still terrifying. Maybe Steve will respect me for holding back. Maybe it will make him want me more.

"Christy, stop staring at your phone!"

Mom drives the gold minivan west, away from Connecticut and New York and my friends. I check my silver Nokia window for the gazillionth time, hoping that maybe Steve sent something, anything. Ever since my birthday, he's been ignoring me. He's vanished. And I thought he loved me.

"You'll have plenty to do in California," Mom says as one of the dogs jumps into her lap. "You won't even remember that boy in two weeks' time. This is our new life, Christy." At least she seems happy.

The Pacific Ocean shimmers across the street in the distance, and I know I should be thrilled. I know I should feel like the luckiest girl in the world. I did it. After all these years, I booked a pilot with real money and opportunity. I'm in Los Angeles, by the ocean, with perfect weather and a pool and a hot tub, away from my crazy family. Just Mom and me.

A phone rings, and my heart thrums as I look down to check.

"It's your agent," Mom says. It's her phone, not mine. Not Steve. It's like the stupid phone is taunting me. Mom talks to my agent, something about logistics, and I stare out at the ocean, feeling anything but thrilled. I don't know if it's Steve I'm missing or something else. I put my phone away. Maybe Mom's right. Maybe I'm the luckiest girl in the world, and I should be thankful to be here. I can't help but feel totally alone, though. I wait for the ocean to calm me. I just did a cross-country trip with my crazy stage mom and two anxious dogs. I should be happy to be starting a huge job, but I feel totally trapped.

Dear Girls,

Do you know what a try-hard is? Don't worry, I'll define it for you. It's basically a person who goes into something (a game, a part, a conversation) with a little too much enthusiasm and excitement. They are trying too hard *to be liked. The etymology of the word apparently dates back to between 1980 and 1985. I was born in 1984 and clearly got the memo.*

Do you know how much compassion these people deserve? I do. Because I might as well be Exhibit A next to this term in the dictionary.

Try-hards are some of the most important people in the world, in my opinion. They must be of use or they will die. They must put out maximum effort or they will not survive the night. Their brains will take them down through hellish thought spirals until they manage to pass out from anxiety and fear of failure. No stakes are more intense than those of a try-hard. Or at least that's how it feels.

What people don't see, what they miss when they're busy rolling their eyes, is what's happening on the inside. Try-hards have vast, extraordinary inner worlds. They are constantly rehearsing, advocating, strategizing, playing out every scenario in their minds with a precision and passion that would exhaust most people. All that energy that looks like desperation from the outside? It's a whole universe in there.

As you can see, I put up with a lot of crap from people everywhere I went in the name of acceptance. I was ostracized because I cared too much, which came off as annoying, weak, needy. In a pecking order, I would have been killed by the other chicks because you can smell a try-hard a mile away even in nature.

Try-hards are committed to success at almost all costs. They are tenacious, hard chargers, and full of heart. The flip side of a try-hard is someone who is either apathetic and doesn't care, or someone who is confident enough not to feel the desperate need to try so hard.

Give a try-hard the right ally and watch what happens. They become unbeatable. They are high-value, deeply loyal people and they will outwork everyone in the room. In a team, they are an asset unlike any other, because they cannot phone it in. It's not in their DNA.

Your father is my opposite in handling conflict, which I find extremely attractive. When he transferred to a new school as a kid, some preppy jerk took one look at his discounted school outfit and decided he was an easy target. A few punches later, your dad got suspended for settling that score in the moment (so we are not telling you to throw punches). He never flinches. He never cared what others thought in high school, which made him the most interesting guy in the room. Over the years, we've both learned to balance one another and inspire growth in either direction, but I believe you are born with these traits.

If you find yourself desperate to please, try to harness that try-hard energy into good. Meaning, do it for yourself, because it empowers you. Not because you think it'll make other people approve of you. Always try hard, but know deep down that no matter what, you are enough.

6

The Fame Game

2000–2002

Ages 16 to 18

The green building at 3800 Alameda in Burbank is all the way across the city from Marina del Rey, where Mom and I live. The building is mainly for meetings or press or media training, so we don't go there that often. But whenever we do, it just reminds me that we're on the outskirts of Hollywood, not in it.

I feel that nervous and excited combination about starting the show and living across the country. Mom says it's a huge opportunity, that this show is a big step for Disney and for me, since it's one of the first single-camera comedy shows for them, and it seems like they're all in on it.

Before we moved, Disney cleared me to get braces before we started shooting because, as the executives said, "normal" girls have braces. I'm not used to acting with braces on, so I'll just have to figure out how to speak without lisping or spitting or looking weird. All these years, I've wanted to be a "normal" girl, and now here I am. Playing one on TV.

"Hey, Christy!"

Donna Pescow gives me a big hug before we sit down at the table to read through the script. She plays my mom, Eileen Stevens, a character who is a quirky but strong feminist California state senator. Donna has fiery red hair and was famous for being in *Saturday Night Fever* and her own show, *Angie*, in the 1970s. I felt close to her from the first moment I met her because she's an East Coast Italian. Mom likes her too. I can tell because she doesn't even gossip about Donna, and Mom gossips about most people or finds something not to like about them, unless they can be useful to us.

I say hi to Donna and to Shia, who walks in and practically falls into a chair. He's wearing slouchy, baggy pants, and his hair looks like he hasn't brushed it in, like, eight years.

Shia's character, Louis Stevens, is Ren's annoying little brother who wants to be a real-life comedian. The character has a poster of Kramer from *Seinfeld* on his wall, so he's like a mini Kramer, zany and all over the place. Louis's bedroom is a total mess, and Ren's is perfect, with everything in its place, the bed made, and no clothes on the floor. An older guy, Nick, plays the eldest brother, Donnie, who is like an athletic it boy. Tom Virtue plays our lovable and silly dad. He's, like, the perfect white everyman with nonregional diction. Whenever I speak around any of these actors, I can hear my East Coast accent. I need to work that out of myself now that I'm in California.

"What up?" Shia says, giving me a little nod. He looks like he rolled out of bed and just tumbled into the executive building and up the elevator to the thirty-second floor.

"Hey."

I have no idea what to say to him. We're two totally opposite people.

What he doesn't have in polish, he makes up for in confidence. I can spot this kind of confidence from a mile away, ever since Scarlett invaded my social life. Shia walks into every room with the urgency of someone who everyone is eagerly anticipating, and it works. Even though he's a middle school boy whose voice hasn't even changed, a room of Hollywood executives get giddy whenever he bursts in. He's like a slacker clown saying, *Ta-da! Let the fun begin, I'm here!* But in my opinion, everyone gets dumber when they're around him.

"Okay, people! Let's get to it," says Mick Frost, one of the top Disney executives who oversees the show. Mom told me to make a good impression on him, since once you're in one Disney show, you might get cast in others if the executives and producers like you. I went shopping at Forever 21 to get clothes for the read-through, since it's one of the first times we're all together before we start shooting. Tan pants, a short-sleeve black-and-brown turtleneck, and my black Steve Madden loafers. I wanted to look mature but still like a kid, like Ren would dress. We take our seats, and my heart starts racing, since I'm worried my braces will trip me up or I'll sound like the only member of this California family that has an East Coast Italian accent.

The read-through seems to go okay, and I think I'm nailing Ren's comedic timing. Shia and I banter back and forth and act like a brother and sister who find each other incredibly annoying. It's not really acting, since I *do* find him incredibly annoying. Instead of laughing at my delivery, though, Mick stares at me for what feels like ten minutes while the rest of the cast and executives look on.

"Christy, you know what we call wearing black and brown together here in LA?"

"Um, no?" I say nervously. I'm smiling, but only to hide my terror.

"A fashion faux pas."

I force myself to laugh along with a few other people in the room. I have no clue if he's trying to just be funny, or if this means I'm on the verge of getting fired from the show. It feels like the room is suspended in space, airless, claustrophobic. This cannot be happening. I can feel tears welling up, and my face is suddenly hot. I do not want to cry in this room, in front of this man or any of these people. I take a breath, hoping the tears will retreat. I look over at Donna, my pretend mom, and she gives me a smile so kind and reassuring, I'm able to hold it together.

"Well, I guess I have a lot to learn, then," I say to Mick, trying to lighten the mood, hoping to just get back to reading the script.

"I'm just messing with you, Christy," he says. "Let's get to work!"

I'm mortified, but I just "get to work" like he asks. Why would a grown man say something like that to a kid? I feel a million miles from home. An invisible tape starts playing in my head, telling me I'm not good enough, not pretty enough, my clothes are all wrong. I try to shut it out, but it just echoes louder.

"Christy, Shia, come here a sec," says Gabe Rose, who's the head of talent. He's a young guy with bright blue eyes and has the best on-set gossip. Shia and I walk over.

"What's up, man?" says Shia.

Gabe hands us each an envelope.

"Here you go," he says. "Have you ever been to the Wango Tango music festival? Christy, I guess you haven't, since you moved from New York, but here are some tickets on Disney. Have fun, but keep it clean, okay? You'll also get passes to Disney and Universal with your own plaid."

"What's a plaid?" I ask.

"It's a VIP tour guide in the parks. They take you around, keep fans from mobbing you, take you around back so you never stand in line. They wear little plaid vests, so . . . a plaid."

"Oh, cool. Thanks, Gabe!" I say, taking my envelope. I've never been to a concert before, unless a Broadway show tunes performance counts.

"Thanks, dude," Shia says. "Cool."

I've gotten memorabilia and show jackets and things, but never free concert tickets, and never anything like a plaid. Maybe I'm not getting kicked off the show. Maybe I'm actually going to be famous. Not poster-on-a-subway famous like *Parade*, but like *actual* fame. Maybe this is it. Maybe this is finally my time.

The studio where we shoot *Even Stevens* is on Beethoven, off Lincoln Boulevard, in Marina del Rey, right across from Loyola Marymount University and across the city from Hollywood. I love driving by the college because it's such a beautiful campus and Mom and I have started talking about college, even though I'm still just sixteen. I had my sixteenth birthday on the first day of shooting, so playing a character who's still in middle school is a little weird. I do love Ren, though. I love pretending I have it all together, like cosplaying this normal girl with a perfect suburban life. There's so much structure in her life, so much order, and even if she's getting tomatoes thrown in her face, she always wins in the end. The tomato thing happened, by the way. I was filming a montage where I got to sing opera, and I guess the director told Shia to pelt me with paint-filled tomatoes. It sucked, because when Shia pegged me in the face, my braces cut the inside of my mouth, and it hurt like hell. But Mom's voice inside my head told me to stay professional like always and just finish the scene.

This wasn't an isolated incident. It's like the whole crew is constantly trying to pit us against each other, or pit Ren and Louis against each other, but then it bleeds over into real life. Because I live here now, and this studio is my everyday life. Shia might as well be my little brother, except we rarely interact off-screen. He barely asks about my life, and I don't ask about his. After a few months of dancing around our friction, we now just try to ignore each other. Maybe it makes the sibling rivalry feel real on the show, but in actual, everyday life, it sucks. I try not to care too much, though, and just focus on the work. Mom seems lonely and I feel like she is drinking a lot back at the condo to deal with her loneliness, so I try to stay in my room as much as possible and just study or memorize my lines. I try to avoid any conflict at all, because she sometimes speaks badly about my family and is just sad to be around.

I've started to realize that I'm not supposed to be the one taking care of her. *She's* the mom. I will never ever be like that. I'll never be like Mom. I'll always stay in control. I'm too focused on college to care about partying and boys *that* much. It's so not worth it. No boy is worth losing sight of my goals.

Mandy, the main makeup artist, tells me all the gossip about everyone who's on set. Makeup and hair are the coolest people on a set or backstage, except that asshole Yves from the *Follies*, who tugged on and pulled my hair. Mandy always has my back. She's always telling me to stay away from guys, even the adult PAs I think are cute. She says, "Do not trust ANY of them." Mom says the same thing.

"Guys aren't worth it at this age," Mandy says. "They just want to nut. So just stay away, Christy. Just do your thing, and don't let some dumbass dude get in your way." I cringe and smile at the same time when she uses sexual language so casually. She's like the saucy big sister I always wanted, but some of what she says is embarrassing, even though it's probably true. I know this is Disney and I'm a teenager, but I love that Mandy is so blunt. She's this total feminist and kind of punk chick, and I trust her more than a lot of people I've met in LA. I almost trust her more than Mom. Plus she teaches me everything I need to know about makeup, which Mom could never do. Mom's taste is like a 1980s East Coast housewife. No thanks.

"Hollywood is sexist, Christy," Mom says. "The short, nerdy men get parts no problem, but it's much harder for women. Just remember that. You have to work twice as hard."

Mom is driving me to set, even though I'm about to get my license and can drive just fine. I cannot wait to get it, since that will give me some freedom and some space away from her. When I think about how Shia gets treated compared to how I do, though, she has a point. I feel like he can show up late, disheveled, not knowing his lines, and everyone acts like he's a genius. He'll have bags under his eyes, and he'll improvise lines, which I think throws the rest of the actors off, but they just kiss his ass. Me? I have to come in perfect, like Ren. Page-long speeches memorized, clothes and hair in place, complying with everyone. No panty lines, no zits, no black-and-brown clothes. Just shiny hair and perfect poise.

"I know, Mom," I say as she pulls into the parking lot. "You tell me this all the time. So does Mandy."

"The makeup artist?"

"Yeah."

"Well, she's right. I like her."

Disney recently hired new writers from *Full House* to try to help with the comedy and connect with audiences. The new writers even brought me in to ask what *I* wanted to happen to Ren. I told them she needed more friends and maybe a boyfriend. I told them I wanted to sing. Girls will be connecting with her, so she needs to experience things that normal middle school girls experience, like a first crush, first kiss, friendships. Ren is always trying something new, like pole-vaulting or editing the class paper, and I love it when she tries so hard at something, maybe messes up in a funny way, and then always comes out on top. It's the best kind of fantasy. A girl who has everything work out for her. Even if that's not happening for me in my real life, it's nice to play the part.

I miss my friends in Connecticut, though. Dad calls Mom a lot, and sometimes I'll say hi on speaker. Every once in a while, I'll hear from my siblings, but they're all busy with college and work. It feels like we're not really a family anymore; maybe we never were. The only time I see them is Christmas break or during the rare times they visit us in LA.

We're getting more and more isolated out in LA as the months go on. Mom seems so lonely, and it's worse on the nights she drinks. I feel for her, but I wish she could be stronger. She's made an appointment to find out about getting some plastic surgery. I mean, who is she anymore? I don't know if she's trying to impress Dad or if she's just depressed because she has no friends and keeps to herself and the dogs. She says she wants to "stay youthful" in case she needs to go back to work, whatever that means. I don't like the way she sees herself. She seems weak to me, like she's just lost herself. Our whole condo is full of plastic furniture that looks like it's made from PVC pipes, because she's trying to be frugal, I guess. But then she'll spend money on a huge big-screen TV, and now plastic surgery? I don't get it, and I don't get where the money for this is coming from.

Our condo literally looks like the Polynesian Resort at Disney World, which is pretty ironic. Now that we're finishing filming the first season, I do feel like I've "made it," as they say. I'm almost an adult. I feel like I'm more of an adult than Mom is sometimes. I work full days and still manage to pull good grades at PCS over fax and email. I had to go back to PCS once I started working for Disney because I could do my classes remotely. I'm focused on the show but also on getting into a good college. It's a huge priority for me. I feel like Shia and some of the other actors don't give a shit about school. I feel like our show tutors are completely ineffective, but I do most of my work on my own, so I wouldn't know. Most of the time, he runs around the halls with A. J. and Margo, who play his friends on the show, making up strange rap freestyles and telling goofy jokes. To me, these LA kids are so unserious. They don't know what it's like to commute four hours a day to get a good education or ride a subway with rats, freezing temperatures, and chaos around every darkly lit corner just to get to an audition.

Sometimes I imagine going to Loyola since I drive past it every day, but Mom says I'll go to the best college I get into, not the college I necessarily *want* to go to. I'm going to apply to all the Ivies and see what happens. Wherever I end up, at least I'll get away from Mom. I'll live on my own or with a fun roommate, and I won't have to hear her smacking her food or complaining about her weight or smashing bugs with her hand. It's disgusting. Who smashes ants with their bare hands? She's always making Kinko's calendars and mugs with pictures of the cast and crew on them to give to the Disney executives and producers. She's trying to be wholesome, but it's embarrassing. I'm over having to answer for where I am at all times. She's lonely, so she calls me about every little thing. She scours the casting notices constantly and tells me she doesn't think we should sit around waiting for roles to come my way.

"We have to be proactive, Christy," she always says. "Mick Frost tells all the kids to manage their managers if they aren't doing enough."

Once we go inside to set, Mom starts talking to A. J.'s mom, so I quietly slip into my dressing room to get some time alone before I go to see Mandy. I'm still pretty tired from working and studying, so it takes me a second to realize that I can hear Shia talking to his dad through the open space above our dressing rooms. I'm still not sure why they didn't close that space up. Shia doesn't tell me much about his parents; he just jokes to everyone about them and to me they sound like hippies. They didn't push him into acting, and Shia was the one who wanted a career. He looked in a phone book and found his manager when he was eight or something. He seems desperate for fame, and it's really sad because I wonder if his home life is tough. I think it's a miracle he's even functioning. It's not like my family is anywhere near perfect, though. Maybe it's because we spend so many hours together, but something in me does feel deeply for him, as if we really are related. He still annoys the crap out of me, though.

I'm fixing my hair in the dressing room mirror when I hear it.

"You think you're tough? You're weak. You're not tough enough or strong enough," Shia's dad's gruff, deep voice bellows. I can't tell if they're running lines for something Shia is auditioning for, but that's what it seems like.

"C'mon, Dad." Shia's voice sounds pinched and weak. Like he's terrified, and like this has happened before. Is he *that* good of an actor?

"Well, try harder."

I should leave, but then they'll know I was here. He sounds aggressive, like he might hit Shia. I hear commotion in the dressing room, like his dad is moving toward him.

"I am, Dad. What do you want from me?" His voice is even more desperate, like it's on the verge of tears. I've never heard him scared before. He's just always done these crazy fake shrieks for laughs on set. This isn't that. I am frozen in my dressing room, like I'd get at home when I'd overhear my dad and siblings fighting downstairs in Connecticut.

"What did you say?" More movement.

"Just calm down, okay?"

I've never heard Shia sound vulnerable before, like a kid. Usually, he's bouncing off the walls, acting annoying and crazy, but I feel bad for him. He sounds so small over there on the other side of the thin wall we share. This experience is making me feel like I am in the room with him. I feel as small and helpless as he does.

"Get your shit together," his dad growls. One last movement.

"Okay. I hear you. I hear you."

Whether they're running lines or not, we're probably all just as fucked up as each other. That's why I'm going to go to college to get out of this weird world.

But I can't think about it anymore because we're called to set. Before we start shooting, a Disney exec calls Shia and me over for a huddle.

"Okay, everyone, we have the TCA upfronts coming up. If you haven't been, it's a yearly media event in New York where journalists from outlets all over the world can ask questions, and we'll show clips and teasers of the show, that kind of thing. Since it's our first season, I need you guys on your A game, got it? We'll be setting up press training ASAP."

I know this is our chance to get the media excited about the show before it airs to the public so that we get coverage and hopefully enough of an audience to get us to a second season. I'm told we need three seasons to get to syndication, which is where we will be shown in international markets and can qualify for residuals. I can't make decisions like executives, but I can just enjoy the ride and hit my marks and memorize my lines. I am excited to have an excuse to go back to New York and hopefully see my friends. I'm almost more excited about that than I am about being a lead cast member. I've never forgotten what Hal Prince said to me before *Parade* about not "gilding the lily" by getting my own publicist. I'll never do that again, no matter what Mom says. I just want to do exactly what Disney says, and if I do that, I'm sure they will take care of me.

"What happens during press training?" I ask.

"You'll get a rundown of Disney rules and codes of conduct, things you can and cannot say. Things like that," the executive says.

Oh, great. What if I say the wrong thing? Will I be fired? I don't ask this; I just keep my mouth shut and listen.

"It's such an exciting time for the channel," the Disney executive says. He looks right at me and Shia. "You kids are our big, new stars. So get out there and wow 'em, okay?"

"Sure thing!" I say, as peppy as Ren would have said it. I can feel Shia rolling his eyes as the words come out of my mouth.

We can't say anything "racy." No cussing. No talking negatively about other Disney shows or people, even though the executives sometimes seem to pit the actors against one another by mentioning how well someone else's show is doing or how big their audience is getting. Because of this, Mom is always telling me that Hilary Duff is my competition. She watches how Disney promotes her show versus mine in between commercial breaks. Mom gets so focused on how popular *Lizzie McGuire* is getting and how much the Disney star machine is pushing Hilary to be the next big thing. Now she thinks it'll be good for my career to get to know Hilary.

At TCA, we've been instructed to be upbeat and happy. To "keep it positive." Disney is big on "synergy," playing up how things are happening as they're supposed to and how one good show leads to another, blah blah blah. *Even Stevens*—and the network more generally—is for tweens, kids between nine and twelve (in be-*tween* baby channels and The WB), but Disney is still owned by the Disney family and shareholders, and they want all-American values, wholesome dress codes, and no funny business, so that parents can leave their children in the room with the TV on and not worry about what or who their children are watching. Now Mom is always talking about synergy too and how we will say yes to anything Disney asks me to do to promote the show. "Say yes to everything, and they'll love you for it. Be easy to work with, and they'll put you in more shows and even movies," she always says.

The first day of upfronts is a blur of panels and round tables and one-on-one interviews. Shia and I put on our best "we love each other" act for the press, since we have to "keep it positive." I answer every single question with a smile and talk about how much I love Ren and how great it is working with the whole cast, Shia especially. I talk about how wonderful it is to be part of the Disney family, but all I'm thinking about is hanging out with my friends later. Don't get me wrong. I *am* grateful to be on the show, thrilled to be on TV, to be on the Disney Channel. But I still just want to be a normal high school kid sometimes.

Four hours straight of answering questions about playing Ren, working with Shia, and being a perfect girl, and I'm exhausted. Everyone was telling us we're the "next big Disney stars" and that the show will just keep getting more popular, especially because of the Ren-Louis dynamic. I listened and put on my best "America's sweetheart" smile, acted polite and upbeat, and did all the things they advised us to do in the media training. They told us not to talk about anything personal—or anything outside of the show, really—so I didn't. Shia was funny but off the walls like he always is. Almost all the reporters asked us how we get along and if we fight like Ren and Louis do on-screen, and we did our best to convince them that it's one happy family on camera and off, blah blah blah. It's not that I hate Shia. I just don't *really know* the guy. I'm happy to get a break and hang out with friends my own age and from my hometown.

After the interviews, I meet my friends Carrie and Sybil in the hotel lobby, and Carrie immediately zeroes in on Peter, another actor who's here to promote his own Disney show. I promise I'll introduce her to him later, and we head up to the room to change.

Carrie and Sybil start mixing vodka and cranberry juice from the mini-fridge. Carrie hands me a glass, and I take a small sip. I've seen Mom drinking for so many years, and I just don't want to get like that. Having a drink occasionally is fine, though. Especially since I haven't seen these friends in months.

"Cheers to us!" Sybil says. "The OSBs, the original sexy bitches."

"Let's hit the hotel lounge," Carrie says. "I want to find that Peter guy."

I'm half hoping Peter isn't in the lounge because I just want to hang out with my friends and not have any drama, but there he is, sitting with Shia and some people from his show. Carrie nudges me to introduce her, but before I can get a word out, Peter looks at us and waves us over.

"Hey, Christy," he says. "Who're your friends?"

"I'm Carrie, and this is Sybil. We went to school with Christy before Disney stole her away."

"What's up?" Shia says. We're Disney kids, so it's not like people are underage drinking in the lounge, unless they're sneaking it. Carrie is buzzed from the minibar, though, so she's talking nonstop and flirting with Peter like crazy. Sybil and I are a little buzzed too, and hanging out with them makes me realize how much I've missed them, how much I loved just being a normal high school kid. When I'm on the East Coast, I feel so much more like myself. I'm not Ren, not the actress from *Even Stevens*. I'm just the youngest Romano kid, hanging out with her friends. I didn't realize how much I've missed being home.

"Where's Carrie?" Sybil asks.

I look around and can't find her—or Peter—anywhere. "We haven't even been down here an hour," Sybil says. "She worked fast. I bet she's with Peter somewhere. Should we look for her?"

"Nah, let's go back to the room," I say.

Carrie and Sybil only took two mini bottles, and the drinks had so much ice. Hopefully Disney doesn't notice those on my checkout tab. Or, if they do, hopefully they'll think Mom drank it.

I'm so tired, I feel like I'm sleepwalking, and I have a whole new round of interviews in the morning. I pass out immediately but wake up later when the door opens. I glance at the hotel clock. It's past three in the morning.

"Carrie?"

"Sorry, guys," she says, shutting the door and tiptoeing in. "Didn't mean to wake you up. I've been with Peter. Don't get mad!"

"I'm not mad," I say. I mean, it wasn't me who went to his room. Disney won't care what Carrie did. Plus I think it's funny that she's being so wild. "How was it? Did you have sex with him?!"

"Almost, but no. It was awesome, though. He's an amazing kisser, *and* he's funny. It's too bad he lives in LA."

"Yeah. Well, maybe that's a good reason for you to visit me," I say. "I miss you guys."

"We miss you too!" they squeal.

It's so nice being back with them.

Carrie and Sybil have to leave early in the morning, so I get ready and meet Mom for breakfast in the hotel before the interviews start again. The first two go well, even though I feel like I have bags under my eyes from not sleeping. When we're about to start our third, our press executive walks in, looking serious.

"Christy, can I speak to you alone?"

Crap. Did I say the wrong thing? Did I not look or act "Disney" enough?

I follow her into the hall. It's never good when an executive pulls you aside like this. I'm pretty sure she's not bringing me into the hall to tell me how great I am at doing press.

"So, it seems a friend of yours went into the hotel room of one of the actors last night. How old is she?"

My throat feels like it's about to close up, and my stomach churns. I can't lie, but I don't want to get Carrie or Peter in trouble.

"Um, she's sixteen. Like me."

"You know he's twenty-two years old?"

Shit. I am about to lose my job, be kicked off the show, and get sent home forever. I just know it. Mom will kill me, and I'll be mortified.

"I, um, thought he was a little younger than that." It's true, but I don't think that will save me. "She went home this morning. She seems fine and isn't mad at him or anything."

"You need to watch it, Christy," she says. "Disney is very specific about how you kids behave at TCA. You know this."

"I'm so, so sorry. It'll never happen again, ever. I promise."

"Just think about your reputation, okay? I know it wasn't you, but still. Guilty by association, right?"

"Right," I say, even though inside I want to scream, *WRONG!* Why is this always the girl's fault? Why is this on me and Carrie, and Peter probably didn't get in trouble at all? It's bullshit.

"I totally understand. I'm so, so sorry."

As soon as the words come out of my mouth, I feel like a fake, but I don't want to lose this job. Plus I'm used to this. Ever since I was little, I've been under a microscope and judged by adults in a way that most normal kids don't have to deal with, but that's part of being a kid actor. You have to just suck it up and be professional. And I'm not a kid anymore anyway, even though they are treating me like one.

"Thanks, Christy," she says before I head back to the day's interviews. "Oh, one more thing."

"Yes?"

She glances down at my stomach and squinches up her forehead in a disapproving way. "I can see your belly button. You gotta make sure we can't see your belly button."

"Sure," I say, pulling down my blue Forever 21 top that is *barely* showing my belly button. "Sorry."

I bet The WB actors never get told how to dress.

For the last month, all the Disney executives keep talking about is the *Lizzie McGuire* show and how Hilary Duff is the "next big thing."

They want me and Hilary to make a movie together during my *Even Stevens* hiatus. It's called *Cadet Kelly*, and I would play Hilary's rival at a military school. The executives keep saying we'll be "perfect rivals" because we're so opposite.

Of course the blond girl is the sweet, fun one, and the brunette (me) is the bad, unlikable one. But *Cadet Kelly* has a fun premise, and we get to shoot in Canada, so why not?

It'll be nice to get out of LA for part of the summer. Mom could probably use a change too, since she's been so quiet, so alone. She actually got some plastic surgery. I couldn't believe it, but she's all of a sudden concerned with looking young—or at least younger. She's swimming at the gym constantly. Maybe LA is getting to her. I don't want her to be sad. I just want her to be her own person without me and still love me when I'm not under a contract for something.

She spends money on surgeries but keeps it cheap with everything else.

I know that 15 percent of whatever I make goes into my Coogan Account since that's the law, but I'm worried she might be using some of my *Even Stevens* money for the surgeries. I haven't really asked. Truth is, I'm too scared to ask, since she's sacrificed so much for me to come this far. I'm not going to judge her for trying to take care of herself. I'll be old someday too. Who knows what I'll do?

I also recently got one of my favorite roles I've ever played on an animated show called *Kim Possible.* It is so much fun to do. It's so freeing and creative, and I love playing someone who feels empowering to girls. Kim kicks ass. She's this fiery redheaded cheerleader who saves the world and goes on secret missions. When I was asked to audition, Mick Frost told me I was on a short list of girls that Disney was considering. He said they saw it as my next big thing after *Even Stevens.* He said there was "synergy" during my audition, where I provided the voice-over to an animatic of the character. Mom tells me to say yes to everything (Hilary's mom would *not* approve), but *Kim Possible* was an easy yes. Even though I'm studying for the SAT, going to tutoring after ten-hour days, faxing my homework to PCS, working on my college essay, and prepping to shoot *Cadet Kelly*, I'm excited to be on my own more and more. To be my own person.

I must be getting bolder with age, because I decide to tell the *Cadet Kelly* director that I don't want my character, Captain Jennifer Stone, to just be some villainous person. It'll be more interesting if she changes in the end and if she and Kelly become friends. I don't want to play just a one-dimensional mean girl. I've been in this business long enough; I can't be afraid to speak up anymore.

At breakfast with the director, I explain my idea and tell him why it would appeal to girls more to see me and Hilary coming together in the end, like a form of female empowerment. I'm shocked when he says he'll talk to the writers and change the script a bit. I want to give her a backstory and make her feel real. I want to play a strong person, someone girls can maybe be inspired by. If I'm being honest, I also just don't want to be disliked. I know *Cadet Kelly* isn't like Shakespeare, and Shia probably thinks it's a dumb movie, but whatever. I might have been a bit mad when

I found out that Shia was playing a person with learning disabilities in a dramatic role in this movie *Tru Confessions* and filming at the same time as us in Canada. Disney must take him more seriously than they take me. By the end of our first *Even Stevens* season, he's gone from annoying me to filling me with anger. When we're in the same room, the tension is palpable. I need this break.

Having the director and writers rework the script is a huge win for me. I don't have to be just the good little Disney girl. I get to have an opinion. Finally.

"Excuse me, Sharon. You're in Hilary's chair."

Hilary's mom, Susan, stares at Mom, waiting for her to move. The chair *does* say "Hilary Duff" on the back, but it's not like Mom is committing some huge crime by sitting in it. I'm embarrassed but also a little angry at Hilary's mom. I mean, it's a chair, not a throne.

"Oh, sorry about that," Mom says, hopping off. "I didn't realize."

"It's fine. It happens. There are more chairs over there."

We've been shooting for two weeks after a month of military training for background prep. I like Hilary a lot. She's not at all the ditzy blond Shia seemed to make her out to be. She's sweet and hardworking. I mean, I wanted to get a purse at the Coach store with our per diem money, and she laughed and said she was going to Louis Vuitton, so we're not *totally* the same. My mom says her parents are oil-rich Texans, but I'm not sure that's true. I can tell by her tone that Mom is a little jealous that they don't have money problems. Some people in the industry say Hilary's mom is difficult, and that she got someone fired from Hilary's show because the mom didn't like them. My mom might have her faults, but she's chill compared to some parents on sets. Then again, stage parents can never win. They either do too much or too little. I wonder what rumors are told about our cast.

One thing I learn from listening to Hilary and her mom talk about Hilary's career during a visit to her massive hotel suite is that she has some pretty smart people giving her advice about money and ways to market herself. For starters, I think Hilary has a bigger suite than I do at the hotel, and a personal bodyguard/acting coach. She says she has the coach because supposedly her mom made Disney pay for it. She pressured the producers, and they listened. I feel like her mom sees her as a brand that's already successful, and I don't think Mom even knows what being a brand means, really. For us it's just job to job, without a big master plan. I'm starting to think we are behind the curve, and being agreeable "team players" isn't the right way to go. My goal, though, is still college. More than performing, more than any show. I still want to work, because like Mom says, I can always defer, but college, for me, means independence, normalcy. It means a life that doesn't revolve around me beating out a blond for a role. Granted, Hilary is perfect casting for Cadet Kelly.

These last few months, I've been trying to stay away from Mom as much as I can. I just need space. I need to be my own person, and all her loneliness and her beauty obsession this past year have been freaking me out a little bit. Even though I wouldn't *mind* getting breast implants one day. When I see myself in my military uniform costume, I look so flat-chested on the video playback that I cringe. I don't feel good about it, so a little surgery might have to be the answer soon. It's my money anyway.

"Christy, come with us!" Hilary, wearing super-low-rise jeans, a baby tee, and her Louis Vuitton bag, waves me over from the entrance to the hotel one afternoon. I'm about to go upstairs and take a nap, but I walk over to where she's standing with her older sister, Haylie, who's visiting for a few days and dressed in an identical outfit. "We're grabbing sushi, then shopping. Come on!"

I text Mom and walk out of the hotel driveway with the Duff sisters.

"Let's do it!" I say, tossing my new Coach purse over my shoulder. Hilary threads her arm through mine, and we're off.

During this entire shoot, Hilary has been easy to be around. I'm older than her, but she is very mature for her age. I also might be starved for friends who are at the same stage of their careers as I am. It feels good to have some community. We're having fun shooting our scenes together, even though I can't shake that feeling of competitiveness that swirls around us. Maybe Disney thinks it'll benefit our performances or something, like with Shia, since we're playing rivals who eventually become friends.

We're settled into an outdoor area at a sushi place down the street from the hotel. The three of us smoke Parliament cigarettes and try to be discreet so we don't get caught. Usually, I hate smoking, and yeah, I was the no-smoking girl in that PSA a million years ago. But they're smoking, so why not? Smoking seems fun, and Parliaments taste kind of minty. We get to some light gossiping, talking about boys, mainly—which costars and extras we have crushes on. I tell them about my most recent date with Shawn, our costar in the movie.

Haylie has tons of wild stories. She tells one about some people she knew who were using the end of a cigarette to snort cocaine, which I never knew was possible, because how would I? I've never been around cocaine, and I'd definitely never try it. Ever.

After that sushi lunch, I hang out with Hilary a few more times before we finish filming. Close to the end of shooting, I have a weird lunch with Hilary and her mom. We're talking about careers, and her mom is staring at me from across the table, which makes me feel uncomfortable. Like she's quietly judging me. She leans in and focuses right on me and tells me I seem like a pretty agreeable person, like a "yes-woman" type.

"I don't know about being a yes-woman, but I guess I'm agreeable most of the time? Or I try to be."

Then she leans closer, and I swear she says something like, "When someone sits forward, you should sit back."

My thoughts are racing to figure out what this woman is trying to say to me. Does she mean don't be too eager? Don't try too hard?

"Um, I think you mean . . . Well, actually, I have no idea what you mean."

She sits back and takes a sip of her drink. She's only about five feet tall, but sometimes she can seem intimidating. She tells me to get more confidence, and to learn the power of saying no to people. That Hilary and I are successful young girls, and we should get what we deserve.

At that moment, I know I'm in trouble. It feels like these people are playing chess, and my mom and I are barely playing checkers. It seems like Hilary has so much support, people who know how to play the game and win. Not to mention I feel like she has a fallback plan since she was born into a good family, so she can keep her standards high without being desperate to keep working. I feel like I still have to fight for attention or relevancy even inside Disney, even after I've been on a big show and been the first in Disney Channel history to be the star of an animated show, a movie, and a single-camera series. No matter how hard I work, I feel like I won't be able to keep up.

"Christy, are you okay? Can you keep going?"

Two Disney executives watch from behind the camera. I want to be professional and finish the job, even if my whole body is screaming for me to run out of the room.

"I'm fine," I say, wiping away tears and catching my breath. "I don't need to stop. I want to tell my story."

Donna Pescow grips my arms tighter. She's seated on the velvet couch next to me. Cameras dolly around my testimony.

"Okay, tell us more about that day. What was it like being in New York?"

It's only a few weeks after 9/11, and Disney Channel is filming a commercial about patriotism to help give kids some hope. It's me, Shia, Donna, Andy and Joey Lawrence, Melissa Joan Hart, Frankie Muniz, and a bunch of others. We're holding up American flags and talking about the importance of patriotism. Shia hasn't really asked how I've been doing since I got back, but Donna has been like a true second mom, comforting me when I lose my shit. Makes sense. She's from New York, so she gets it, even if she wasn't there that day.

That day. It was awful for everyone, but since the show was on hiatus, I was in Manhattan that morning, at PCS, just starting the school year. All the students and teachers were gathered, crying and terrified. Dad sent a friend, Lorenzo, to get me in the city and rush me through the eerily quiet avenues to Grand Central and then home. I remember ash everywhere and the look of shock on people's faces. I wish I could wipe it all away, but I can't. The red line back to Milford was my happy place for so long, and now that's all changed.

After that day, I made Mom take a train across the country to get back to LA instead of flying. I had a debilitating fear of flying before, and now I cannot imagine getting on a plane. So we spent five days stopping in different American towns and cities, seeing how people were feeling, how they were coping. Back in New York, cabbies with turbans were getting pulled out of their cabs and beat up because locals thought they were terrorists. The city was on fire, there were toxins in the air, and the rest of the country just seemed to move along with quiet caution. They couldn't understand it if they weren't there. Not fully.

It feels weird to be filming something about patriotism and acting all positive so soon after such a horrible event. I can't say no, though. Of course I comply and just spill out all my feelings about this terrible day. I hyperventilate in front of a crew of strangers during hair and makeup. I guess I didn't learn that power-of-saying-no lesson that Hilary's mom talked about after all.

When I finally watch the patriotism commercial, I see that Disney cut 99 percent of what I said that day. I guess they didn't want to scare kids. But *I* was scared, and I poured out all that emotion on camera for them. And then they just threw it away.

"Is this really what you want to send?" asks Myra, the tutor who's been helping me with my college essay. "Is this the deepest you can go?"

"Well, I'm writing about my life and juggling being a working actor with trying to be a regular kid," I say, not sure how she wants me to answer.

Myra is in her late twenties and is extremely serious. I can't imagine this girl ever laughing. She wears her hair in this perfectly coiffed 1960s flip with a big headband, mod clothes, black tights, and Mary Janes. She's almost psychopathically put together. The first time she came to the condo, Mom blurted out, "Christy wants to go to an Ivy League school, and her extracurriculars are off the charts, so we're hopeful," which was totally embarrassing. Ever since then, I think Myra has assumed I'm some bratty child actor.

"I get that you're an actor, but what have you ever done for anyone but yourself?"

"Excuse me?"

I'm not trying to be rude, but I'm so shocked by what she just asked in such a blunt way. Is she challenging me? Does she think I'm a spoiled Disney kid? She probably thinks I'm just some dumb girl who can buy her way into college or something. She hates me. I know it.

"Think about your life. I'll say it again: Have you ever once done something for anyone but yourself?"

"I've done a ton of charity events. Make-A-Wish and AIDS awareness performances. I've been a role model for little girls in some of the work I've done."

"I'm pretty sure that was all for you."

Maybe she's right. Maybe I have been living in a world where things are done *for* me, and I'm just thinking of myself and my career. Maybe I have nothing to offer in college at all. I was feeling so positive about things, so hopeful about the future. And now I'm not so sure.

"I'll work on it," I tell Myra. And I will.

When I tell Mom how intense Myra got, she fires her on the spot, and I never have to see her again. But I don't think I'll forget what she said to me.

~

I hate the Warner Bros. lot. Every time I drive past it on my way to an audition or a meeting at the green building in Burbank, I want to puke or scream or flip it off. Sometimes I actually do. Scream and flip it off, not puke. They put up these huge murals with the casts of *Dawson's Creek* and *Roswell* and *Smallville*, with all these gorgeous actors who are way more beautiful and perfect than I'll ever be. I hate it. It feels like you have to be stunning to even walk into the gates of the lot, and I am not stunning.

"You're striking," my mom would say. Which is code for *You're not conventionally pretty, aka a blond with a perfect nose and blue eyes.*

The murals constantly remind me of a level of success I feel destined to never touch. I wonder if other actors feel the same.

There's that tape playing in my head, getting louder and louder, telling me I'm not pretty enough, not talented enough, not interesting enough. Telling me I'll never be invited into those gates. One of the best things about Ezra, my boyfriend, is that he makes me feel confident, so I can turn off the tape. He tells me I'm beautiful, takes me to dinner, treats me like a princess. I met him at Universal CityWalk one night when we were out with some mutual friends, and he's not the hottest or tallest guy. In fact, he's incredibly short. But he's super smart and funny. I haven't dated anyone since Shawn in Canada, so it's nice to be with someone who makes me feel good about myself. Except for that one time he jokingly tried to drop me off at the strip club and said, "Time to go to work, sweetie." For someone who thinks he's a comedian, he sometimes isn't very funny.

I did finally get my boob job, so that's helped with my confidence, with not feeling like that flat-chested girl that boys in school called "Triple A." When I saw a screening of *Cadet Kelly*, my chest was so flat that my shirts just fell straight down, and I looked . . . like a kid. So I decided to get implants, and I'm glad I did. Disney didn't care. They would care more if I wore a miniskirt that was "inappropriate." I think Ezra would have liked me whether I got my boobs done or not, but I did it for me, not him. He's a pretty good boyfriend, and we have fun, so I'm just taking it day by day.

Not all of Ezra's jokes land, but he knows every comedian in LA since he was on a high-profile comedy series, and he hangs out at The Comedy Store all the time and will occasionally attempt to do stand-up. We've been seeing each other for almost eight months, and I finally feel like it's time to lose my virginity, so we do it. It feels like the right thing to do. I'm in a good place: College applications are in (even though Myra the evil tutor is out of my life), I feel better about my body, and we're making an *Even Stevens* movie this summer, so losing my virginity just feels like the next box to check. I *think* I love Ezra. I mean, I tell him I do. I'm not sure what love is supposed to feel like, though. So maybe this is it?

I don't tell Mom about having sex, even though she's told me many times to "use a rubber" if I do. One of my sisters had a baby pretty young. Since I was living in LA with Mom at the time, I stayed with Mandy the makeup artist while Mom flew to the East Coast to help right after the birth. Mom and Dad *love* being new grandparents, but Mom warns me that my career will be over if I have a kid so early. Being grandparents has softened my parents and reunited them across the miles. I love my little nephew, I love babies, but I know for sure I'm not ready to *be* a mom. Ezra used a condom, of course.

Right after we have sex for the first time, Ezra calls.

"Hey, Christy?" Ezra is hesitant over the phone.

"Hi, babe! What's up?"

I'm guessing he's calling me to tell me how much he loves me, to see how I'm doing since he knew I was a virgin and now . . . I'm not.

"So, about last night."

"Yeah?"

I suddenly feel hot in the face. Is he about to break up with me? Was he using me like Mom and Mandy always talk about? "Don't trust men," they always say. But Ezra is supposed to be different.

"I really think you should get the morning-after pill. Just in case."

"But you used a condom."

"Yeah, of course, but I feel like maybe it fell off? I'm just saying, just in case. That's all."

I feel a pit in my stomach. "Ezra, I'm Catholic! Those pills are like getting an abortion, and I would never! How could you?!"

I'm obviously not *that* Catholic since I had sex before marriage, but the idea of taking those pills goes against everything I've been told my entire life. Tears are now streaming down my face. I don't know why I'm this upset, but I am. I feel betrayed. I was always taught that dirty girls and sluts got abortions or took pills. I feel marked, like I've crossed some sort of line. I thought nice guys would be more dependable and that he was a safe bet. And now I'm supposed to go to Planned Parenthood to get a morning-after pill? I instantly hate him.

I just want to get away from Ezra and Mom and make my own life. I want to get far away from Mom's bad habits and this depressing condo. I don't want to get played by guys. I want to be the player now. I want to feel in control for once, if that's possible. I want out. I want change. More than anything, I want to feel like it's not always other people dictating what, when, and how things happen to me.

I did it! Screw Myra.

I'm going to Barnard College in the fall. The idea of going back to New York sounds exciting. It'll be a new kind of life there, a new start that I have been working toward for years.

Ezra and I made up, sort of. I never respected him after that "incident," though. I mean, we're still dating, *technically*, even though I left for Hawaii to shoot *The Even Stevens Movie* and I leave for school in August. The movie also marked the end of the show forever. Before I left, Ezra gave me a thin promise ring from Tiffany's, which was so sweet, even though Mom and Dad said it was ridiculous.

"What do you see in him, Christy?" Dad keeps saying. "He's short. He's not a prince. You deserve to be with a prince."

I know a lot of dads say this to their daughters metaphorically, but I'm pretty sure Dad thinks I should be with an *actual* prince. What Dad doesn't know is that I've been hooking up with Clint, who's in the movie. We just had instant attraction, and we're in Hawaii, and . . . well, why not? I'm young and about to start a new chapter. I need to leave Ezra behind. I want to break out of the "perfect" Ren mold and maybe even be a little wild. I can be anyone I want to be, just a girl in college, making normal friends and studying and riding Jeeps to the beach during the summer. At least, that's what it looks like in movies. And that's what I want.

Ezra calls almost every day, and I feel guilty about Clint, but not enough to stop. Truth is, Ezra broke my trust, and I just can't see him in the same way. Mom and most everyone on the shoot knows what's going on. Mom once again tells me to "use a rubber," and Donna, always the maternal one, tells me to be careful. "I've had showmances before, Christy," she tells me one day at lunch. "That's what this thing is with Clint. You're about to go to college, so don't get too serious. Have fun, but think about your future, okay? Showmances usually last until the director yells 'Cut' for the last time. Got it?"

I trust Donna. She's played my mom for three years, and she's always given me good advice. She gets it. She's so kind, and I'll miss her. She even once spent three hours helping me run lines for an audition that I desperately wanted. It was for *The Princess Diaries* with Julie Andrews, one of my heroes. It was a perfect role for me. When I read the script, I felt like maybe this was the one to break me out of TV and into film. But after all those hours memorizing and running lines, the shoot went late that day, and I missed the audition, and I couldn't reschedule it.

Everyone keeps telling me that if I leave Hollywood right after being in *two* Disney Channel shows, I'll be ruined. I'll always just be a Disney kid. Maybe they're right, but my mind is made up. I have no clue how much money I've saved in my Coogan Account or elsewhere, but Mom says it's enough for school. When this movie wraps, an entire chapter of my life will end. A new one will start, one where I'll get to be the thing I've dreamed about since I was small. I'll get to have a regular life.

The writers wanted to give Ren and Louis a sweet goodbye scene at the end of the movie since the characters had been so combative (in a funny way, I guess) during all the seasons. It's goodbye for me and Shia too. Who knows if I'll ever work with him or even see him again? I'm headed to college and am so ready to leave fake-ass LA, and he's all about making it big there. I think he will too. But you have to be such an ass-kisser in that town, and I'm over it. Other actresses are doing college too: Natalie Portman is at Harvard, Claire Danes got into Yale, and Julia Stiles is at Columbia. Unless there's an amazing opportunity, I never want to go back to the West Coast.

"Christy and Shia to set!"

I leave my trailer and head to the beach, where we're filming the last scene of *Even Stevens* ever. We're sitting on a stone wall by the ocean, and it's gorgeous out. A warm breeze blows through my hair, and a hibiscus flower grazes my right ear. The whole cast and crew are here because it truly is the end of this thing we built together for three years. Shia has on an oversized Hawaiian shirt per usual, and I'm wearing turquoise pants and a coral shirt. We look like typical suburban tourists, not cool at all.

Shia/Louis walks over and sits next to me/Ren on the wall. We've been in vacation mode during the shoot, and I think we bonded more during these few weeks than we ever did in LA. Last night we ended up judging a Hawaiian Tropic bikini competition together with Clint. Our location manager wanted us to experience Hawaii nightlife, so we all went out to a bar, where the locals thought it was funny for some actors to judge a bikini contest. The Disney executives can't watch us 24/7, so we had drinks, even though most of us are underage. I was drinking Malibu and pineapple juice and couldn't stop laughing at Shia's face as each beautiful woman took the stage and strutted down the runway. There was even a wet T-shirt contest. All the women were given tens across the board.

"Okay, kids. Scene thirty-four, take one!"

"Roll sound! Speed!"

"Mark it!"

The second assistant camera slams the clapper, and I find myself feeling emotional—not just as Ren but as myself. Shia and I might not have been superclose over the last few years, but we did kind of grow up together. He started as a kid and is now practically six feet tall. I take in his face for what feels like the last time, and for once, he is looking back at me.

"Sorry about blaming you for everything," says Ren.

"Ren, look. I'm your brother. I love messing with you," Louis says. "But I would never do anything to hurt you."

Our final hug in the scene is like a true goodbye too. And then he pratfalls off the stone wall we're sitting on, and I roll my eyes. That was not scripted, but our Ren-Louis dynamic always felt like our real-life dynamic anyway. Whether I see Shia again or not, I'm so ready to shed the "perfect" Ren persona. In college, I'll reinvent myself, on my terms.

Dear Girls,

Children are born innocent. It's the world that corrupts them, shapes them into whatever they become. Sure, there are genetic predispositions for talent, hair color, or height, but all kids start out carrying this uncorrupted light inside them. Adults are supposed to protect that light, make the world livable for innocence, at least for a few years. Otherwise, who wants to bring a baby into complete chaos?

Around age ten, I felt this crushing pressure to kill off my sense of wonder. The world started to seem unfair and maybe a little scary, so I made a choice to seek protection in childhood magic while projecting this mask of maturity to survive. My emotional growth became performance art. I was split between the kid I was inside and the precocious actress everyone expected me to be.

This binary existence created resilience in me. When I got knocked down (which was a lot), I'd bounce back up like a jack-in-the-box. I learned to smile through pain and make sick jokes about trauma. My goals were simple: Be likable, be funny, be shrewd, survive. People called me "relatable," and I still can't tell if that's a backhanded insult. My young Hollywood peers, however, weren't "relatable." They stood out, leveraged their talent and their resources, and became very wealthy. The more I wanted security, the faster it eluded me, since I sanitized myself to be palatable and safe.

Here's what I wish someone had taught me and what I'm teaching you now: Having a plan handed to you isn't the same as having dreams. Adults love compliant children who listen without questioning, but that compliance can cost you your authentic self. I spent years changing myself to make everyone else comfortable, dialing down my weirdness and intensity so people wouldn't feel threatened. It was shortsighted to try to change myself to please others.

The entertainment industry—and society—rewards this kind of self-erasure in children, especially girls. They want you to be manageable, grateful, and willing to morph into whatever sells. But, girls, you need to stick to your guns about who you are, even when it's inconvenient for the people in power.

I learned to be charming and agreeable because it kept me working, but it also kept me small. The peers who didn't learn that lesson, who stayed difficult and demanding, often got bigger careers because they never apologized for taking up space.

Your innocence isn't something to be ashamed of; it's not something you should be in a rush to abandon, because you can't get it back. When people pressure you to grow up faster, to be more serious, to stop being "childish," that's usually about their *comfort, not your best interest. Hold on to your wonder as long as you can in this complex world.*

Being relatable might keep you safe, but being authentic will keep you whole. And when people can't handle your authentic selves, when they try to dim your light or pressure you to be smaller, accept that as the red flag it is, not as a reflection of your worth. Leave them where they stand and go play mermaids.

7

Ivory Towers

2002–2003

Ages 18 to 19

Barnard's Sulzberger Hall is about as opposite to our wooden Marina del Rey town house as you can get. It's a red-and-white brick high-rise dormitory that could easily be a hospital or an office building. It looks out onto the Quad, which is basically like a grassy meeting area, and it's where I'll be living, *by myself*, without Mom for the first time in my life. Mom, Dad, and my siblings all drive me into Manhattan to drop me off and get me settled into the dorm. Driving up to Sulzberger, seeing the buzz of other girls coming to campus, I feel like this might be the best day of my entire life.

"Christy, let's get a photo." Dad is beaming. He keeps telling me how proud he is of me. He tells me he's proud of my career, but even prouder that I'm focusing on college.

Between the success of *Cadet Kelly*, the buzz on *Kim Possible* launching soon, and *Even Stevens* still running, I am a household name for younger kids. Plus I've always kept my GPA up, and I have eight thousand extracurriculars, so I worked hard to get in. I think my essay ended up being pretty good too, even if that evil tutor Myra thought I'd never done anything for another human being. I'm surrounded by brilliant people here, people who will want to talk about politics or art or poetry. I feel so much more myself here in New York, on this campus, than I ever have. It's just where I'm meant to be. Everything I've done, from the *Follies* to *Even Stevens*, every school and tutor and test I've taken—they all led me to this.

"You're still wearing that thing?" asks my sister, pointing at the promise ring Ezra gave me.

"I tried to give it back to him this summer, but he wouldn't take it," I say with a shrug. "He's sweet, but we're on opposite coasts now, so it'll never work. But no matter what I say, it's like he just ignores it."

"Christy, if I give you one piece of advice at all about college, it's this: Do not get serious about anyone during your first year," my sister says. "It always turns into drama, and you'll be miserable."

"Well, that's depressing," I say as Dad asks a student walking past to take our photo.

"It's true, I promise. Have fun and date, but I am telling you: Don't get serious about a guy."

"Fine. But what if the Columbia version of Leo DiCaprio walks up and wants to get serious?"

"Walk away! You're going to be busy."

"Okay, Romano clan, smile!" Dad throws his arm around me, and we all pose for the photo. After being away from home for so long and not really feeling like we were much of a family, this is nice. My sister knows I exist, and Mom and Dad are *mostly* getting along. I think the grandparent thing is good for them.

I love the feeling that the students at Barnard are like a tribe. "BC '06! BC '06!" Students chant this over and over at orientation beneath the cherry blossom trees, and I join right in. I'll graduate in four years and just focus on school the whole time. Unless an incredible role comes along, something we can't pass up, it's BC '06 all the way for me. Mom even told my manager not to contact us about auditions this year unless an "unmissable opportunity" comes up. "Give Christy at least this year," she told them during our last meeting. "Let her be a kid." A little late, Mom, but the thought was there. I don't think I'll miss acting at all. Singing, maybe. But I am so over being with tween actors and actresses in LA who just care about being famous and walking red carpets. As far as guys go, I'm sure Columbia is full of cute ones who don't care about celebrity, even though my sister practically made me take a blood oath that I wouldn't become some dude's girlfriend for an entire year. We'll see how that goes. My braces are off. I got my boobs done. For the first time in my life, I don't feel awkward or ugly or flat-chested. Anyway, these are college guys, not Hollywood assholes. It's a whole different world.

I scored my fake ID on Alvarado Street in LA last year, so it's easy to get into clubs in the Meatpacking District, like Lotus and Bungalow 8. My sister takes me out some nights too, which is crazy, because when she was in high school, she'd barely speak to me. Now I'm like her little protégé, and it feels like we are making up for lost time.

My sister studies hard and aces all her graduate school classes, but she also has fun. I guess she's figured out how to balance it, so I kind of use her as my guide to my new adult New York life. We head into a crowded club. A live saxophonist toots near my head, and a bongo drum is beating loudly over a sped-up version of Wham!'s "Everything She Wants." My sister takes my hand, and we sit at her Russian model friend's table with a massive bottle of Belvedere vodka and a few juice mixers. Everyone is dancing wildly, and it's clear you have to drink to get on their level. I'm handed a screwdriver and sling it back, fast. It feels like we're in a circus, and time stops and speeds up all at once. I reach for the vodka bottle, and an older businessman in a suit touches my hand before I lift it up. He locks eyes with me as he smiles flirtatiously and pours the vodka for me in my glass. I smile back. I feel so different from Disney's good little girl. Within these nightclub walls, I'm a woman.

Of all my friends at school, Nicolette is the one I'm closest to. She's from DC, and she's beautiful, mixed race, and super smart. Her dad's a Fulbright scholar, so I guess it runs in the family. I go out nearly every night, and money isn't an issue, since I'm still getting *Even Stevens* payments and anything on campus is connected to my campus account (which I also pay for). I'm still recording *Kim Possible* here in a studio on Fifth Avenue. Some people at school recognize me or know I was on a Disney show, but *Even Stevens* was for a much younger audience, so most of the time, I blend in. Besides, my classmates are all the best and brightest of their hometowns, so it's like they are just as famous as I supposedly am in their minds. It's a strange new feeling of being away from that whole world but still in it on some days of the month when I record *Kim Possible*.

I feel so much freer here without Disney watching or giving me "media training" or executives telling me my clothing is too revealing. I dated a few people at the start of school, but I listened to my sister and never got serious. But then I met Giovanni.

We were at West End, a dive bar near campus where all the Columbia students hang out. Giovanni was with his varsity hockey team, and the minute we started talking and flirting, we clicked. He's a green-eyed Italian guy who smells like Dior cologne and is a star athlete and totally different from Ezra. He's always with his team, which means I'm always with the team too. Honestly, most of them are dicks and misogynistic. But sometimes they're fun. And it doesn't really matter, because I'm so focused on Giovanni.

After four months together, Giovanni and I have been fighting a lot, and I'm starting to worry that he's hooking up with other girls when he goes out without me. Sometimes he'll wait hours before he calls back or replies to a text. It's weird. I'm trying to be cool about it and not be "that girl," but it's getting hard. In the time we've been together, I don't think I've had one intellectual conversation with him. I made the dean's list the first semester and am trying to stay focused, but it's not easy when everyone's out at least five nights a week. It's also not easy when I'm constantly thinking and worrying about Giovanni. Who he's with, whether he loves me, if he's with another girl. It's exhausting. It also reminds me of my parents. It made me so angry watching Mom accept how miserable they were, and now here I am, doing nothing.

Giovanni calls. Instead of asking where he's been or who he's been with, I agree to meet him at West End. I already have plans with Nicolette and some others, but we'll wind up at West End anyway. I wear tight low-rise jeans, a midriff-baring top, hoop earrings, and a black puffy jacket with a fur collar since it's cold. I meet my friends at their dorm to pregame.

"You need a night out," Nicolette tells me. "Make him think you've been totally fine without him."

I'm drinking whatever my friends are pouring. Mainly shots of 99 Bananas, a banana-flavored liquor that's ninety-nine proof, whatever that means. I've never had it and it's sweet, so I'm able to down two more shots. Why the hell not?! I'm done freaking out over this jerk.

West End is packed like always, but tonight it seems even more charged with intensity. My friends and I stumble inside, and I spot Giovanni and his buddies sitting in corner booths. 50 Cent's "In Da Club" is bumping, and the beer pong room in the back is packed with people I know from Barnard and Columbia. I pretend not to care that he's in my orbit, but I'm keeping an eye trained in his direction to see if he notices me. There are always girls around him.

"Just be cool, Christy," Nicolette says. "Do your thing, and he'll come by eventually."

I buy a Corona and focus on my friends, or I try to. Eventually, though, I see Giovanni sauntering toward us and do my best to act chill.

"Hey." He smiles, draping his arm over me as if nothing has happened. He's holding a full pitcher of beer in his hands.

I roll my eyes and stumble a bit into his arms from the shots I took before. The problem is, he *does* look hot. If he looked like crap, it would be easier to ignore him.

"Where've you been, Giovanni?" Nicolette asks, and I shoot her a look.

I do not want her to bring the drama. I just want to have a fun night. I want college to be what I expected it to be, fun and free and romantic, not dark and full of chaos.

"Are you my fucking mother? Calm down," he says, pretending to be clueless.

She rolls her eyes.

I follow Giovanni over to the corner where all his hockey buddies are being rowdy and telling one another animated stories of the most recent Harlem bum fight they filmed or binge-and-purge regimens. My vision is blurred from all the 99 Bananas shots, plus I purposely didn't eat dinner so I could get a better buzz.

Soon, for reasons that are unclear, Giovanni is pulling me out onto the street. It's frigid now that we are deep into winter, but I feel hot with alcohol and jealousy. I'm trailing behind Giovanni, who's rushing because he's not wearing a jacket.

"Giovanni, just stop!" I pull my hand away and stop walking. He turns to face me, his face looking red and sweaty.

"What?! It's fucking cold!" He jumps up and down to stay warm.

"Are you fucking another chick?! You're such an asshole. I know you are!"

"God . . . You're such a bitch!" he yells without skipping a beat.

I didn't realize just how angry I was with him for bringing me down and ruining my first semester at school. This was supposed to be my time at college. I'm not some ornament that he can toss away. I hate him.

"Yeah, keep talking. I would murder your fat-ass dad and your pussy-ass brother. Shut the fuck up."

We're in the middle of the freezing cold street, but I don't even care. Giovanni has told me about his family, about their toxic dynamics and awful fights, so I'll use that. Even though, deep down, I know it's probably wrong.

"Is that what your dad said to your mom? Did he hit her too?" I say this with more venom than I have ever said anything in my life.

That's when I see it. White-hot anger lights up in his eyes, passes across his face. His palm slams into my throat, and he pushes me against a brick wall until I choke and cough.

"Never talk about my mother again," he says before removing his hand, walking off, and leaving me alone, doubled over in fear.

I can see the streetlamps and hear the bass from the closed doors of the West End, and I can finally feel the bitter cold of the late-evening air. I cry, glancing around to see if anyone witnessed what just happened. But I'm a drunk college girl alone on a street corner, and New York doesn't care about drunk college girls making it home safely. I pull myself together and walk back to my campus through bitter cold gusts of wind, vowing two things: One, to never drink 99 Bananas. Two, to never speak to Giovanni again. To never get treated this way again.

"I'm coming into the city with my friend Lorenzo, and we'll handle this," Dad says.

After that awful night with Giovanni, I called my parents to tell them what happened and ask them what I should do. They said to report it to the dean, so I did, but now Dad wants to come to the Columbia cafeteria with me and his buddy Lorenzo to "make a statement." Instead of feeling afraid or embarrassed, I'm thrilled. Fuck Giovanni.

Dad and Lorenzo show up in black leather jackets, looking tough. I love it.

"Show us the way to their cafeteria," Dad says, "and show me his dorm building. We're not going to do anything—just make our presence known and give him and his hockey buddies a little scare."

"Yeah," says Lorenzo with a sinister laugh.

We walk from the Barnard Quad over to the Columbia dining hall. I scan the room for Giovanni and don't see him, but a bunch of his teammates are there. I know they hate me because I reported what happened, and after that, Giovanni was banned from the Barnard campus. That's not a massive punishment for choking a girl if you ask me, but at least I spoke up about it. After the ban, the team printed out flyers with a photo of me from a Disney Channel promo and the words "CHRISTY ROMANO IS LYING ABOUT GIOVANNI BRANT." They were posted all over campus, and I only found out because a nice guy I friend-zoned was yanking them down, and he called to tell me about it.

I feel empowered to be sitting there with Dad and Lorenzo in the main dining hall of Columbia University, but I'm also a little embarrassed. I'm a Disney kid with a tough-guy dad trying to intimidate a bunch of college hockey players. My dream of this perfect college life, like you see in all the movies, doesn't feel so perfect now. All that talk at orientation about this being a "safe space" doesn't feel so true anymore. It's not the school's fault. Barnard is like *the* place to be for feminism and women's empowerment, but somehow I got mixed up with the worst kind of guy. I fucked up. My grades aren't stellar, and one of the *Kim Possible* producers called the other day to tell me they're "concerned" because my voice is changing, and not for the better. I don't know if it's all the partying and smoking, but I know it's not as strong, and honestly, after this whole year of college, I don't even care. I don't want to leave school, since I worked so hard to be here. It would take a lot to get me to leave.

The minute they sing, "We'll beat up your ex-boyfriend for you," in their rush recruitment song, I know Alpha Beta Delta is my tribe. I never imagined I'd rush a sorority, but I want my second semester to be different. I want a community, and not just some asshole hockey players and random drinking buddies. I picked the artsy, inclusive girls who smoke weed over the rich Alpha Beta Delta girls with Tiffany necklaces and a few, it seems, who have eating disorders and coke problems.

I started seeing a therapist at the student health center after my breakup with Giovanni, and it's helped a little. I've been learning to unpack my anxieties around being perfect all the time. Because I'm certainly not being perfect. For starters, I'm failing sociology, which I'm terrified to tell my parents about. I've never failed a class or a test in my life. I haven't heard about any auditions in so long that I'm wondering if I'll ever act again, or if it even matters. Over the summer, *Vanity Fair* magazine came out with a big young Hollywood issue that featured Amanda Bynes, Hilary, Mandy Moore, the Olsen twins, Lindsay Lohan, Raven-Symoné, and a few other girls, and I was and still am *pissed* that I wasn't included. I've worked so hard for so long, but I'm out here with what I believe is a weak management team. I'm still on Disney shows and have a name out there, but they didn't even ask me to be part of it. It's not that the other girls don't work hard—I'm sure they do, because anyone in this industry has to bust their ass, but it will haunt me forever that I wasn't on that cover. Is this a sign of what's to come? What did anything add up to anymore? Mom says they have more aggressive managers or agents than I do. But I'm sure Susan Duff was right there on set, managing her daughter's outfits and position on the cover. Whatever it is, I've been back at school, but that magazine thing makes the old negative tape in my head go into overdrive. *You suck. You'll never make it.* It makes me think I'm an imposter, a fake, both in school and in Hollywood. It messes with my confidence, and I need to make it stop.

But things change again the next time Mom and I catch up. "Christy, Geoff called." My most recent manager, Geoff, hasn't called me or Mom much in the last year. I thought that he'd given up on me or that Mom telling him to give me space had scared him away.

"What did he say?" I ask. I'm surprised by the rush of excitement I feel. I'm just now starting to *like* college again after all the shit that went down last year. Do I really want to act again? It's like that line from one of Dad's favorite movies, *The Godfather Part III* (of course): "Just when I thought I was out, they pull me back in."

"He said the producers of *Beauty and the Beast* on Broadway are looking for a new tenth-anniversary Belle, and they want you to audition. What do you think? If you get it, you'll be the youngest actress to play Belle on Broadway."

"Ever?"

"Ever."

I've always wanted to play Belle. Her solo "Home" was one of my first go-to audition songs, and I know how to sing it backward and forward. This makes perfect sense. I look like her, and I have a ton of cache because of all the Disney work. My GPA at Barnard is a 2.8 right now, and if I take a role like this, either I'll have to defer, or my grades will for sure get even worse. I'm tugged in two directions. But who am I kidding? If I have to choose between getting back on the dean's list and playing Belle, it's Belle.

"Just give it a shot and see," Mom says. "I think you should do it."

"Okay, I'll do it," I say quickly. I know the songs by heart already, but I haven't done any singing in so long, and I already know that all the drinking and late nights are making my voice iffy, because I can hear it when I record *Kim Possible.* This is one of those roles I can't pass up on, though. I know in my bones I can do this.

On the day of the audition, I had been preparing the material for about two weeks. I know this role so well, Mom says it's mine to lose. "You were born to play Belle," she says over the phone that morning. "The songs fit your voice perfectly. Just remember to be friendly with the producers—"

"Mom," I say, cutting her off in a warning tone, as if she were my employee. "I'm nineteen, not six."

She goes silent on the other end of the phone and then just tells me good luck and hangs up.

When I walk into the rehearsal room, I *do* feel like it's mine to lose. I have three Disney shows on the air right now, including *Cadet Kelly*, and I've been on Broadway before. I have training and an actual Broadway background. I know that after almost ten years, they've been losing their audience for the show, and they need to bring in a younger audience, which means the *Even Stevens*, *Kim Possible*, and *Cadet Kelly* fans.

I walk into the audition room with confidence. When I start singing, I figure, what can go wrong?

And then it does go wrong. So very wrong.

My voice cracks and stumbles. I can't hit the notes. The veins in my neck pop out as I belt out the notes.

"Sorry," I say in a rushed, chipper voice to a table of producers and a director with a perplexed and disappointed face. I clear my throat and flush what I'm sure is tomato red. "I can do this. Can I just start again?"

This is something you should never say in any audition, let alone a Broadway audition, but I feel myself becoming desperate. I want to play Belle, but maybe even more than that, I need a reason to leave Barnard. As much as I dreamed about college and how amazing it would be, I realize, at this moment, I want out. At least for a while, especially after Giovanni. I guess it's like the devil you know versus the devil you don't. And I know acting. It seems easier than trying something new.

"Sure," says one of the producers. "Go again." I can see the disappointment spreading across their faces.

I'd practiced the songs, but my voice is something I don't recognize anymore. As a child, I'd been taught to belt it out, to sing as loudly as possible. And now here I am. Failing at the one thing I felt most confident about. I can't even look at myself in the large mirrored wall behind them.

"Thanks for the opportunity," I croak out when it's over. The vibe in the room is not jubilant. If I walked in cocky, I'm walking out totally defeated and on the verge of a mental breakdown. I should have been humbler. I'm a loser. I'm nothing. I'm a piece of shit. I should have nailed this, but I just lost my dream job.

The following week, a long, thin black hose with a camera on the tip is inserted into my nose. It stretches to the back of my throat to view my vocal cords. A kind man in a white lab coat asks me to sing, and so I do.

"Eeeeeeeee," I sputter and cough to the key of C flat.

I feel the camera line grazing the side of my esophagus. Before I gag uncontrollably, I choose to effectively dissociate and breathe through my nose.

"I recommend surgery ASAP," says Dr. Woo to Mom and me as he lifts the camera line back through my throat and out of my right nostril. I feel sick and entirely vulnerable as I stare at the pictures of my throat.

Dr. Woo is the best voice doctor in New York. He's worked with tons of A-list singers, so when he says I have nodules on both of my vocal cords that need to be removed so I can keep singing, Mom and I trust him. I'm also scared shitless because this is the same surgery that mutilated Julie Andrew's voice for good. It's risky.

"How soon can we do it, and how long until she's healed?" Mom asks. In the wake of me not booking the *Beauty and the Beast* audition, Mom has been frantically trying to get me another shot. The production manager had worked with me when he was young and starting out on *The Will Rogers Follies* and took pity on my situation. He said he'd convince them to see me again if the part was still open when I recovered.

"We can do it next week, but she'll have to completely rest her voice for one to two weeks. Then two months of post-op speech pathology."

"Let's do it," Mom says, without even asking me. I do want to do it, but I hate not even being *asked.* It feels like I'm six again.

I spent my entire childhood singing my heart out onstage. I'm coming to realize that it's not such an easy thing to give up, even when your body decides it hates you. If I were an athlete, this would have been the time I'd have decided to start juicing. I don't have much of a choice.

Right after the surgery, I meet with the hospital's voice pathologist, who is one of those New Yorkers who might seem like a total bitch but is actually all about tough love. Her name is Dr. Erhat, and she was in the Israeli army and is now taking out her aggression on post-op patients, I guess. Her technique motivates me, since it feels similar to how Mom got me to commit myself when I was a kid.

"You suffer from Y-and-S disease!" Dr. Erhat yells during our first session. "Young and stupid! The way you use voice? ALL WRONG! It's perverted. Your natural voice isn't that low, see?"

Dr. Erhat manipulates my larynx with her dainty but fierce hands.

"Um." I feel a bit uncomfortable with her hands on my throat.

"Toughen up!" she growls. "You will learn to modulate and do the exercises every day. No exceptions."

I try to respond, but my throat is in a vise grip.

After my sessions with Dr. Erhat, I try to rest my voice as much as possible. Dr. Woo hooks me up with a steroid inhaler before my *Beauty and the Beast* audition, and after six weeks of warnings, he clears me. My vocal cords are feeling squeaky clean when I speak, and I'm willing to do the audition just to redeem myself. I keep going to classes and hang tight till the audition. I don't drink or smoke. I write down what I want to say as much as possible. I stay focused on what's to come.

If I was overconfident in my first audition, in the next one I felt totally humbled. I also felt like I had something to prove since the last one was so bad. I may screw up in life, but I've been in this business long enough to know what's at stake. I prepared and felt totally locked in when I entered the room, focused but fully knowing I could blow it again. But I didn't. And now I get to leave school not because I was defeated but because I have something better to do.

So much happened at school that my illusion of a perfect, normal college life is obliterated. The reality is that it's like the worst of Hollywood, like Mom and that makeup artist Mandy and other women told me: Be careful of men. Not all men are bad, I know that for sure. I remember being so excited to chant "BC '06" during orientation. I was so sure I'd finish college in four years with a 4.0, but I can't get away fast enough.

The bubble that was my dream of a carefree college experience has gone bust. Giovanni was the final straw, the way he and his friends were and are. There's a rumor that the forward and the goalie recently got suspended for raping someone I knew from the bars. I need a change. I'm ready to get back onstage and pretend to be a princess in a magical castle for a while, because I got this part. I'm going to be the Belle of Broadway.

Dear Girls,

Millennial pop culture set my generation up for disappointment. Popular movies like National Lampoon's Van Wilder *and* Road Trip *sold us on a version of college life that was wild, free, fun, and aspirational. I was no different in my idolatry of the fantasy while I was filming in LA in the years before starting Barnard. Those college films are, in fact, super problematic. They endorse an acceptance of predatory behavior in young men and downplay the sheer financial commitment that it takes to attend college in the first place. It's not real.*

One thing I learned at college: DON'T date a Giovanni. It's just a cry for help. And don't pressure yourself to go to the "best" school. I would rather you take a gap year than push on and move yourself into something that isn't right for you. I desperately wanted to have a positive social experience my freshman year. But I was greeted with the raw truth that if you don't have a balanced base of support and a firm grasp of your identity outside of school, you can suffer and break under this system. To that end, gap years make sense. College is a microsociety and social experiment all in one. It's the Hunger Games with tailgates. Women have to look out for themselves, stick together, and fight back against misogyny and inequality. That's just the truth.

There is a reason your dad and I are so protective of you both. Men change after becoming girl dads when they reflect on the male mind. This world doesn't treat women equally, and it is up to us, your parents, to bring that to light at the right time so as not to scare you but to wake you up. I want you to walk in the world with confidence, whether you're in college or at work. Not everyone (or every guy) is a Giovanni, and there are amazing people out there for you to meet. I just want you to meet them with both feet firmly planted on the ground.

8

Poster Girl

2004–2005

Ages 19 to 21

Beauty and the Beast is a huge deal, and Belle is a role I've wanted to play since I was a little girl. It's a dream part. The gorgeous ball gowns, the romance, the spectacle and publicity of it all. Once I booked it after my disastrous first audition, we negotiated that Disney would pay for my apartment close to the theater, on top of my salary. Because of *Even Stevens* and *Kim Possible* and all the other things I've done to make Disney money, I think they see me as a "sure thing" as Belle. At least, that's what Mom says. She's not as involved in my career now that I'm over eighteen, but she still has opinions. And *sometimes* I still listen.

I'm going to be Belle for the show's tenth anniversary on Broadway, and I'm taking over for Megan McGinnis, who I know a little bit because she had a small part in *Parade* when I was in that show. I don't remember her having such a beautiful voice back then, but hearing her sing "Home" and "No Matter What" is a little intimidating now, especially after my surgery. I've been working with Dr. Erhat, the tough-love voice pathologist, as well as Joan Lader, voice coach to the stars. My range is definitely better since my totally embarrassing first audition, but I'd be lying if I said I wasn't a tiny bit nervous. Still. I'm a pro, right? I've been doing this since I was six years old. If Megan can do it, I'm going to do it.

Even after I've only been on set for a little while, it's clear that the cast and crew love Megan, and she brings so much energy, wholesomeness, and spirit to the role. I feel like I need to kill it, to go big or go home, to be the best Belle that Broadway has ever seen. I can feel my old competitive streak rearing up, and I can't help it.

"This role is really physical," Megan tells me when I start shadowing her for the week. "You're running and leaping. The dresses weigh a ton. You're onstage ninety percent of the time. So take care of yourself. Get sleep. Drink water. Don't party too much. Not that you would, but trust me. You'll be exhausted."

I'm nineteen years old and living alone in Manhattan, so I want to go out to clubs *sometimes* at least. But I don't tell Megan this. I want her to know I'm here to work. To take on this role with all the seriousness it deserves.

"Totally!" I say.

Megan is not kidding about the dresses. When I go in for my fitting for Belle's iconic golden-yellow ball gown, it feels like it weighed forty pounds. Megan teaches me to chug water whenever I exit the stage and get even a short break, like while the Beast is singing "If I Can't Love Her." I trust Megan, since she's been playing this role for eight shows a week for close to a year. She's not leaving because she's doing a bad job—it's because they need to sell more tickets. At least, that's what my agents told me. Basically, because I have three Disney shows airing, they see this as "stunt casting." Because kids, little girls especially, know me from all the shows, they're hoping my name will drive up ticket sales. No pressure or anything. Or, as Kim Possible would say, "It's no big!" Except, unlike Kim, I'm human and scared shitless.

I hate that term, "stunt casting." It's insulting. I *started* in theater and Broadway. I'm not some teenybopper TV actress from LA who is getting a random shot on Broadway. This is my *home*. I've been working my ass off for years. My entire childhood has been spent working and commuting and auditioning and hitting my marks. I didn't just stumble onto this.

I guess stunt casting is the trend now. Mel B (aka Scary Spice) and Joey Fatone from NSYNC have been in *Rent*, one of my favorite musicals of all time. Deborah Cox is taking over for Michelle Williams from Destiny's Child in *Aida*, and now "Ren Stevens" is Belle. Unlike in *Parade*, when Hal Prince told me not to "gild the lily" and get my own publicity, this time I'm encouraged to do as many interviews and press events as possible. They want me talking to *Playbill*, BroadwayWorld, and the *New York Post*, so I do. It's like a full-time job. The PR team is great but also super gossipy. I wonder if Mel B or Michelle Williams struggle with their voices like I do. I've heard of so many singers having to do steroid shots and I pray I don't have to go that route, and that I can keep my voice up and not be the subject of some PR person's gossip. Every time a journalist asks me about being the youngest Belle on Broadway, I smile and say what an honor it is, but inside, I'm hell-bent on proving wrong anyone who thinks I can't handle this part.

Playing Belle is like having the previous year's Miss America pageant winner hand you the crown, only I'm getting a yellow dress instead. It's like joining a sorority of all the girls who've come before, and now that crown, that dress, is in my hands. It's an honor, honestly. The one problem is that I'm pretty sure the director, Robert, doesn't like me. Or he doesn't believe I can play the part successfully. He's super strict with me during and after rehearsals and treats me like a kid sometimes. He did tell me about another actress who played Belle in a production he directed in Spain, and she was so honored to take on the role, she got a huge tattoo of a rose winding around her arm to represent the magical flower in the play. I think he told me this to intimidate me a little, to show me that I need to take this seriously. And I do.

We rehearse about eight hours a day for about a month before I officially take over as Belle.

I finish rehearsal for the day, and Robert motions for me to come talk to him. I'm covered in sweat, exhausted. I walk over, pasting a big everything's-just-fine! smile on my face like I always do.

"Hey, Robert," I say. "What's up?"

"Christy, listen. You're the youngest Belle we've ever had," Robert says. I can sense a few cast members lingering across the room, trying to make out our conversation. "You'll be onstage ninety percent of the time, and we rehearse six to eight hours a day before opening night. Some of us are nervous you won't be able to stick to the plan, so I need you to step up the effort, got it?"

"Sure, got it," I say, straining to keep the smile on my face when what I really want to do is burst into tears and punch him.

"Belle means a lot to kids all over the world," he says, as if I need more pressure. "Not to mention how much the longtime cast and crew depend on this job. You know Calvin, the guy who plays the spoon? He's one of the original cast members. This has been his bread and butter for a decade. This is a *job* for him. It's how he feeds his family."

He stares at me, daring me to say something dumb. I'm no kid, though. He has no idea what I'm capable of. I'll keep Calvin the Spoon in business if it kills me.

"I won't let you down. I promise," I say. "It's important to me too."

"I know you will," he says with a subtle nod.

The thing is, I don't want to let Calvin the Spoon down, or anyone else working on the show. One thing I love about New York theater is that the crew and the ensemble sometimes work a show their entire career, and they get health benefits and provide for their family. It's work. They commute in from New Jersey or Connecticut, do the job, go home. So I take that responsibility seriously. The last thing I want is for Disney to write this off as a failure because of me. But it's starting to feel like a pressure cooker.

The makeup artist, Vicky, has been teaching me how to apply Belle's makeup for weeks. Megan gave me some tips too, since there is a certain way to do it with exact colors from a very specific brand. Disney even has a notebook, like a Belle makeup bible, that explains exactly how to blend these intricate colors, how to put them on, where to apply blush. They did it for the big photo shoot a few weeks ago, which was the first time I got to really get used to the iconic ball gown. I haven't been partying during rehearsals at all, since I feel like I'm under a microscope constantly. I think I'm hitting my stride, though. I also just signed with a new agency, ICM, and the agents say they have high hopes for me.

This week was a big moment. Megan pulled me into Belle's dressing room to officially hand the room and the role off to me. I could tell it was bittersweet for her. It's this historic dressing room with lavender paint on the walls. It's so old and tiny but still pretty, with furniture that looks like it's been handed down over generations. I'm honored to take over that room, and I even have my own bathroom. The Lunt-Fontanne Theatre opened in 1910, so there is so much New York history in the walls. And more than ever, I feel like I'm about to become part of that.

"Look up!" Mom says. We're in Times Square, and she said she had something important to show me. I closed my eyes like she asked, and she led me down the street and told me when to stop. As soon as I look up, my breath seizes. There, towering above Times Square, is a massive poster with my picture on it, smiling in my Belle costume and clutching a red rose. It says:

Disney Channel Star
Christy Carlson Romano
Is Broadway's New Belle!

"What?! Holy shit! This is crazy!" I gasp. The billboard looks like it's a hundred feet high. I feel a hot tear run down my freezing cold cheek. Mom is beaming.

"I'm so proud of you," she says.

I cannot believe it. This feels like the moment, the pinnacle of my whole career. A little girl from Connecticut worked her way up for this exact moment. This is it. Instead of just "Christy Romano," the poster says "Carlson," which was Mom's idea. She got it into her head that just "Romano" was "too ethnic-sounding." So I added her maiden name for a broader appeal. I'm embarrassed by how long it is. And there it is. Looming over Times Square. It's not even my real name, but now I'm stuck with it.

I take it all in for a few more minutes, and as we hurry off for dinner, I shut off the tape in my head that's saying, *You're not worthy of this, not good enough. You're going to fail . . .* I pray for the sounds of New York City to drown it out forever.

I have some money in the bank, and even though Mom has a debit card to the account too, I don't think she uses it much. She told me that a CPA once advised her to use my money to get an apartment and a car because they could be tax write-offs if she used them to help my career. I do pay for my parents' meals a lot, and my Coogan Account money paid for college, so I have some cash to burn but no time to splurge. Plus I don't pay that much attention to the money. Mom has always handled that, and Disney pays my rent, so I think I'm probably saving and doing fine. My new agents want to package me as "the next Jen Aniston." Finally! I've been watching Shia and Hilary and so many other actors I grew up around get these bigger and bigger film roles or merch lines at Target, and I worry I'm stuck in Disney mode for life. I'm focused on Belle but hoping for even bigger things.

The shows have been going well and capacity is up significantly, so the producers are happy. Even Robert, the director, has been a little less stressed, his brow a little less furrowed around me. The producers send me to Joan to keep my voice up and it's helping, but I wish she could be a little less condescending sometimes. Still, she's a big deal, so I want to impress her. She's a legend in the theater world. I wish I could speak up for myself or defend myself from people like this, but I just act agreeable, like I always have. Clearly, they have all the answers that I don't.

At least my costar isn't condescending. Jeff McCarthy, who plays the Beast, is way older than me, but it's not awkward at all when we kiss because he's goofy and not at all creepy. He's a sweetheart, and he's made me feel comfortable from day one, so I can have fun with the role at least, even though the pressure can be intense. He's one of the original Beasts, and so they paired us as a joint PR stunt. Despite the pressure, we can joke around. During a matinee, one of his bushy eyebrows popped off right in front of me during our emotional garden scene, and I nearly lost it. I was supposed to cry in the scene, so I just disguised my laughter as sobbing, and it worked.

I was also told to see the "acupuncturist to the stars," Cathy. She has an apartment near the Flatiron Building. I think she ionizes the air in the room, so every time I walk in, it feels electrically charged, crisp and metallic and energizing. She rubs my larynx and gives me a massage that activates pressure points. I hope it's all worth it, because it's probably expensive and Disney is paying. I don't want them to think of me as the actress who costs them too much.

I see some of my sorority friends and hang out with my siblings sometimes, but mainly I'm running from appointments to shows to press events to bed. Mom comes to press events here and there, almost acting like an assistant, which helps. But I don't need her like I used to. She keeps saying how proud she is, how "we've made it," especially since the billboard was unveiled. She seems almost content now. She doesn't try to run my career or push me to do things. Dad, though, has gone into full-on obnoxious mode. He's always having dinner at an Italian place near the theater, asking me to come meet him so I can sign autographs for friends or people he does business with. He acts like he owns the place, orders off menu. His cologne, which is now Dolce & Gabbana, still overpowers any room. It's how he announces himself. Some people might wince at it, but to me, it's just Dad. It's comforting, a way to know that he's here.

"Christy, come talk to me after you get changed," says Robert. It's Saturday night, and I'm exhausted from nonstop work. I just want to go home and crash, but as soon as I change and get some of the makeup off, I find him talking to the stage manager. When I walk over, nervous he's going to lecture me about my voice or my performance, Robert tells the stage manager he'll see him later before he heads my way.

"Hi, Robert," I say in my typical I'll-just-pretend-everything-is-fine voice. "What's up?"

He takes a big sigh. Another bad sign.

"Well, I know you know that you're our youngest Belle," he says. I know what's coming next: I need to step it up, get with the program, try harder, sing better.

"Yes," I say, my voice sounding a little less chipper.

"Well, I wasn't sure if you could pull it off, especially after that first audition, but you pulled through, Christy. You're the star we needed you to be. So thank you."

Now this I was not expecting. I try not to jump up and down and scream with joy like a kid. I act as mature as possible, like a pro, like a star.

"Wow, that means a lot to me, Robert. Thank you!"

"I'm leaving town to direct the touring production for a few months, so I know you'll keep it up and keep the seats filled."

As relieved as I feel to hear all of this, that he has confidence in me *finally*, I know there is a subtle "Don't fuck this up" underneath the compliment. I know I have to do whatever it takes to keep my energy high, my voice healthy. And I will.

It's like *Groundhog Day*. Every day, every week, feels like a grind now that the newness of Belle has worn off. Every week feels like a reset to more of the same: tough-love voice coaching with Joan, acupuncture with Cathy, meeting Dad at the Italian restaurant to sign photos, Mom asking for more comp seats to shows, cortisone treatments with the doctor. I feel like everyone is watching me, yelling, "Dance, monkey, dance!" And I'm of course complying. But some days I want to rebel from Mom and Dad, from Joan, from everything and everyone. Some days I want to disappear. It's strange that you can feel so lonely when you're surrounded by people looking at you with stars in their eyes.

I swore I'd never take steroids for my voice, but now I get it. I get why other singers supposedly do it, or why anyone would do it. There is so much pressure to perform constantly. It's not like it's a hard drug or something. But it feels like an athlete using performance-enhancing drugs.

It's sad that Jeff left for another show. He was such a good Beast, so easy and fun to work with. My new costar, Zane James, is one of the longest-running Beasts on Broadway. He's also over twenty years older than I am. The minute he walked into rehearsal, it was like the air in the room shifted. If Jeff was light and funny, Zane feels heavy and borderline toxic. His energy reminds me of Shia's dad's energy whenever he was on set during *Even Stevens.* He's much older and unlike with Jeff, when we have to kiss at the end, it doesn't feel safe. It feels creepy.

"I've seen it all, sweetie," Lottie always says. "Zane is one of those bad boys of Broadway, so watch out. When it comes to women, I think he's an alley cat." Lottie, my personal dresser, is a former dancer, and she's hilarious. She's got bright red hair and emerald-green eyes, and you can tell that in her day, she was probably the kind of girl who made guys trip over themselves in the streets.

Women like Lottie always have the best gossip, especially when it comes to guys like Zane. It bums me out that I now have to pretend to love a Beast who actually does supposedly sometimes act like a beast, but that's why it's called acting, I guess.

Afterward, I have to change and go outside the stage door to sign autographs for little kids for an hour, like I do after every performance. I don't have to sign autographs every night, but these little girls who show up with their parents are the reason I'm even here. They're the reason my face is on a hundred-foot billboard in Times Square, so I don't want to let them down. It's exhausting doing it every night and every matinee, but I get to see how excited they are. So even though I'm tired, even though I just want to collapse into bed, I do it because I know that it really matters to them. Every single day and night.

Dad did tell the production to get me some security when I'm signing. There is always a mob outside the door, just tons of kids plus their parents. One of the guys who works at the theater told me he heard that Hugh Jackman, who's doing *The Boy from Oz* down the street, saw the crowd outside our door was bigger than theirs and asked, "Who the hell is *that* for?" I'm so grateful for the fans, and I'll always, always stop to say hi or sign something for them, but I am burning out, fast.

There are always those fans who get a little scary, and I think what sent Dad over the edge was the guy in Florida. He sent me a letter to the theater saying that he was getting out of jail and that as soon as he got out, he was coming to see me. What Dad didn't tell me was that he flew to Tampa to "talk to the creep." Not the safest thing to do, but it must have worked, because the letters stopped. So now I have Raul, the security guard who watches out for me when I'm out on the streets. After the highest highs—performing onstage, taking our bows, hearing from all these little kids about how much they love Belle, and then getting into the car with my driver and going past the giant Times Square billboard—I go home. Every night I crash. And I just feel totally depleted, totally alone.

Even though I'm working constantly, I do go out to a club called Vinyl a few times. I meet Joey Fatone, and he is super funny and shows me his inner lip tattoo, which I'd seen in a teen magazine. But then another night, I have a not-so-sweet run-in with Lindsay Lohan. It's totally my fault and so embarrassing. I don't know why I even do it, but it backfires. When we were making *Cadet Kelly*, I feel like Hilary mentioned that she didn't like Lindsay. So I figured if I told Lindsay that, maybe we'd bond or something? So, so dumb. I walk over and ramble some lame, drunken bullshit that sounds like I am some superfan.

I immediately regret walking over to her.

Lindsay stares at me blankly for a second and smiles, but I can tell she's annoyed by me. I have no clue what else to say. I'm so humiliated that I just walk back to my table and refill my drink. I gotta admit, I'm a little impressed. Lindsay's energy is unlike anything I've seen before. She radiates darkness, danger, sex, and chaos, and everyone LOVES her for it. She's seventeen years old, mind you. I feel like I always have to present this perfect-princess front for Disney, and I wish I could be myself as much as Lindsay is herself. She's unapologetic, and it seems so freeing.

I feel like I've been living so many different lives. There's the professional Christy, hitting her marks onstage and singing to the best of her ability. There's the downtown Christy at clubs like Vinyl and Caine, the one who is totally free to say or do anything she wants. And then she wakes up and goes back into professional Christy mode. It's a cycle that's wearing me out.

After the show one night, I'm outside the theater, signing autographs for all the kids, and a tan woman with dirty-blond hair and a blue skirt suit stands a few feet away, watching me among the crowd of excited mini princesses and their parents. At first I assume she's a fan. Once the crowd begins to thin out, she puts a white business card in front of my face. It says:

Yvette Chevalier
Psychic Healer and Clairvoyant
I see your future!

"You have a heartbreak in your life," she says. "A curse has been put upon you, you and your family are in danger, and I can help. I have answers for you."

"Thank you so much," I say, running my hand over the blue-and-white card. This feels like a sign, like something I need. Maybe this woman does have answers. Maybe she can just help me feel better about where I'm headed, because right now, as positive and confident as I felt when I first saw that giant billboard in Times Square, as high as I feel when an audience erupts in applause, I'm scared. When I see Shia or Lindsay or Hilary blowing up and getting bigger and bigger parts, as grateful as I am for Belle, I'm also freaked out. I don't want to get left behind anymore. I don't want to get lost.

"Call me," Yvette says before taking off down the street. The rest of my signing is a blur, and I can't get what she said out of my mind.

"You okay?" asks Raul, my security guard.

"Yep, I'm great!" I say, feeling, for the first time in a long time, a little hope. Maybe someone has the answers I need.

I don't tell anyone where I'm going. Not Mom or Dad, not friends. I'm doing something just for myself, and keeping it a secret makes it even more satisfying, more fun. Maybe even a little scary, in a good way. I drive my red convertible out of the garage under my building and into Jersey City, where Yvette has a shop/condo. I don't immediately think of Jersey City when I imagine a miracle fortune teller or spiritual healer, but a girl's got to live somewhere, right? And Jersey City is a hell of a lot cheaper than Manhattan. I take the Lincoln Tunnel out of the city and follow the directions I'd written on a piece of paper from MapQuest. I see the sign for Yvette's shop, which is on the bottom floor of a row of town homes. There's no crystal ball or anything cheesy on the sign, just her name, plus a neon sign in the window that says *Crystal Readings*. I park and head to the door. Yvette opens the door before I have a chance to knock.

"I *knew* you were here," she says, before dissolving into laughter. "Just kidding. I heard your car pull up. A little psychic humor for you, sweetheart. Come inside."

I walk into a small shop with different-colored crystals scattered on shelves, incense burning, and tarot cards on a small table. A few candles burn, and there are posters on the walls with images of what I *think* are supposed to be symbols for your third eye and the heart chakra.

"Sit, sit," she says. She has a thick Jersey accent and big hair, and she's wearing a power suit that's similar to the one she wore that night after the show. No flowy skirts or gold bracelets like you'd imagine a psychic to wear if this were a movie where a slightly depressed, overly exhausted actress drives out to see a psychic in hopes of curing all her woes. It makes me trust Yvette. She's not playing a part.

"Take a deep breath, close your eyes, and we can begin."

It feels so good to actually take a deep breath. I didn't even realize how tense I've become, how much I just need to *relax.*

"Now," she says, "give me your hands."

I move my hands across the table, and Yvette clasps them in her own, like a cocoon. We sit that way for what seems like forever, but it's probably just sixty seconds. She squeezes my hands.

"A curse has been put upon your family by your ancestors," she says. "On your father's side, there was a coven of witches who practiced black magic, and they cursed you in love. You've met the love of your life already, but you've lost him and need to get him back. It's not who you think it is."

I think she means Giovanni. Maybe I can save him. Maybe if we just give it another chance, he'll change!

"He has dark hair. He's strong," Yvette says.

"Yes," I say. "That's my ex Giovanni. He hates me."

She also tells me that my career will take off but that there is someone who might surpass me if I don't watch out. It makes me feel like a sitting duck.

It might seem ridiculous to have this woman tell me she can see the love of my life and that I need to reverse an ancient curse on my family, but I was raised Catholic, so this isn't that weird for me. I've seen my mom hold prayer beads and pray a novena for days in a row just so I could book a job. Magical thinking is not new to me. Mom has also always said that our hundred-year-old farmhouse where my siblings and I grew up is haunted by ghosts, and all of us tend to believe her. I'm playing a character onstage who falls in love with a magical beast. So this moment with Yvette doesn't feel like a joke. It feels incredibly real, like anything is possible. If she can help bring love into my life to make me feel less confused and lonely, I'm all ears.

"What do I do?" I ask, my eyes still closed. I decide at that moment that Giovanni is the love of my life and that I will get him back so we can succeed at life together. If I don't, Yvette says, our lives will amount to nothing.

Yvette says that she needs to get me a few "curse-reversal" candles and several "love-spell" candles and sand and that only she can purchase them, or else they won't work. She has to bless the candles before giving them to me. I write her a check for two hundred dollars.

"Make it out to cash," she says as I sign the check. "I'll get the candles tomorrow and set the plan in motion. In the meantime, don't mention this to anyone. Speaking about it can cause the curse to become permanent."

I hand over the check, and Yvette walks me to the door.

"I'll drop off the candles at your apartment, and we can discuss. Maybe you can buy me lunch. Then you'll come back at the same time next week for some blessings to cleanse you of the curse," she says.

"Thank you, Yvette," I say. "Thank you!"

I drive back toward New York through the Lincoln Tunnel, blaring music that I know Giovanni would listen to, imagining my wedding, a regular life, a beautiful dress. I imagine being loved, feeling normal. I truly believe I will get everything I want as long as I listen to Yvette.

I've been visiting Yvette in Jersey and burning her candles for two months when it happens. I've burned so many love candles and reverse-the-curse candles that once I almost set my apartment on fire. You're not supposed to blow the candles out or it's bad luck, and one day when I was out, the smoke set off the sprinklers and fire alarms, and the whole building was evacuated. Since my brother lives in the same building, he found out it was from my apartment because the doorman told him. When he questioned me, I just told him it was an accident, just a regular old candle I forgot to blow out. I beg him not to mention it to Mom and Dad because they'll just worry for no reason. I still trust Yvette, but something tells me that my parents might ask me a million questions if I tell them about her, and I am doing this for me, not for them. Plus it's my money. I've earned every cent. I'm so desperate that I've been buying crystals and candles and anything Yvette tells me I need. I'm sure this is the way to change things, and I'll do whatever it takes.

Still, sometimes it does feel like I have this dark secret, like something is wrong with me, but then I get the text. Out of the blue, two months after I first visited Yvette and burned her candles and held her crystals, Giovanni's name pops up on my phone.

What's up, stranger?

For a split second, I worry that it's a trick or that I'm just imagining it, but there it is, on my screen. As real as it gets.

Been thinking about you. Come visit?

This is it! I've heard through some of my old Barnard friends that Giovanni has a girlfriend, but I figure that this is just the spell being lifted. I run a lap around my apartment, almost screaming with excitement. I wait twenty minutes to reply, just to keep him on edge.

Hey, you . . . What's the address?

It's nine p.m. on a Monday, so I quickly change out of my pajamas, throw on some makeup, and pick a sexy but not over-the-top outfit. I put one of Yvette's crystals in my purse for good luck. This is it! It all worked. Yvette was right about everything. Why else would Giovanni text completely out of the blue? It's a sign. I'll never be alone again. This is only the beginning.

Over twenty thousand dollars. That's how much I've paid Yvette over the last few months for her stupid candles and her useless spells. When I confess this to Mom and Dad, they're more worried than angry. Well, Mom is worried, and Dad is livid.

"Give me this con artist's address!" he yells, his face red.

"No, Dad. I just want to be free of her," I say. I'm sitting in their kitchen in Milford, feeling like a little girl who's just gotten caught doing something bad. Giovanni and I did see each other, and then he just dropped off. I found out he'd never even broken up with his girlfriend. Figures. So my bank account was drained of over twenty thousand dollars for what? A bunch of useless crystals and stupid love candles? When I told Yvette about the night with Giovanni, she said we needed to "double down," so I started buying even more things. Or she did. With my money. Yvette kept making me promise not to tell my parents about her, but then Giovanni blew me off, and I figured out what was happening. I had to. How could I be so dumb?

"She's been getting even pushier," I tell my parents.

Yvette even accused me of "seeing another psychic," which freaked me out. How would she even know that? I didn't seek anyone else out, but a few weeks ago, I walked into another psychic reading shop on St. Mark's. I don't know why I did it. Maybe just to see how it would compare to Yvette's place in Jersey City. The woman inside, Agnes, really did look the part. Flowy dresses, tons of bangles, an eastern European accent. She said she was Albanian and told me she didn't want my money, but she could tell I was spiritually confused. Is it that obvious all the time?! Do I have "Save me, I'm totally adrift and directionless" written across my forehead? At least Agnes just talks to me and has never once asked for money or told me she can reunite me with the love of my life. I never even hinted to Yvette that this was happening, but she still figured it out. Had she been spying on me? Each coincidence that happens makes me feel like I'm losing my mind. When I admitted to Yvette that I'd been talking to this other psychic, she demanded that I stop going there. She told me to write her a check for twenty thousand dollars, and she would finally get the "magic" crystal she'd been promising, and wouldn't ruin my life.

"You know I can, dear."

As soon as I gave her that check, I knew it was wrong. Which is why I had to tell Mom and Dad. I'm in over my head. They know more about my finances than I do, and I'm scared.

"Do not give that woman another dime!" says Dad. He's pacing around the kitchen, looking like he wants to punch a wall. "We need to do this legally. I'll call my buddy Frank Calder and see what to do. He's a detective. What's her address?"

"Dad, you have to be careful," I say. I'm finally realizing that Yvette is a fraud, but that doesn't mean I'm not scared she may curse us. Getting ignored by Giovanni was my first clue that Yvette is sketchy. Talking to Agnes was the second. Here was this woman literally dressed in rags and living in a shitty studio off St. Mark's, and she charged me nothing. It made me question everything about Yvette, from her long red nails to her poofy blond hair. It made me not trust anyone. Especially not myself. I'd never spent that much money before, except for college tuition maybe. I'd never been that dumb.

"This is your fault, Shar," Dad says. "I should have been more involved with Christy's finances from day one. I would have paid attention."

"Oh, like you paid attention to our finances all these years," Mom yells. "How well has that gone for us?"

"It's my fault," I say. "I'm an adult now, not a kid. I should have known."

"No. Christy, I should have been paying attention," Mom says evenly. I can't believe she's not angry with me, but then again, that's Mom. She may have her issues, but she's ride or die. She'll always be there, no matter how much I fuck up.

I think about the little girls who stand out in the winter cold or in the heat of the summer, waiting to meet me—or to meet Belle. I love them so much. What kind of role model am I for them if I'm paying off fake psychics and falling for some asshole's proclamations of love? I have to make this right. I feel so much shame standing there in the kitchen with my parents, the kitchen I ate thousands of meals in as a kid. I feel even more lost and alone than I did before Yvette came into my life. I wonder how many actors or dancers she's targeted over the years. I'll never know, because I won't ever speak about her again. I just want to forget it ever happened. That's impossible, though. It's impossible to forget. I truly believe I'm cursed, thanks to Yvette. The tape playing in my head keeps telling me that I'm destined to fail. I hope it's wrong.

I try to move past Yvette, but some nights I get scared that she'll try to find me and harm me out of revenge. Dad thinks she'll just move on to the next sucker. The stress of the last few months has caused me to be hyperaware of my acid reflux, and I'm always running on fumes. I need to reset after all the drama with Yvette and the strain of eight shows a week.

At least I have some things to celebrate. I met with Nancy Josephson, who is a massive power player in the industry. She also reps Raven-Symoné, who is starring in her own popular Disney Channel show. Maybe Nancy can help me get to that next level. I never thought I'd want to move back to Los Angeles, with its sunshine and fake smiles, but now I know what I have to do. That's where the TV jobs are, the ones that can make me "the next Jen Aniston," as my agents keep saying. It's their job to have high hopes for me. To build me up. I just need to try to believe them.

Dear Girls,

Being a role model isn't something you can learn in a few meetings or in some half-assed course run by network executives. Becoming a public person recalibrates your DNA. You're born as bright-eyed "normal" kids, and then, somewhere along the way, you get trapped in what I call a "narcissistic purgatory," where your entire life is about preserving what you mean to people. If you don't, you have to start from zero in a new career. Once you become a public person, you'll exist on a spectrum of relevance for the rest of your life, depending on how your fans feel about you at any given time and what is trending in the world. Your fans, who adored you when they were little kids, grow up and learn to judge your every move through either rose-colored glasses or critical eyes. Fame can be a bitch, but being famous while you're growing up can be so much worse.

According to several different sources, Gen-Z's top career choice is being an influencer, and honestly, I get it. Using technology to brand yourself gives you the autonomy to evolve as an artist and a person. Even if you're a sorority girl showing off dress hauls, you can make millions if you capture the hearts and minds of your demographic. But you two are Gen Alpha, and I can't even imagine what the implications of AI and the evolution of social media will have for your generation. The landscape is changing faster than I can keep up with, and that terrifies me in ways I can't fully articulate yet.

Girls, we could make you social media famous tomorrow. That wouldn't be hard. But robbing you of your anonymity would be the deepest cut for me. True, you occasionally appear in the periphery of my content because I'm proud of you, and you've definitely borne witness to my ridiculous video shoots and silly props and products I film with my tripod. But the spotlight will never be on you unless you choose it yourselves.

I don't see my *experience as a family business you're inheriting. I see it as a way to help provide for our family. A means to an end and an honest living for someone in my situation with my set of skills I've sharpened. Life is about perseverance, and you are cut from my cloth. You have the fabric, the material, the DNA of performers and artists from both your father and me. But whether you stitch that cloak is entirely your choice. You get to decide if you even want to try it on. There is an entire world out there that needs peacemakers, helpers, society fixers—not influencers. That's the difference between being pushed into fame by a narcissistic parent and being protected from it until you're old enough to understand what you're choosing. The cloak is there if you want it. But your anonymity, your childhood, your choice to be private citizens—I believe that that's my greatest gift to you.*

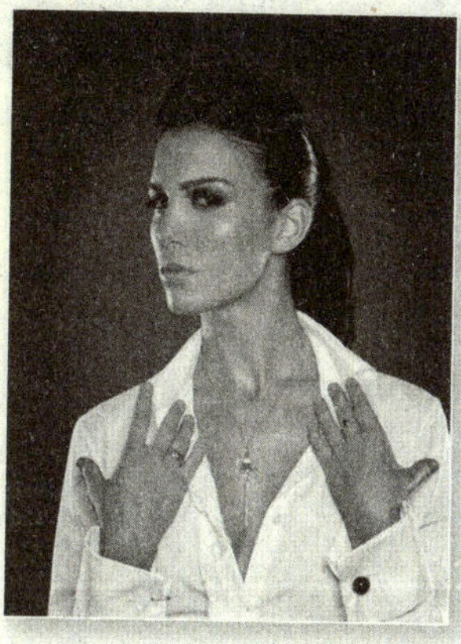

9

Dream World

2004–2010

Ages 20 to 26

I'm still trying to forget that, at our last performance, during the final kiss, Zane's tongue felt like a plunger going down my throat. It seemed like total beast behavior. If he was trying to surprise me or gross me out, it worked. I had to be a "pro," though, and stay in character as Belle and smile and bow as if nothing happened. When my eyes popped open from shock, Zane was smiling. I wonder if he does that to all the Belles before they leave. Then again, that's just how theater is, right? Instead of getting pissed at Zane, I just laughed it off. I wanted to end on a good note, but that moment made me glad my contract was over and I could move back to LA, even though I thought I was totally finished with that city. But like Mom says, go where the work is. And right now it's in Los Angeles. I hope.

It's my time to be an adult in LA, but Mom moves out there with me again. I guess it's to manage my career, even though I'm almost twenty-one.

Mom said that Dad wanted to manage my career when I was doing Belle, but she told him, "Over my dead body." She says Dad would ruin my career and my finances, and to never trust him with those things.

"It's you and me, Christy," she always says. "I'm moving back out there with you because I don't want people to take advantage of you. I can look out for that."

I've wanted her to leave Dad and stand up to him for so long, but now I just want her to have her own life. She leased a smaller apartment one floor below my loft in this building called the Palazzo, which is super high-end. There's a gym and a yoga room and a pool, and I'll probably never use any of them, except maybe the pool. Mom said I can afford both apartments—the *Even Stevens* money plus *Kim Possible* and all the million other things I'm doing are keeping my bank account full, I guess. I never check it; I just trust Mom to make sure everything is fine.

I'm not working that much yet. We've only been settled back in LA for about a month, but it feels a little slow, even though my agents keep saying they're going to package me with showrunners to try to get me a huge show like *Friends* or *The O.C.* I had a disappointing lunch with Mick Frost from Disney, and he told me that I'm too old to play one of the Disney Channel kids and too young to be a mom or a teacher or anything, so really there's no place for me there anymore.

Mom keeps saying I need a recording contract, so I'm working with an LA attorney who represents huge people like Gwen Stefani and the Black Eyed Peas. He's setting me up to go to sessions with some big songwriters so I can create my own hit single before I get signed.

I've never created my own music, unless it was something I wrote in my bedroom alone at home. I recorded "Teacher's Pet" and some Disney songs for a greatest hits album, but nothing original. It's awkward for me to write my own music, especially with people who are such pros. I just hear the tape in my head saying that my lyrics suck, or this isn't what I'm meant to do. But I *want* it so badly.

We've only been in LA for a few weeks, but Mom and I get invited to a fashion event to kick off LA Fashion Week. It's nowhere near as huge as New York or Paris Fashion Week, but I still feel like it's a big deal to get to go. It's in West Hollywood, and I'm eager to meet some new people, so I pick a fitted black shirt, boots, and a turquoise-and-purple skirt layered over jeans. We get to the venue, give our names, and walk into a room packed with beautiful people: actors and models and agents and musicians. When I was a kid, Mom went everywhere with me. It was normal then, but now it just feels odd, like she's my handler or something. It's embarrassing, but I feel bad saying anything to her about it. She needs this.

I go to the bathroom and come back to find Mom talking to a tall, good-looking guy in a brown suit. He's tan with blue eyes, and when he looks over at me, I pretend not to care. But I do. He's got to be a model or an actor. No one this good-looking is an accountant.

"Christy, this is Ravi," Mom says, giving me a look that says, *He's cute, right?* "Ravi, this is my daughter Christy. The actress and singer. She was just starring on Broadway."

"Hey."

"Nice to meet you, Christy. Your mom was telling me you just moved back to LA. Are you working on a show?"

"Not right now," I say, wishing I could instead tell him I just booked a lead in a major sitcom or I have a record coming out in the spring. "I do voice the lead in this show, *Kim Possible*, and I'm going on a lot of auditions and recording some songs for a record."

"Very cool," he says.

"What about you?" I ask, trying to deflect from the fact that I have zero work right now, except for *Kim Possible*. "Are you an actor?"

"I'm a filmmaker mostly, and sometimes I act," he says, which makes Mom perk up, of course.

"Oh, interesting!" she gushes. "Maybe you can write a part for Christy."

"Mom!"

"What? I'm just putting it out there."

Ravi laughs but not in a mean way. He's easygoing and charming and more sophisticated than most LA guys that I've met. He reminds me of an East Coast person, someone who's cultured and refined, not some surf bro. He tells us he's from Brazil. His dad is some sort of high-powered guy, and he's related to a famous fashion designer. He's supposedly Ravi's great uncle. The way Ravi describes it, it's hard to understand the connection, but the guy *looks* like he'd be related to a famous designer. His suit is perfect, and his watch is upscale, especially for a twentysomething. His class and refinement stand out, even in a room full of gorgeous, stylish, rich (or trying-to-look-rich) people.

Mom wanders off to get a drink, and Ravi and I talk nonstop. We hang out with a few people he knows, and photographers buzz around the room, snapping pictures of the crowd. We talk about my love of political science, my time at Barnard, missing the East Coast, and his love of musical theater. Boxes are checked. His intense eyes look right into mine. As we talk, we lean closer to each other until our arms touch. I get a thrill from being so close to him, but I try to play it cool. His charisma is hard to resist.

"Want to hit up the Chateau?" he asks.

"What's that?"

"You don't know the Chateau Marmont?"

"Oh, yeah, of course," I lie. Ravi looks amused, as if everyone should know what it is.

"Well, then, we're definitely going," he says.

"Let me just tell my mom. I'll be back."

I find Mom in the crowd and run over to her, so excited that I can barely breathe.

"Ravi wants to take me out to some place called the Chateau Marmont."

"He's a nice young man, Christy. I like him. You should go. Have fun."

"You sure?" I'm a little surprised Mom is being so casual about this. She must love this guy.

"I'm fine. Go!"

We hop into Ravi's sleek black Mercedes and head down Melrose, onto side streets, and then onto Sunset Boulevard, past huge billboards advertising every new movie and show coming out. It's like each ad is mocking me, reminding me of my lack of work. Ravi navigates through the streets like he's a NASCAR driver, and I love it. I know he's showing off, but it feels rebellious and a little dangerous, and I'm here for it. He takes a long drag from his Marlboro Red, and when his phone rings, he turns down Pearl Jam's "Yellow Ledbetter," which is blaring from the speakers. He starts speaking Portuguese heatedly into the phone on speaker and I don't understand anything he's saying, but his confidence is sexy. He puts his hand on my leg, and I suddenly feel flustered. He hangs up the phone, shifts gears, and the car lurches itself up the Hollywood hill and pulls in front of a classy neon sign that reads *Chateau Marmont* in a font that reminds me of old Hollywood or a European chalet. A wall of ivy spreads behind the sign. It's magical, a place that looks like it has history. Ravi tells me everyone from Clark Gable and Marilyn Monroe to Keanu Reeves and Kate Moss have stayed here. Ravi seems to know a lot of Hollywood gossip, which feels like a weird thing for a straight guy to care about.

Ravi zooms up to the valet, gets out, and walks around to my side of the car to help me out. I feel like a princess, and I love how he seems so confident, tossing his keys to the valet like he owns the place. There are paparazzi lurking in the corner of the driveway, against a wall. He leads me into the lobby bar, which is full of dark wood and chandeliers, like a Spanish-style villa. I wonder if any superfamous people are sitting in dark corners, huddled up and talking about their next projects. Ravi pulls a chair out for me and orders red wine and steak frites for us both.

"So, Christy, what do you think?" he asks, gesturing around the room. "This place is my second home. I can't believe you haven't been."

"It's cool," I say, staring into his intense eyes. Everything about this guy seems intense, but in a good way. He's hard to look away from. "I've mostly lived in New York, so I'm used to clubs in Manhattan, but this is way nicer."

I didn't eat anything at the party, so I'm starving. Ravi tells me about growing up in Brazil, how his dad is on his fourth wife but his mother was "the first." He seems a little bitter about it. I tell him about my parents always arguing, how I wished for a long time that Mom would leave. Ravi lives in Hollywood and is working on a few film sets and going to auditions, but it doesn't seem like he has a regular day job or anything. Judging by the way his watch is gleaming, it looks like he has plenty of money. He makes me feel like the most beautiful, fascinating girl in the room, and I don't want it to end. This is the kind of guy I want to be with. Sophisticated, successful. He makes me want to level up.

It's been three weeks since our first date to the Chateau, and Ravi and I haven't really been separated since. I spent the night with him that first night, and Mom didn't even question me the next day. She just did her usual I-hope-you-wore-a-rubber speech, which was so embarrassing. Who calls condoms that anymore?!

Ravi's apartment is nice, but the only weird thing is that he has stacks of gossip magazines lying around, like Hilary and her mom did during *Cadet Kelly*. I don't understand wanting to read those if you're *in* the business. Don't they know they're all fake? I guess it's not that big of a deal, though. I'm also trying to tell myself that it's not a big deal that Ravi's dad is possibly under fire for money laundering or something, and the FBI is supposedly investigating him. I know Ravi is stressed about it, but he tells me his dad is completely innocent, and the charges are all lies. I just want to have fun with this guy. It's moving fast, but who cares? When you know you know, right? When I told Dad about Ravi and his family, he said he sounded "suspect," but Ravi's the most refined guy I've ever been with. He's not some LA douchebag. Dad is hung up on the fact that Ravi doesn't have a "regular job" and that his dad paid for his condo, but it's not Dad's life or his relationship. It's mine.

We're walking the red carpet at a music awards show, and Ravi is acting distant and weird. I'm trying to pose for photos and answer the reporters' questions, but he's over there sulking and side-eyeing me. He looks classy while he's doing it, but still. It's hard to focus when I can pretty much *feel* that he's pissed, and I have no clue why. We've been together for a few months, so by now I can read his moods, and this one isn't great.

I move toward him and take his hand so we can go inside finally. I smile for the cameras, but I have a nervous feeling in my stomach that I don't love.

"What's wrong?" I ask under my breath, still smiling. "You seem angry or something."

Ravi leans down to whisper in my ear.

"You know I was asked to be Penelope Cruz's red-carpet handler at another event, and I said no so I could be here with you. And you're icing me out of the photos."

"Icing you out? I was just talking to journalists. I didn't know you cared. I'm sorry, babe. That's totally my fault."

Maybe I'm being selfish, leaving Ravi out of the photos and making it all about me. I remember that awful tutor who accused me of never doing things for others, only for myself. Maybe she was right.

"I could have been out there with an A-list actress, but instead I'm here with you."

"Babe, I'm so sorry. I didn't know. I'm so happy you're here," I say, squeezing his hand. I *am* sorry, but he's also making me feel small, like I'm some has-been actress. Someone he's wasting time with. "It won't happen again. Promise."

Sometimes it feels like he's holding a scorecard that I can't keep up with. I like that he's so assured. He's cultured and aware of the world. He wants me to be better, to learn about wines and art and film. Yes, he's loud and he talks about himself a lot, but that's part of his confidence. He challenges me, which is probably a good thing. I'd rather him be confident than meek or insecure.

Ravi squeezes my hand as we walk into the auditorium, and the knots in my stomach dissolve. The next time we're on a red carpet, I'll keep him close. I won't disappoint him.

"It's disgusting in here," says my brother after I puke for what feels like the fifteenth time in an hour. "No offense, but we can't be in here. It reeks."

"Fine," I say, so weak that I can barely get the words out. "Go stay with Mom and Dad."

We're spending Christmas on a cruise as a family, and I wanted it to be a blast for everyone. We haven't gone on a trip together in forever, and when the cruise company asked me to perform on this ship in exchange for a free vacation for my whole family, I felt like I could do something cool for everyone. It felt good to be able to bring everyone together. And now I'm covered in puke, stuck in this room with norovirus, while my parents and siblings are eating at the best Italian restaurant on the ship, of course, where Dad orders everything off menu and they drink top-shelf cocktails, which Disney *hates* paying for. At least I got to perform for two days before it all went, literally, to shit.

I call Ravi for some sympathy.

"Hey, babe," I croak into the phone.

"How're you feeling? Any better?"

"Not really. I'm stuck in the room, and my family is out there eating and drinking their way through the ship. I mean, I want them to have fun, but they barely even come by to check on me. I miss you. I'm over this."

"Your family doesn't have your best interests in mind," he says. "They're there on your dime. You're the one who had to work for the trip. This has to stop."

Ravi has started questioning my relationship with my parents lately, asking how often I pay for things and whether or not they contribute anything. He thinks it's "weird" that I pay for their plane tickets and pay my mom's LA rent when I'm an adult and she doesn't need to be in California anyway. When I tell him I have no clue about my finances, he tells me I'll "never be an adult" until I handle my own money and find out how much my parents actually take.

"When you get back on the twentieth, why don't you come to Aspen and spend Christmas with my family? Take a break from your family."

Ravi wants me to meet his dad. I want to scream with excitement, but I'm too weak from puking nonstop to emote.

"Really?" I croak. "I'd love that! I can change my ticket to Connecticut to go to Aspen for a few days. A break from my family sounds pretty good right now. And they probably won't even care, since they're not paying any attention to me here anyway."

"I'll fly you out, babe," says Ravi. "My dad can send his plane. It's not a problem. You deserve it."

"I love you, babe," I say. "Can't wait to see you. And I promise I won't be sick by then."

"Love you too," he says.

Now at least I have something to look forward to. I wanted to bring my family together with this trip for once. I thought this cruise could help us bond again. Maybe Ravi is right. Maybe they just love me for my money. When I go back to LA, I'll start looking at my finances. I *hate* math and accounting, but I'm an adult now. It's time for me to grow up.

"I don't think your dad likes me," Ravi says as we leave the Fox Theatre in Atlanta. The January cold here isn't as bad as Aspen's was, but I still shiver when we walk outside. "He kept eyeing me like he was sizing me up or trying to see if I'm good enough or something."

I'm doing an eight-day run of *Beauty and the Beast* back at the theater where I got my start in *Annie*. It's wild to be back, and it brings up so many memories of being this tiny six-year-old just wanting to belt it out for the adults. I wanted Ravi to come to meet my family, even though he's always telling me how terrible they are.

"He likes you," I lie. Truth is, I'm pretty sure Dad doesn't like Ravi, but no way am I telling him that. "He's just extremely protective of his daughters. He looks out for us, so he just wants to make sure you're a good guy, which you are."

I know hanging out with the Romanos isn't as posh as having aged Cabernet with Ravi's family, but it's important to me that he gets to know my family. I imagine marrying this guy. I think about him proposing and us having a beautiful wedding. I know it's only four months in, but I feel it.

"Thanks, babe. You were great tonight."

"Thanks!"

"Have you asked about the money yet?"

"I will when we get back to LA, I promise."

I'm getting a little annoyed that he keeps bringing up my finances, but maybe he's thinking about a future with me also, and knowing that I'm not bleeding money is important. He's like my white knight, protecting me and making sure I'm not getting taken advantage of. He did get me to start staying at hotels like The Ritz, and he's gotten me to stop shopping at places like Forever 21. I also started getting bikini waxes, which I absolutely fucking hate. Women do the most brutal things in the name of beauty. But Ravi said that classy girls wax, so I'm just suffering through the appointments like millions of other girls, I guess. He says I'm a successful woman and I should be buying finer things, like Chanel or Prada. Like Hilary when we were in Canada. If only Hilary and her mom could see me now.

I'm trying to get Ravi and Dad to bond, but I think they may be too much alike with their machismo and their alpha-type personalities and their charisma. In private, Dad said that Ravi seems pretentious and flashy and that I should watch out. I don't tell Dad about Ravi's dad having legal troubles, because then he'd for sure lose it. He'd probably have one of his shady friends "look into him." Ravi might have family money, but he did tell me that he pawned his Patek Philippe watch for cash and that his dad wasn't giving him as much money lately. Ravi says that it's "backward" that I'm the one giving my parents money, and his dad helping him out is "the way it should be." I guess it's time I know exactly what I have or don't have.

A week after that trip, I finally sit down with my accountant, Barry, at his Beverly Hills office to talk about money. It isn't good news. Well, it's good and bad. The good news is that I made my first million dollars with all the *Even Stevens* and *Kim Possible* money plus checks from a record deal that's in the works with Atlantic. I also made money from a young adult novel I'm writing for a big publisher. So I guess I can afford to shop on Rodeo Drive after all.

The not-so-good news is that it seems like I've been giving Mom tens of thousands of dollars a year, paying for her apartment and her car and whatever plastic surgery she's gotten. When I look at that plus the fact that I'm paying a percentage to a lawyer, a manager, agents, and a business manager, I'm giving away most of my money. *My* money. Plus I finally sold my red Cabrio, even though I loved that car, and got a Mercedes G-Wagon, which wasn't cheap. So here I am, driving this fancy car, wearing tight Frankie B jeans and Dior wraparound shades. Sometimes I feel ridiculous but also, I have to admit, pretty cool. I mean, I worked for this lifestyle, and I need to play the part to keep it going.

I'm scared to tell Ravi about Mom's salary because he will for sure freak the fuck out. I have to do it, though. We're getting serious—we just moved in together! If I'm going to have a future with this guy, I can't lie about my finances. It feels like it's us against the world. I do want Mom to leave LA. It's time. There's no reason for her to be here. I don't need babysitting, and it's a huge waste of money to pay for her condo and car. How do I tell her? I don't want to break her heart or make her think I'm not grateful for all she's done, but I'm over it. I'm gearing up to tell Ravi because I don't want anything to come between us. Because everything feels right with him. The only thing that's been bothering me is that he used to date this model, Savannah, and when I looked her up, she's this gorgeous blond-haired, blue-eyed goddess with massive tits. I look nothing like her.

I finally got up the courage to confront Mom about the money. I didn't cut her off, but I did tell her that Ravi and I are concerned about how much I'm spending on her condo and that it's a lot of money I'm giving her each month. She said she could scale back, but she hasn't offered to leave. I have to get up the courage to just tell her to go, but it's not easy. We haven't spoken much since I confronted her, so when she calls and tells me that Dad is flying out to LA because he has something he wants to tell me, it freaks me out a little. I ask if they're divorcing, and she says no.

"Whatever he tells you, don't let them manipulate you about money," Ravi says as I get the condo ready for my parents to come. "Just be strong, and remember, that's *your* money. Not theirs."

"I got it, babe," I say. I'm hoping it's not about money and not some desperate ploy for me to keep being their gravy train. When the buzzer rings, my stomach lurches. It's been three months since I last saw my parents and it was so tense with Dad and Ravi there. I'm not looking forward to more of the same.

I buzz them up, and when they come in, Dad is wearing an eye patch and holding a large yellow folder.

"What's wrong with your eye?" I ask as we hug hello.

"I'll tell you," he says. He shakes Ravi's hand awkwardly and asks how he's doing, but I know he doesn't care about the answer. I've laid out cheese and crackers for them, and we head to the couch to sit down so that Dad can spill whatever news he's got. I motion for Ravi to sit, but he shakes his head.

"I'll be upstairs," he says. "This is family business; you guys can have some privacy."

"Thanks, babe. You can come down anytime. You're family too, you know."

As soon as I say this, Dad shoots me a look that says, *Like hell he is.*

Ravi disappears upstairs.

"I can't stand the suspense, Dad. What's so important that you had to fly across the country to tell me?"

Dad and Mom look at each other, and he hands me some papers, which turn out to be X-rays that I can't understand.

"What's this? I don't know what this means," I say.

"Christy, I have a rare eye cancer," Dad says. "I love you so much—so does your mom—and we just wanted to tell you in person. We told your brother and sisters. I'm going to do radiation, and there's a clinical trial that sounds promising too."

I feel numb with a tinge of hotness behind my eyes. How is this real? He's supposed to be the invincible, tough guy, and now he's got cancer? I can't comprehend this moment. I'm scared for Dad, for all of us. My parents aren't perfect, but I don't want to lose them. Before I can say anything, though, Ravi comes running down the stairs, screaming and pointing his finger in my father's direction.

"This is ridiculous!" he yells, rushing right up to Dad, who stands and faces Ravi as if he's gearing up to fight him. "This is bullshit. You're manipulating her. How dare you pull the cancer card right after she confronts you about how much money she's been giving you!"

It looks like they're about to punch each other right here in the living room. Even though Ravi is taller and younger, Dad, who grew up in the rough streets of 1960s Italian New Haven, would drop him in a second. I'm in utter shock about how this is playing out. For starters, Dad just told me he might die. Tears stream down my face. I'm not sure if I'm crying because Dad has cancer or because I know Ravi and my parents can never repair things after this.

"You don't deserve my daughter," Dad yells. "You're a fake, and she'll see that soon enough! You don't work. You're a freeloader. Where's your paycheck, besides the money your trust fund gives you? If you even have a trust fund!"

"Ravi, Dad, stop!" I yell through my tears. "Stop screaming at each other!" I rasp breathlessly.

Ravi puts his arm around me. Dad's face flushes purple with rage.

"You've never really been there for her except when you've needed something. And now you're playing on her emotions. It's disgusting!" Ravi pulls me closer. I don't know how to even process any of this—Dad having cancer, my parents taking advantage of me. It's all too much.

"Just leave!" Ravi yells, opening the door for them to go. Mom and Dad grab their things and walk out the door. Ravi slams it shut. I'm sobbing, and he takes me by the shoulders and looks right into my eyes.

"This is too much drama," Ravi says. "I'm going to stay with a friend tonight. Listen, it's them or me, Christy. Don't call me until you figure this out."

The door slams again, and I feel totally, completely alone.

Less than a week after that awful night, Dad calls. I haven't spoken to him since then. It's just been me and Ravi, and I've been agonizing over how to handle things. This is my family, after all, but it's been toxic for so long, and that night was a breaking point. And now here's Dad, reaching out. Ravi is out running an errand, so I answer. I mean, Dad does have cancer.

"Dad?"

"Christy, I know you don't want to talk to us, but this Ravi guy is bad news."

"What?" I laugh, even though I'm suddenly full of nerves and don't find this funny at all. "What are you talking about?"

"Look, don't get mad. I hired a private detective. Remember my buddy Frank Calder, who used to work for the NYPD? He's legit."

"Dad! Why would you do that?" I peek out the window to make sure I don't see Ravi pulling in. If he hears this, he'll lose his shit. "Ravi is from a good family."

"His dad is some crook, and he's being investigated by the FBI. They're not 'refined,' Christy. They're money-hungry phonies. Look, Frank ran a search, and he sent me the preliminary findings, and this Ravi has all kinds of charges and mental health issues. Aggravated assault, multiple violent offenses. He's been in and out of mental institutions. It's bad. I don't want you anywhere near him. Come home, and we'll figure this out."

I knew Ravi got in trouble in his younger years, but this doesn't sound like him at all. He's never been violent, not once. Except when he and Dad almost came to blows.

"Dad, are you sure? This sounds crazy. Maybe it's another Ravi?"

"Frank says he has some more digging to do, so hold tight. And in the meantime, why don't you tell this boyfriend of yours what we found? See how he reacts?"

"I'm not holding tight, Dad! This Frank guy is full of shit. This isn't true! I'm DONE!"

I hang up, and when Ravi walks through the door, I'm sobbing. I don't have enough time to try to hide what's going on, so I just blurt it out.

"My Dad just called. He says you have all kinds of criminal charges against you, violent crimes, and you've been in mental institutions, but I don't believe it! He has some private detective looking into you. I told him he's full of shit, and I hung up on him."

"What the FUCK?!" Ravi yells, dropping his bags. "I hope you know me better than that, Christy. I'll give him anything he wants. My social security, references, anything. I have photos with the Clintons and Shakira, for fuck's sake. I'm not some lowlife. I have nothing to hide."

"I know, babe," I say sweetly, trying to calm him down. "I will never question you again."

He grabs me in his arms, and we start to kiss. I feel dopamine coursing through my body, and I don't resist.

It was all a fucking mix-up.

Two days after Dad called with Frank's "findings," he called back to say it was a misunderstanding. The wrong Ravi was profiled. And that was all I needed to give me the courage to send an email to my entire family calling them out for every horrible thing I feel like they've done and cutting them out of my life. I tell my siblings I feel distant from them, tell Mom and Dad their marriage is a sham. I just let everything I've been holding in for years out in that email.

Ravi stands over my shoulder as I hit send.

"Good for you, babe," he says. "Screw your family. You'll be better off. You'll see."

A few hours later, Mom responds simply with a very corporate, cold email, and she cc's my lawyer:

Christy, I will be moving back to Connecticut. I need to know if I should sell off any furnishings and if there is any final business to address before I leave.

Please advise.

As powerful as I felt finally saying all the things that have been building up over so many years, I now feel a deep loss. I've lost my family—literally overnight—and it's of my own doing. I have Ravi, though. At least I have him. It was cathartic in the moment to hit send, but in the pit of my stomach, there's shame and fear. Maybe this is just what freedom is supposed to feel like, and in time, I won't feel so nauseous and afraid.

He's all I need. Forever. I finally know he is the only family I need.

~

My agents are doing an okay job getting me work, but I'm still hungry for something edgier, something that shows my range. I've gotten cast as characters in video games, the coolest being the voice of Yuffie in *Final Fantasy VII*. She's a beloved character in a huge game and the biggest thing I've gotten since *Kim Possible*. I don't think the director loved me, though, so I'm not sure I'll get asked to voice her again. I've had some guest spots on shows like *Joan of Arcadia* with Amber Tamblyn and *Summerland*, but no big Aniston-in-*Friends* moment like they kept promising when they signed me. I did book two movies, though: *The Cutting Edge: Going for the Gold*, where I play an ice skater, and *Campus Confidential*, a TV movie we'll shoot in Louisiana. I play the brunette (of course), paired with Keri Lynn Pratt, the blond (of course). I play teenagers in these movies, but since I've just turned twenty-one, I'm itching for more mature roles.

I do miss my family, even though I'm still so angry at them. I don't tell Ravi that I miss them, since he pretty much hates my parents. I want to call Dad to see how he's feeling, but I can't. I've been spending more money since I cut them off and cut them out of my life. Ravi keeps encouraging me to spoil myself a little. So I drive my G-Wagon to Rodeo and shop whenever I feel like it. My days of Abercrombie and Forever 21 are long gone.

Even though he's loving and protective, Ravi's also crazy jealous and pretty strict about how I should act around other guys, and I hate it. In *Campus Confidential*, there's a scene at the end where I have to kiss my costar Teddy Dunn. Teddy is totally sweet and there is nothing going on between us, but every time Ravi and I talk, he's freaked out about this kiss. I explain that it's all business, that this is what actors do, but he's not having it. Being long-distance in Louisiana while he's in California doesn't help. I'm by myself down here, and I can't call Mom for advice. So how do I tell the director or Teddy that I'm freaking out about the kiss? It's so unprofessional, but I also don't want to piss off Ravi. I know he cares about me and his jealousy is out of love, but I just want to get this shoot over with and go home.

~

Fuck.

This cannot be happening. The past few days, I was so crampy and not feeling right at all. I've been trying to hide it by taking Aleve and just gritting my teeth through my scenes. When I finally took a pregnancy test and it was positive, I knew I was screwed. I felt sheer terror and total shock, not knowing how I'd manage, scared to tell anyone. My first thought was to call Mom, not Ravi. But I kept it secret. I knew Ravi would blame me and make me feel like I'd done something wrong. He wouldn't be gentle or caring. I know he's not ready to be a father now because he's told me a hundred times. Maybe it's wrong, but I don't know how else to handle this.

I don't feel comfortable telling the director or producers, and definitely not my costars. I've been acting emotional between takes and sometimes combative, because I'm scared. I'm afraid to confide in the other actors, even my old Disney friend Brandon Baker, but there is one person I think I can trust.

I find Marvin, the location scout, smoking a cigarette near craft services. I feel like I can trust Marvin to help me out. He reminds me of some of Dad's take-charge, burly friends at home. Not the scary ones. But the ones who get shit done quietly.

Talk about awkward, though. Marvin is like a kind, hilarious older uncle, but still. Asking him to take me to a Planned Parenthood in the deep South for an ultrasound is mortifying.

"Hey, kiddo," Marvin says when I walk up.

"Hey. Can I talk to you in private?"

"Of course, hun." He stubs out his cigarette and follows me to a quiet area away from set.

"So, this is a little embarrassing to ask," I say. I'm sure my face is pale since I feel like I may throw up.

"You okay? Did something happen?"

"Yeah, I guess that's one way to put it. You've met my boyfriend, Ravi? Well . . . I'm pregnant, and I need to get to a clinic. I have the address and already talked to them. Do you think you could take me and not tell anyone? I found the address of one not too far away, and we wrap in about an hour. I'm so sorry, but I don't know what else to do. I hope this doesn't put you in a bad position."

I start crying, and he pulls me in for a bear hug. I can just hear my Catholic ancestors wailing in agony, knowing their descendant is unwed, pregnant, and about to go to a Planned Parenthood. I know I'm not the first Catholic girl to go through this, but years of church and catechism have me feeling even worse.

"I got you," Marvin says. "You'll be just fine. Do you want to tell anyone in your family? You shouldn't be alone."

"I haven't talked to my mom in, like, two months," I say. But I *have* been so tempted to call Mom. She's always been there for me. Always. A piece of me is missing.

"Why don't we meet at my car when we wrap, and I'll drive you over?" Marvin says.

"Thank you. Truly."

I find a secluded spot away from set and make the call I've been so scared to make. It rings twice.

"Christy?" She sounds excited and scared, almost like she's been waiting by the phone.

"Hi, Mom," I say as more tears stream down my face.

"What happened? What's wrong?"

"Please don't get mad at me, Mom. Promise?"

"I promise."

"I'm . . . pregnant." Choking out the words makes the tears run faster. Thank goodness I have a weekend off after this, so maybe she can come stay with me. Mom is silent for a few seconds.

"Where are you filming?" she asks. "I'll get there as soon as I can."

"Thank you, Mom! Thank you." Relief washes over me, knowing she's coming. At least somebody will be there to help.

My mom might be a lot of things—bad with money, a little controlling—but she *always* has my back. As angry as I've been with her, I know at this moment, she's my ride or die.

Marvin drives me to the clinic, and I have to walk inside past angry protesters shouting horrible things. I lie down for the ultrasound, having no clue what I will do once it's confirmed for sure that I'm pregnant. I can't even be very far along. It must have happened right before I left LA. The ultrasound tech squirts cold jelly on my stomach and starts checking for signs of life. My heart is thumping through my chest.

"Hmm," she says.

"What is it?" I say, more terrified than I expected myself to be. "What's wrong?"

"I'm so sorry to tell you this, Miss Romano . . ."

The whole aftermath was horrible, but it was so good to see Mom. I hadn't realized just how much I missed her and my whole family. How much I needed her. She took care of me after they told me it was an ectopic pregnancy, which means the embryo implanted outside the uterus and wasn't viable. I would have been terrified without Mom there to help me through taking the medication and dealing with the whole process. I cried when she left and felt the loneliest I'd felt in my life. Even though I'm not ready to be a mom, I want to someday, and it's still sad to think . . . what if?

As the shoot goes on in Louisiana, I become more and more terrified of Ravi leaving me. I told him about the pregnancy, and it's like he blamed *me*. He gave the baby a name, Grace, and a birthday. He eventually acted more caring, but I can't help but think he'll somehow hold it over me like he does with so many other things on his growing list. Midway through our time apart, he went to shoot some independent movie in Nebraska—some slasher thing for no money. I'm happy he's getting work, because all he wants is to be a famous writer or an actor featured in one of his gossip magazines he devours. Maybe that'll make him less jealous of my success.

I know my agents are not happy with me screwing up the kiss scene or with the feedback they are hearing. They don't like Ravi at all, and they keep hinting that he's bad—not just for me personally but for my career. I told him I hated doing the kissing scene, which I did, and he's calmed down about it happening. So it's back to LA, back to my life with him. Hopefully back to more work and a record deal finally. I'm so tired of waiting for one to happen.

One amazing, not shitty thing that happened when I was in Louisiana was that I got my first Daytime Emmy nomination—for *Kim Possible*! I called Ravi immediately, and he was so supportive, and then I went straight to this Italian jewelry company, Valobra, to see if I could wear their jewels to the event. And they said yes. Ravi asked his uncle the designer if I could wear one of his gowns. It's a gorgeous nude-colored bejeweled dress, and I love it! I felt like royalty when I tried it on with the jewels in their boutique. The night will be amazing, except for one massive thing: Mick Frost, the president of Disney Channel, invited my parents. And they are coming. Mick has no idea about our rift. When I tell Ravi they'll be *at our table*, he says, "Don't even look at them. Don't speak to them. Just pretend they don't even exist."

We leave the Carlyle Hotel in Manhattan, where Ravi's family has an account, and a driver takes us to the Emmy venue. Ravi looks handsome in his dark suit, and I love my whole look, but in the pit of my stomach, I know it's going to be a tough night. We pose for photos, and I make sure to keep him close, even when reporters ask me questions. I don't want to give him a reason to be mad at me like after some of our previous red carpets, when he was so pissed. I try to appear calm, even though my heart is racing with anxiety.

Inside the ballroom, I say hi to Mick and a few other Disney executives. I feel like I've known them my whole life by now. As I'm hugging Mick, I see my parents already seated at the table. My face flushes bright red. My heart pounds.

"Hi, Romanos!" Mick says, giving them both handshakes. "You must be so proud of Christy. I know I am."

Ravi pulls my hand, and we sit at the far end of the table without acknowledging my parents at all. Mick looks totally confused, and Mom and Dad look hurt and embarrassed. I feel so ashamed, but this is the right thing to do to give myself autonomy from them. Right? I try to remember all the money I paid out, all the ways I thought they took advantage of me over the years. My hands are clammy, and I don't even care if I win. I just want this to be over with. I'm scared Dad will lunge across the table and punch Ravi in the face.

Ravi keeps his hand on my back under the table pretty much the whole time, except when I get up to present with Donovan Patton from *Blue's Clues*. I make sure not to stand too close or look too cozy with Donovan, since I know Ravi is watching. I manage to smile and do the bit without flubbing a line, despite my nerves. I've barely eaten, so I feel a little lightheaded, and when I sit back at the table, I'm almost a little jealous to see Mick having a good time with my parents.

"And the Daytime Emmy for Outstanding Performer in an Animated Program goes to . . ."

Ravi squeezes my knee, and I can barely breathe, not because I need to win, but because of this fucked-up situation.

". . . Henry Winkler for *Clifford's Puppy Days*!"

I clap, even though I want to cry. I can feel Mom and Dad looking at me, and Ravi leans in and whispers, "You deserved it," but it doesn't help. I mean, it's Henry Winkler. He's a legend, and he's also one of the few actors to have a reputation for being *actually* sweet and kind. Here I am, in jewels and this gorgeous dress, ignoring my parents, pretending that everything is fine. My heart feels like it's being squeezed in a vise. Not because I lost but because I feel so totally alone in this room full of people.

The summer following the Emmys, I'm sensing it again. That feeling that my peers are blowing past me in their careers, and I'm just trudging along with no direction. I'm scared that being with Ravi is hurting my reputation, but I don't dare say that to him. People just don't seem to like him, which obviously worries me. But I know him. I see his good side, the moments he's loving and attentive. I'm getting way too thin from stress. I'm just not hungry. I'm always anxious, and it's hard to focus. I'm so scared he'll leave me for someone else, someone blond, like his ex Savannah.

I had friction on *The Cutting Edge* set because Ravi was jealous of my costar, just like he was when I did *Campus Confidential*. I feel like

I disappointed Sean McNamara, the director, since I'm pretty sure he cast me to boost my career a little. He executive produced *Even Stevens*, and he knows me so well, and I just couldn't deliver the type of professionalism he was used to from me. There were a few times I was late to set because I was fighting with Ravi in my trailer. My reps hate him. The most fucked-up part of it all is that right after Ravi got so pissed at me, I found out that when he made that stupid slasher movie with his friend, he had a scene where he fully had simulated sex with an actress. I mean, what the hell? I was livid when I found out. Not because I was jealous but because he got so angry at me to the point that I sabotaged not one but two projects. He got so dramatic about it, it was like we were living in some telenovela.

"How dare you kiss me with that dirty mouth," he screamed after coming home from our big final *Cutting Edge* scene where the characters fall in love and win the Olympics. "Go wash your mouth out!"

I didn't, of course. It wasn't our best day, that's for sure.

While I wait around for Ravi to get home one night when we're both back in LA, I find myself getting antsy. I haven't found any evidence that he's cheating or anything, but something is nagging at me, telling me he might be. I open the cabinet of his bedside table, just for a little peek. There's a camcorder, which I didn't even know he owned. I have a little time, so I hook it up to our big-screen TV to see what's on it.

As soon as I hit play, I want to throw up. There's a grainy video of two people having sex, doggy style. One is Ravi. The other one is Savannah, his ex. My whole face and body feel like they're in flames. The room starts to spin. I keep watching, even though I want to throw the camcorder into a fire or out the window. I can't stop. Just then, I hear Ravi's keys in the door. I could scramble to hide everything, pretend I wasn't snooping, but fuck it.

"Hey, babe—"

As soon as he sees himself on-screen slamming Savannah with her crystal-blue (and bored) eyes, he stops, frozen.

"Christy . . ."

I run over and start yelling.

"You piece of shit! How dare you!"

He takes me by the arms.

"Hold on, hold on! I can explain!"

"You asshole! You lying asshole!"

"Christy, it's old!" he yells. "It's an old tape from a few years ago. I don't even talk to her anymore. You know this."

I stop for a second, trying to process what he's saying. Part of me is relieved, but then a new reason to be pissed wells up.

"Then why the fuck do you still have it in a table by OUR BED?! I pay our rent, Ravi!" I point to the screen.

I stare at him, waiting for some sort of explanation. Nothing comes.

"Burn it!" I scream.

"What? Why are you being so crazy? You're acting like your family!"

"Don't say that. I am nothing like them! Fucking burn it! Fucking deal with it. NOW!"

"I'll take care of it."

Ravi pulls me in and kisses me, hard. I let my anger fuel my passion, and I give in. He's all I've got now.

"Will you marry me?"

I'd been dreaming of hearing those words from Ravi for so long, and when it finally happened, it felt like a dream. After the sex tape incident, he did a one-eighty. He even suggested we go to couples therapy. He did get angry when he caught me texting Mom, since he thought we weren't in contact, but I explained that I do need my family. I promised not to give them any money, not a dime.

Because of this shift, of course I said YES! He proposed with an eternity band full of cushion-cut VVS diamonds, and it was so sweet and casual. I was waking up, and he knelt by the side of the bed and made a whole speech about how much he loves and needs me, how we belong together. He apologized for his jealousy, for our fights. He was romantic and vulnerable, and I saw truth in his eyes. I really felt like it was right, even though after a few sessions, the couples therapist flat-out said we were not in love. She said we're just codependent, and then I had to ask her what that even meant. It reminded me of Mom with Dad. So we stopped seeing that therapist.

Since I haven't been working a ton after I got back from Louisiana, I've been taking a few classes at the Beverly Hills Playhouse, and I love it. I need it so much—the community, the artistry. I'd had lunch with Donna, my old *Even Stevens* mom, and she'd encouraged me to try it, since it's been her school for years. "I think it'll be good for you to learn the process of how to break down a script and approach character work. The coach, Milton Katselas, is the best," she said.

When Ravi found out, he got angry.

"Christy, that place is supposedly all Scientologists," he said. "I don't want you to go."

I haven't heard one thing about Scientology, though. The classes are giving me confidence and a community that I need so badly, probably because I don't have a ton of structure right now. I feel for Ravi because I see him struggling as a writer and actor, and I want to help him. I just don't think he's that talented. I bring him to events and red carpets in hopes he'll figure out his next steps in life. I introduced him to Shia when we went to the premiere of his movie *The Greatest Game Ever Played*, and it felt like a full-circle moment. Like part of my past was coming together with my future. I was invited by some Disney marketing people who probably thought me and Shia reuniting would be a good photo op. It felt so good to see Shia. We hugged, and I was genuinely happy for him. More than ever, I've been rooting for him. He's been through so much. I think he'll really make it if he can keep it together.

Ravi loves for me to show off the ring in red carpet photos, which I do, even though it's loose. He even grips my hand to present it to cameras for close-ups. I think he thinks our engagement might be newsworthy or something. We don't even have a wedding date yet, but I already ordered a Monique Lhuillier lace wedding dress with the back out. It's stunning and definitely not cheap. But it's my wedding! It's a dream come true for me.

I asked some of my old sorority sisters and a few friends from Connecticut to be my bridesmaids, but no one from PCS. I feel like Ravi and I are just floating in this bubble of romance and love. I think about our wedding and our future. To one day have kids—at the right time. I'm still getting big residual checks, so money isn't a problem. Well, it kind of is. I'm not bringing in as much as I should or as much as I have in the past, so I should probably slow down on shopping. After putting down the payment on the dress, I need to go easy for a little bit.

It's been a few months since we got engaged, and I'm feeling bit like that bubble of bliss has popped. Maybe Ravi is just worried about his career, but he's been distant. I'm staying busy with acting classes, but he seems adrift. He needed a few days away from LA, so he went to Aspen to hang out with his sister for the weekend. I think the fact that the investigation into his dad is heating up isn't helping things. The break has been good, and I'm eager for him to walk through the door. I've missed him.

The door opens, and I run to give him a kiss hello.

"Hey, babe!" I say, hoping he'll notice that I'm all dressed up for him on a Sunday night.

"Hi," he says, throwing down his bags. "Hey, Christy, can we talk?"

My smile fades, and my heart drops to my toes.

"Sure," I say, sitting on the couch so my knees don't buckle. "What's up?"

"Christy?"

"Yeah?"

"I don't want to get married."

My mind races. I'm not sure what he even means. He just proposed.

"You mean, soon? We can have a long engagement. We don't have to rush," I say, even though I don't want a long engagement. My voice sounds terrified and shrieky.

"No, I mean I don't want to get married. Ever."

I try to let this sink in, but it's like my brain is pushing it away. I do not want this reality. I want our bubble back. This can't be happening. I've given him everything. Who is this person in my living room?

"How is that possible? This is BULLSHIT, Ravi." I start to cry.

"It will be hard now, but you'll see it's the right thing," he says.

"What am I supposed to do? Celebrate?! What the fuck happened in Aspen?"

He looks away from me, guilty.

"You're just not from the kind of family I'm from. You'll never be. My sister doesn't think we're compatible. And neither did the therapist, remember? And I just don't want to marry anyone."

"This is insane," I yell, standing and finally accepting the reality of the situation. "We have problems, but I'm working on myself!" Maybe it's something I did. Maybe I need to be more elegant. More refined. "I'll do anything," I say. I hate the words as soon as they come out of my mouth. I feel like Mom. Where the fuck is my backbone?

"Please, Ravi!"

I try to take his hand, but he moves toward the bedroom.

"I'm leaving," he says. "I'm moving out. You can keep the ring."

"I don't want this ring if you're leaving," I say, pulling the loose band off and shoving it in his face. How will I tell my family about this? My friends? I just wasted over a year with this person. For what?

"I'll pack now," says Ravi. He pockets the ring and starts pulling out a suitcase. I feel totally hollow, watching this level of betrayal play out like a movie in front of me. Once again, I find myself floating above the room, because my heart is breaking into a million pieces and it's safer from up here. I am frozen in an echo chamber. Something in me cracks open. I don't have my family, and now I don't have Ravi. I scream and plead with him to stay. I tell him I love him, and as I do, I feel pathetic. But I say it anyway. He slams the door behind him, and I scream before dropping to the ground.

As soon as Ravi gets all his things out, he ghosts me. I don't hear from him anymore. I even helped him move out, and like an idiot, I bought him an eight-hundred-dollar Hermès ashtray as a housewarming present. I realize I bought him a lot of things over the year and a half we were together. Like the time I rented him a Ferrari for a day for his birthday since he was big into F1 racing. Why? I have no clue. As if that would've made him stay. I guarantee he'll hock my ring. With his dad's legal troubles, he needs the money.

When I tell Mom what happened, she says to come home for a little bit, and I know I finally can and should go to see my family in Connecticut. But if I'm being honest, I don't know where I belong right now. I thought I belonged here in LA with Ravi, doing my best to make music and be a member of "young Hollywood." Now I'm totally adrift. I can barely eat because of the stress and am almost 105 pounds.

I can't figure out what to do, so I distract myself by going out to the Chateau Marmont, even though I know I may see Ravi. And one night I do. He's walking through the parking lot with two girls who look like models, dressed all boho chic. I pretend not to see him, pretend not to feel totally broken. But I am. I don't think he even notices I'm there. I'm hollow.

Dear Girls,

It would be super easy for me to say, If I ever catch you making concessions for a man like Ravi, I'll lose my mind. *But what would be the point? You're going to make your own choices. We're raising you to be strong, so you'll hopefully learn faster than I did.*

Here's what I wish someone had told me: Ask questions, and then listen for the answers. People, especially men, tell you *who they are. Women hear what they want to hear and try to change the men. Izzy, I was reading you a bedtime story, and you mentioned that your teacher talked about how every story has a problem and a solution. When someone consistently shows you who they are through actions, even* if *their words are saying something different, believe what you're seeing. Find the solution within yourself and leave.*

I wish I had taken all that time obsessing over toxic young men and put it toward traveling, learning about investing, building healthy hobbies. But I was young and scared and desperate for a semblance of love, family, and community to fix what was broken in me. To Hollywood, my emotional struggle came off as entitlement. But in reality, I was just a confused young woman who didn't know her worth yet, performing for scraps of affection, exactly as I'd been trained to do since childhood.

My family, as flawed and messy as they were, loved me the best they could. Did they suck sometimes? Absolutely. But I was old enough to set boundaries, and I was maybe a little complacent, too afraid of disappointing people to protect myself. I thought keeping the peace meant swallowing my needs whole. Classic good-girl syndrome.

Girls, if you ever don't like something about our dynamic, tell me, and we'll work it out together. I want to help you build conflict-resolution skills so disagreements don't feel like catastrophes. I'm building something with you that I hope is strong enough that you'll never feel like cutting contact is your only option, but if you ever do need space, I'll respect that boundary, even though it would gut me. Self-awareness, accountability, and open dialogue—I'm trying to model this for you so it doesn't feel impossible when you face your own big decisions.

My relationship with Ravi was like playing Jenga. I was carefully building something I thought was real while he casually pulled out pieces whenever it suited him, just to see if the whole thing would collapse. And it always did, because he never loved me. I was playing for keeps while he was playing for entertainment. My career, my reputation, my professional relationships—everything was at stake for me. His stakes? Nothing. He could disappear into the night whenever he wanted to, and he did. There was nothing my mom could do to protect me from what she'd already put into motion by role-modeling her own poor decision-making with men. The Ravis of the world will always exist. Men who make you feel like you're one wrong move away from losing everything and who keep you nervously placing blocks on top of a wobbling tower because the foundation was never stable to begin with. My job isn't to prevent you from meeting them. It's to make sure you recognize when someone's treating your heart like a game piece before you waste any time trying to win a game that was rigged from the start.

10

Fallout

2008–2010

Ages 24 to 25

"Place your fork facing down like so to indicate that you're finished with the meal. That's right. Delicately and quietly."

I place my fork down gently, just like Lizbeth tells me to do. She smiles in approval. It's been three months since Ravi dumped me, and after a few weeks of crying at gay bars around West Hollywood and lurking at nightclubs with the smorgasbord that is my fair-weather party friends, I decided to get my shit together and work on myself *for* myself. So I hired an etiquette coach. I signed up with Lizbeth because I wanted to finally iron out my weaknesses. I just need a little self-improvement to be the kind of woman a guy like Ravi would want to marry.

"Wonderful, Christy. Now, show me how you pour the teapot," Lizbeth says in her clipped, polite tone that's helped her become hugely successful at elevating high-profile people's etiquette. We always meet in a conference room at the Beverly Hills Hotel. She's dressed impeccably in a sleeveless Chanel dress and pearls. She did a color analysis on me at our last session and asked me to wear something that incorporated my best tones: TRUE WINTER. The only thing she's missing is white gloves, but I wouldn't be surprised if she elegantly whipped a pair out of her purse. I delicately tilt the white ceramic teapot.

"Perfect!" She claps quietly, of course, and bows her head in approval. "You're doing so well."

Mom and Dad taught us basic manners, like being respectful to our elders and cleaning our room, but nothing like this. If Ravi and his asshole younger sister thought I wasn't good enough or refined enough for their family, well, screw them. My money manager keeps telling me to go easy with the spending, but this course has been worth it. I'm not doing it to get Ravi back. I'm doing it as a fuck-you to him. Plus Lizbeth's approval feels pretty good. I feel like there's a secret society I can finally gain access to. I can rise above the doubt and inner voices telling me that I am never enough. Ravi and his family made me feel like I had no class, so spending money on these sessions is worth every penny.

I know I'm spending more than I'm making, but I tell myself that I've worked hard and I'm getting over a breakup. What else am I supposed to do?

In addition to seeing Lizbeth, I've spent most of the summer partying in Malibu with older rich men and model friends and at clubs like Hyde, where I now know the promoters on a first-name basis. A lot of my girlfriends have sugar daddies, but I refuse. No matter how low I get on finances, I swear to myself that I will never let a guy pay my way, and I will never do a nude scene. I don't judge other women, but that's a hard line in the sand for me. I could never go back to Barnard with my head held high and call myself a STRONG BARNARD WOMAN again. Mom always said nudity was the "bottom of the barrel" for actresses. So I did learn some class growing up, I guess.

I did finally go see my family after the breakup, and we repaired things, for the most part. I was so lost and distraught, barely getting out of bed, so they told me to come to my cousin's wedding. So I did. We all drank, danced, and bonded again. Dad has a radiation patch behind his eye, and he's trying some of the latest experimental treatments, so he seems good. I know I cut them out because of Ravi, but I do need them. Especially at a time when I have nowhere else to turn. It was a little awkward at first with Dad and my siblings since I hadn't seen them, but it didn't take long for us to fall back into old patterns. It was so good to actually have *fun* with them.

Ravi hated the Beverly Hills Playhouse, so I've doubled down on those classes too. Yes, they talk about the "BHP way" and we do "admin," which is when we take stock of things we have and have not done for our careers each week. But it's community and it's creative—so what if it's a little spiritual or even possibly based on Scientology? I go to the class in Los Feliz every Monday and Wednesday night, and I do think it's helping my approach to acting. It's also helping me feel like I'm a part of something, like being on Broadway or in a touring production. It's family. I need the structure of it; otherwise, my days and nights bleed into each other, and I get way too lonely. I can't party *every* night. At BHP, I love that the teachers break us down to build us back up like they're the military. I love being pushed outside my comfort zone. I'm not getting naked onstage like some people do, but I'm pushing myself emotionally. One of the teachers, Blake Glenn, tells us crazy stories that are borderline inappropriate, like the time he fucked a pig while growing up in Louisiana, but the students idolize his authentic approach. He goes right to the edge, I guess in the name of art.

"Romano," says Blake. It's a warm Wednesday evening in September, and we've all just settled in and finished our warm-up exercises. I'm not expecting to be called out like this since I wasn't supposed to prepare a scene for tonight. Or maybe I was, and I forgot? My stomach tightens, even though I know this is a safe space. I just want to get it right. Show them I'm a pro.

"Yes?"

"You're a singer, right?"

"I am," I say. I don't mention that I'm struggling to get a record deal or that I'm starting to feel extremely insecure about the sound of my nasally voice, to the point that I'm getting anxiety whenever I think of performing.

"Why don't you give us a song?"

"Um . . ." I look around the room at all the mostly familiar faces, people I've gotten vulnerable with and who've gotten vulnerable in front of me. I have to contribute to be a part of this tribe. There's one attractive guy who's new, so that makes me a little nervous because I've been eyeing him. He's tall and kind of scruffy, with light eyes and sandy hair. He's wearing a Raiders cap and an old T-shirt that shows off his muscles. He looks a little bit like an older Shia but way cuter. I look away from the Raiders cap guy and sit up in my chair.

"A song? Right now? Which song?"

"Anything that lights you up. Lay it on us," he says, his voice as smooth as it is authoritative.

I think for a minute and take a breath. For some reason, I start singing "Summertime" from *Porgy and Bess*. It's a song that I have in my theater repertoire, and it's soulful—plus it's quick. The class isn't used to people singing, and they seem to be impressed with my performance. For the first time in a very long time, I am lost in the song, and the riffs come easily. I choose a lower key so I don't sound nasally like I did with Belle. When I finish, the class erupts in loud, supportive applause. This is what art is supposed to feel like. I am safe in this room, and I can finally take risks. I sit back in my seat as Blake finishes class with an inspirational speech, citing me as the evening's example of one's ability to commit to a moment.

"That was dope. I love that song. I love that you sang Sublime." The Raiders cap guy is now smoking a cigarette next to me and a few stragglers after class. His presence is incredibly masculine and nerve-racking. I keep it cool, though. I'm not looking for another relationship, not so soon after Ravi.

"Oh, yeah, I love that song," I say. I don't correct him and tell him it's the famous aria from Gershwin's Tony Award–winning *Porgy and Bess*, and that bands like Sublime have covered it for decades. I stifle the geeky theater girl inside me and just take the compliment.

"I'm Caleb," he says, extending his large, calloused hand. The hand of someone who works hard and doesn't pawn his daddy's watches to play pretend screenwriter and fuck Playmates.

"I'm Christy." We lock eyes, and almost immediately, I regret it. This guy is so hot. I have to be strong.

"I know who you are," he says. "Look. I got this script for a film, and I'm directing it in a few months. Can I give you a copy? I think there's a part you'd be perfect for."

"Sure," I say, trying to sound totally casual. "Send me the script."

"Cool. I'll email it to you," says Caleb. I feel a few eyes from other classmates on us as we talk. I'm quietly reading his body language: He is loose but strong, casual with his cigarette, and his face maintains a friendly grin. His eyelids droop ever so slightly. Is he high?

"Thanks," I say with a pleasant but aloof smile as I stomp out my own cigarette. "I'm leaving to shoot an indie in Utah next week, but I'll check it out when I have time."

"Cool. Later," he says, throwing up a peace sign.

We part. I breathe. I haven't been this excited about a guy since . . . Ravi. It's not going to be easy to play it cool.

While I keep waiting to get cast as an adult, I'm in Utah, shooting this movie called *Taking 5*, where I play a big sister. At least I'm like a sexy, wild college girl, but still. I dyed my hair black partly for the role and partly because the teachers at BHP keep telling us that we need to "find our archetype," meaning "find our character." What that is exactly, I'm still trying to figure out. Maybe black hair will help me get there. I'm working on channeling an Angelina Jolie type, dark and dangerous. The opposite of Disney.

I'll dye my hair, but I refuse to get a nose job. My reps had the nerve to suggest that I might get more and better roles if I "fix" my nose because of some "feedback" they've gotten from casting agents. I have a Romano nose like my dad. I'm sort of proud of it, and I don't want to hack my face up. Also, what if a nose job changes my voice? That's what scares me the most. I could tell my agents at ICM were frustrated on the call when I said no, but screw that. I haven't been getting a lot of parts, but I'm not going that route for a role.

As months go by without landing anything big, I can tell my agents are getting worried, and honestly, I am too. The feedback from casting directors was that I wasn't "model pretty." But something big will come. I'm out here in California, doing all the right things, saying yes to everything, and going to the best nightclubs with famous people and producers. But I'm still not invited into the *Gossip Girl* or *Entourage* worlds. Until something better comes, I'll play the sexy older sister in *Taking 5.* It's scary thinking that this industry I've devoted my whole fucking life to might not want me anymore, but Mom tells me to "never give up" and to "keep pushing" and it'll all work out. I hope so, but I can feel my overall confidence in my talent shrinking, which is death for a performer. I feel like I've been grinding it out in this industry for a hundred years. I have to focus. I have to keep going. What else can I do?

"Hey, Christy. It's Caleb. Remember, from class?"

Of course I remember. Raiders cap, Cheshire cat smile. I'm pretty wasted since the whole cast and crew drank and smoked weed at the hotel after we wrapped shooting on *Taking 5* for the day, but I'm together enough to hold a conversation.

"Hey, you!" I say, maybe a little too excited. "What's up? I'm at my hotel in Salt Lake."

"Cool. What's the movie about?"

"It's about some teen girls who kidnap a boy band. It's . . . pretty whatever."

"Sounds like it." He laughs. "When do you get back to LA?"

"End of this month," I say. "We wrap November 22, so I fly back right after that. Why?"

He asks if I had a chance to read his feature script, and I tell him yes. It's a romantic comedy, and there are no teenagers in it, which is a good sign. I promise Caleb that we'll meet when I get back to do a read-through and some rehearsals. We talk for another half hour after I promise to meet up with him, and the time flies by. He's so easy to talk to, and it feels totally natural, even though the alcohol is probably helping me keep my guard down. He loves filmmaking and horror and directors like Tarantino and Robert Rodriguez. Caleb isn't pretentious like some Hollywood kids I've met. He worked at a Maggiano's restaurant and grew up deep in the Valley. Unlike Ravi, he understands what it means to be an artist and to work. He's passionate, professional, and ambitious. The whole conversation is a total turn-on. Or maybe I'm just drunk.

"You're an interesting person, Romano. Therefore, we're interested in *you.*" This is the feedback Blake gives when I finish scene work from *Girl, Interrupted.* The Angelina Jolie role, of course. I have always wanted to be just like her since I was at Barnard. Before I started college, I read that she'd started doing human rights work when she wasn't making movies, so I wanted to study that. She is the epitome of edginess, vulnerability, chaos, and sex on a stick. I'm trying to channel her energy per the teachings of the BHP to manifest a more adult, *Maxim*-cover-worthy appeal. As ridiculous as it sounds, if I get on *Maxim* like Jamie Lynn Sigler in a black bra and white shirt, or even Hilary Duff with her new brown hair (ironic) in white lingerie, I'll be deemed appealing enough to cast. Everyone talked about Jessica Biel changing her image, cutting her hair, and doing a *Gear* magazine cover to get out of her *7th Heaven* contract. That's what I want. To shake the Disney image for good.

"Thank you," I say as I exit the stage.

"That was great," whispers Caleb when I sit down next to him. I've been back from Utah for a few weeks, and I am not trying to get into another relationship right now. It is nice to hear Caleb compliment me, though. We got so drunk the night we finally read through the script together that I chucked an empty glass off my balcony at the Villas and into the street for no reason. He laughed and kissed me, hard. He didn't mind that I was out of control. He even stayed over that night. There's something about Caleb that makes me want to unleash my wild side. He does not criticize my table manners or my lack of wine knowledge, and he doesn't expect trips to Aspen. He hates that stuff and thinks it's posing. He doesn't think I'm less than. He doesn't try to change me. He's got his own career going, and that feels good to me. He's an aspiring artist, he paints too, and he's "about the work," as our BHP teachers have termed it. Ravi always made me feel like talent was transactional, but this guy gets it, and our connection feels deep. I let "I love you" slip out one night while we were in bed together. He said it back.

Instead of going to Hyde or partying at Malibu mansions, I've been smoking Caleb's weed and happily eating Chipotle, finally gaining weight back, and listening to him critique horror movies in his small apartment in the Valley. He's about to break out as a director, making films with this company called The Scary Studio, which specializes in crazy sci-fi horror TV movies. It's not highbrow or Oscar-worthy in the slightest, but the movies this company makes are all strangely cult classics within the horror community.

I'm getting some voice-acting gigs but not much else. I voice-matched Angelina Jolie in a *Kung Fu Panda* video game she couldn't do, so maybe this BHP manifesting is working after all. What I never managed to get was a record deal. Atlantic never renewed my contract, and they dropped me, cold. After all this time. I really feel like my career is officially stalling, like I can't get a real role or a record deal, but Caleb is so full of confidence and positivity, so I feed off that energy to stay blissfully optimistic. I need it.

I'm focusing on my BHP classes and taking whatever voice work I can get. I'm spending a lot less because Caleb is so much better about saving money than Ravi was. We went to Marshalls, and I filled the cart with fun, cheap clothes, and he told me to put it all back.

"Chill out, Christy. It's too much."

He's right. It's just scary going from making huge residuals off Disney or getting put up in a Manhattan apartment, to thinking that a shopping spree at Marshalls is indulgent. Every time I call Mom and Dad, it's "keep going, Christy. Don't give up." I'm trying, but that tape starts playing in my head again, the one that says I'm not good enough or blond enough. Like the BHP teachers say, though, I need to find ME. I need to find my type, who I really am. Am I a Disney girl or an indie actress? I'm not Ren Stevens. The closest I've felt to a character is Kim Possible, and I'm proudest of that role. I can't play Kim forever, though.

Even though Caleb and I have only been together six months, it just feels right. It started casual and fun, and we just feel like friends who are insanely attracted to each other. He calls me "Chris," which I love. No one else calls me "Chris."

When he asks me to move in with him in his new house, I don't hesitate. My lease is up at the Villas, where they are now filming *The Hills*, so it's perfect timing. I feel like I've finally fallen in love with a kindred spirit. Probably because of what happened with Ravi, I'm secretly jealous of girls Caleb dated in the past, and I have checked his phone a few times. He was dating his famous costar before he met me, and I couldn't help but feel super jealous. They still seem to be in contact. But these are my own insecurities. We're solid, and I need to get used to that.

But still, something's not right. I'm too thin. I'm at 105 pounds again, and even my new agent says that I need to gain weight. I've always been thin, but I have been stressing—about Caleb, about my career.

"I don't usually say this to clients, but you need to *gain*," my agent keeps telling me. "Just a little."

While with Caleb, I've left ICM for Global Artists, even though ICM is a top-tier agency. It didn't feel like they were interested in getting me any work or cast in any big shows like they promised a few years ago. Nothing was happening, and it seemed like they lost interest in me as a client. I figure that a smaller agency might give me more time and attention. At least, that's what I'm hoping for. At bigger agencies you can get lost in the shuffle, since they're paying more attention to the top stars. I don't want to be some has-been. I am struggling to do it all myself, including making it to auditions on time. I get so turned around on the freeways. Mom used to drive, but now it's just me, and the more anxious I feel, the worse it gets. Mom once said I wasn't ready to do this on my own, and maybe she was right. My agents are always reminding me to be on time, but I am always, always late. It probably doesn't help my chances.

Caleb is laser-focused on directing, which is inspiring. We've been together pretty much every day, smoking pot and watching movies, hiking Runyon Canyon, meeting each other's friends. It's just been so natural. No games. He's not judging me or trying to control me. There's no pressure to be "better." I can actually breathe. Our relationship is so much deeper than anything I've experienced before, even if he does pull away and act distant sometimes. I think it's just because he's so dedicated to his work. We can talk about art and creativity and our hopes and dreams. I'm really starting to see a future with him, and it feels so much more real than it ever has before. That doesn't mean we don't have our issues like any couple, I guess. We had a huge fight at an American Film Market party, and it didn't help that I was drinking tequila and almost blackout drunk. Tequila makes me a werewolf, I swear. After that fight, Caleb said I should look at my drinking, and I agreed. I've gone to some Al-Anon meetings, which are for people with alcoholic family members or spouses or friends. It's not AA, but it's something. I want to make him happy and not screw our relationship all up because I had too many drinks.

My phone rings. It's Caleb, calling to tell me how his meeting went with the head producer at The Scary Studio, who went rogue and started a new studio. I'm hoping it's good news.

"Hey, babe. How'd it go?"

"It was great," he says. Something about his tone feels off. "They want me to direct two features this year. And make me their head director."

"That's amazing, babe. I'm proud of you. Why do you sound funny, though? I thought you'd be more excited."

"Well, um, the thing is . . ."

"Yeah?"

"I have to move to Louisiana."

"What? Why? You can't go back and forth?"

"It's because of the tax breaks. They're shooting everything down there now. So I'll be in Baton Rouge, and you can come visit."

"For how long?"

"Indefinitely, I guess."

The idea of hanging out in Bumblefuck, Louisiana, again doesn't exactly get me excited. I don't want to be in long-distance relationship, but if this is the guy I'm meant to be with, I have to suck it up. I have to be the cool chick about it and not freak out. I have to pretend, even if I do have a sinking feeling in my stomach.

"We'll make it work," I say. "You deserve it."

In the weeks since Caleb moved to Baton Rouge, I've gotten a little voice work, which makes me feel less insecure about finances. I'm sick of getting feedback like "Christy isn't an actor who gets her own TV show; she's a hot piece of stunt casting." One of the bigger jobs I did get was on a huge adult animated show. It was fun, and I've been seeing Chase, the guy who created the show. I thought Caleb and I were meant to be, but we lasted about four weeks with him in Louisiana and me in LA. Over just a few weeks, he got distant, and then he pulled away completely. Being with him is like emotional whiplash. When I'm physically with him, it's like I'm the most gorgeous, important, talented person in his life. When we're apart, it's like he forgets I even exist. I'm sure he's seeing some local dumb blond wannabe actress, and that's the real reason he ended it. I don't have proof, but I feel it.

Chase is rich, fun, and intellectual, and we're both from the East Coast, so we talk for hours and almost every day. It's weird, though, because he never really takes me out in public. It's always us hanging at his mansion in the Hollywood Hills, getting takeout, and watching random eighties movies. We make out, but it all feels pretty casual, like he's gal-palling me but with benefits. He's been spotted with so many other actresses that he's cast on his animated shows over the years. I told my brother I was seeing Chase, because my brother *loves* his show and wants to see me happy with someone successful. But when I complain about the gal-palling thing, he says, "Christy, you're just his Tuesday."

His comment stings, but I know he's right. Nobody really wants me.

I play it cool and keep it casual with Chase and try not to dwell on Caleb for months, but one day, there it is. Out of the blue: a text from him. He misses me. He saw the photos I posted on Facebook of a fun trip I took. He wants me to come to Bumblefuck, Louisiana. And, of course, I'm going. I love the guy, so I'll go to the damn South.

Lafayette, where Caleb is running a production company, isn't quite a swampy hellhole, but I don't feel like I belong there either. I'm probably acting a little bit like a bitch with my Yankees cap and my East Coast attitude, but I can't help it. Caleb and I fall right back into it—passionate hookups, talking about anything and everything, smoking weed, and drinking Coronas late into the night. He wrote a part for me in this movie called *Vampire Reckoning*, a sci-fi piece about vampires and werewolves. It's a pretty good script, and it's an adult role for once. We're shooting it quickly, so I'm here for the whole month. Now that we're back together, it feels like we're closer than ever. He may have been aloof before, but he gives me the kind of attention I need to feel like a normal person. Truthfully, I know that I'm addicted to our chaotic dynamic, and I think he is too.

The vibe in Lafayette is like if a college frat had a filmmaking scene. They have keg parties and do drugs all the time at one another's small, run-down houses. I find out there is a local blond girl named Tabitha who I'm pretty sure hooked up with Caleb while we were broken up, and so of course I stalk his phone sometimes to see if they're still talking. I know I shouldn't, but I can't help it. I'm super paranoid after everything with Ravi and his ex. It's impossible not to obsess. I feel so out of control these days, and I won't stay here forever. After this month is over, I have to go back to my so-called life in LA.

"So, this is like your film school," I tell Caleb one night after filming. "You're partying and making low-budget movies. Like this is your training to become an actual director."

"What the fuck, Christy?" he says, catching me off guard with his anger. "I *am* an actual director. This isn't college."

I don't mean to offend him, but the scene does remind me of college. It doesn't feel serious, because it's not buttoned-up and official like Disney. It's also insane. They are super unethical with the ways they get shots without permits, which isn't even legal, and make people do stunts with blood, swallow fake vomit to spit it up, and do all sorts of dangerous things without professional supervision. There are also a few kid actors who don't even have the level of protection that I used to get, which bothers me. It feels beneath me. I don't say this to Caleb, though.

Ever since going to Al-Anon after one too many drunken fights with Caleb, I'm able to see how my family dynamics, with all the drinking and dysfunction, probably turned me into a people pleaser. The meetings are like free therapy. My whole childhood I wanted to be "good" and make everyone happy and proud of me. I peed onstage instead of just saying I needed to go to the bathroom! I got pushed around because I'd always been too scared to do or say the "wrong" thing. But at least I'm working on it in Al-Anon. I'll keep going back. *It works if you work it, and you're worth it.* And when I go back to LA, I'll keep fighting for better roles. Because whenever I think of quitting, I hear my mom's voice saying, "Stick with it, Christy. You've come this far." Whatever happened to "Stop when it stops being fun"?

Caleb loves my performance in *Vampire Reckoning*, and we celebrate our last night with a huge wrap party at a local nightclub. That chick Tabitha is there, but she keeps her distance from me and from Caleb. She is the total opposite of me, naturally. Bright blond, bubbly, wearing pastels and bright pink earrings. Very fucking Southern. I glare at her from across the room, so maybe that scares her away.

We promise we'll see each other once a month and not go so long between visits, but long distance sucks. I'm back living at my little place on Argyle, going to auditions, partying. I'm hanging out with friends from the BHP, who drink like fish.

It's one of those wild LA nights when you feel like you could end up anywhere, meet anyone. It's electric and totally free. I feel like I know almost everyone in this bar, The Hook Up—old friends, the DJ, some friends from the BHP. This guy Paul, one of the head employees, is a regular in one of my Al-Anon meetings. He talks a lot about how his mom is bipolar and how he is sober when he shares during the meetings. He is now hooking me up with shots close to last call. Loud eighties music plays in the background.

"Hey, come down here, Christy," he says. "I want to show you something in my office."

Paul looks a little blurry, and I have to shut one eye to focus on his face. Too many shots, but I was in the moment and dancing all night. The bar is closing, the lights are all on, and at least a hundred people are piling out onto the street to buy street meat from the food stand on the corner or wait for their cars.

"What do you need to show me?" I ask. There aren't many basements in LA, not like there are on the East Coast. It's a little weird to be led into a dark staircase below a Hollywood bar. Since I know Paul a little from Al-Anon, I figure it's fine. I follow him down the stairs.

"Come in." I step into a cramped office, and as soon as I do, Paul shuts and locks the door behind me, which freaks me out. Paul has a strange look in his eyes, a totally different look than he had upstairs. I can tell I'm swaying a little, so I try to sober up and get my bearings. I hear a sound that I pray is not what I think it is. I look down and see Paul unzipping his pants.

"You don't want to hurt me," I slur with a strange laugh. "My dad is in the Mafia."

Paul laughs like this is a joke. It's not exactly true, but I need to get out of here, so I try to make him think my dad is dangerous. And who knows? Maybe he is.

Paul pushes me against a wall, hard, and kisses me so aggressively that it hurts. My head hits the brick wall. He's got one hand at my neck, and I try to get free, but I can't. He's too strong. I'm even more scared now, and I try squirming and pushing his arm off my clavicle, but it's no use. His arm and fingers get heavier on my chest and shoulder, and I know I fucked up by coming down here. I try something else, something I've always said I would say if I was ever about to be raped. Paul has his dick out and is stroking it against my belt. I'm utterly humiliated and pissed at myself at the same time. I'm also terrified.

"Hey." I manage to move my face away long enough to speak. I let him kiss me as he keeps stroking himself faster, but his arm presses me against the wall more violently. He reaches for my belt to take it off. "Whoa, baby, whoa," I say. "I have my period. I have a tampon in. Let's hook up another night, okay, baby? Give me a call, and we'll make it happen."

I feel fully disgusted even saying this, but it's the only thing I can think of to get this guy off me. I pray that I was convincing enough—my greatest acting role in years. Paul miraculously backs away and finishes jerking off in his hand. As soon as I'm free, I unlock the door and race up the steps to the blaring lights and empty bar. My heart is pounding so hard, it feels like it might burst out of my skin, through muscle and bone. I get to the bar and find my neighbor Cliff, who had come to the bar with me and my group of BHP friends who have long since split.

"What's wrong? What happened?" Cliff asks. "You don't look good."

"Nothing," I say, holding back tears. "Nothing. Let's just get the fuck out of here. NOW."

I wake up and see bruises on my arms and shoulders. Everything hurts. The night comes back to me in quick scenes, like I'm watching a horror movie where the girls get lured into the scary basement. But this isn't a movie. I don't call Caleb. I call Mom.

"Christy, you're up early." Mom's voice sounds scratchy, like she had a rough night. "What is it?"

I tell her what happened and ask what I should do. Despite all our problems, she's always been there for me when I've needed her.

"What if he does this to someone else?" I ask. "Do I report it?"

"Christy, this is what happens when you drink too much," Mom says. No words of support, no empathy. She is, after all, the same mom who drove me to the police station when I was a kid and threatened me with foster care. She can be cold when she wants to be. Plus she's from an old-school generation that probably thinks that some girls "deserve" it.

"Mom, I have bruises on my body."

"You need to straighten up," she says. "Especially out there. You know how men can be."

It's as if she's calling me a slut. It's true that there are predators in Hollywood, that guys in power take advantage of women all the time, and no one says a thing. People just turn their backs. It's not like Paul is some big producer or agent, but I bet I'm not the first girl he's done this to. I also won't be the last. I take Mom's advice and don't report the guy. I'll just have to be more careful and never follow some random-ass man into a basement ever again.

It's been three weeks since that night at The Hook Up, and I haven't been back there. I'm never going back there. I also haven't told anyone but Mom and Caleb. When I told him, he was pissed at Paul, but it's not like he offered to fly to LA or anything. After I told Caleb, I never brought it up again. Maybe I'm ashamed. Maybe I just want to forget about it.

When Caleb comes to visit for a few days, I still don't bring it up. Until I have to.

Caleb and I are having a late breakfast at Roscoe's, one of our favorite places. And of all the fucking brunch spots in this stupid city, there is Paul, walking to a table with some young girl on his arm. My face goes ghost white. I feel sick. My hands go clammy, and I might throw up. Caleb doesn't seem to notice.

"Caleb," I whisper. "That's him. That's the guy." I can barely look at Paul. Caleb keeps shoveling fried chicken and waffles into his mouth, the sticky syrup covering his lips. "That's the guy who assaulted me."

I gesture as subtly as I can toward Paul, who hasn't seen me. Caleb looks over and keeps eating.

"That dude? Gross," he says, stabbing his waffle with his fork and taking another huge bite.

That's it? My dad would have gotten up from the table and beat the shit out of Paul. Caleb is making me feel like it's no big deal, like I'm a loser, and I got myself into a mess, and it's over now.

"Caleb, I can't eat. I need to get out of here."

"What? Why? I'm, like, half done."

"Are you serious?" I say, standing up and grabbing my purse. "The guy who assaulted me is *right there*, and you want to keep eating fried chicken and waffles?"

Caleb puts his fork down like he's annoyed.

"Fine," he says, standing up. "Fine, we'll go."

I rush out without Paul seeing me. Caleb follows behind me, never saying a word. Not to me, not to Paul. He's right beside me, but I feel totally alone.

I finally did it. I told my manager that if he doesn't find me work soon, I'm leaving. And it worked. I wanted a reason to leave LA anyway, since things with Caleb weren't good and I've been struggling so much financially. I was on the verge of applying to be a bottle-service girl at Les Deux.

I get a job in New York for a few months doing the play *Avenue Q*. Caleb recently pulled away, like always when we fought like crazy because of the distance and lack of trust between us, so we broke up. Again. I needed to get out of Los Angeles for my mental health. New York—and

Broadway—has always been my North Star, for better or worse. *Avenue Q* won a few Tony Awards when it first ran a few years ago, and now I'll be playing two parts, Kate Monster and Lucy the Slut. It's a musical comedy with puppets and is really the atmosphere I need right now. I get to wear all black and hide behind these puppet characters. Disney never let me be crass or sexual, obviously, so playing Lucy, this blond puppet with big boobs and lips, is such a release and so fun. We've been rehearsing, and I'm learning to move the puppets, which is something I've never done. When I was a kid, that would have been a cool skill for my résumé, next to ice-skating and twirling: puppeteering.

The production put me up in a place called the Archstone for the two-month run. I know I'm "stunt casting" again since they want to fill the seats with people who were fans of *Kim Possible* and *Even Stevens*. But I love the work. I'm finally stretching myself and being an adult, and I can channel all my rage over Caleb and Paul into these characters. And my rage over the feedback I kept getting in LA. So, yeah. Channeling all my rage into puppet comedy is pretty cathartic.

Finally, I feel like I'm back on track. Like I'm on an upswing, career-wise. The cast and crew are great, and I've been going to a Buddhist center in Harlem with one of my costars who I love, Carla Renata. I think she could see during rehearsals that I was a little on edge. It's only been two months since the assault and my latest Caleb breakup, and Carla sensed it. I like the temple, which is really just a nice brownstone. It helps me feel centered during a chaotic time. And unlike the psychics and the crystals, the Buddhist center doesn't want anything from me. I'm not sure what I'm searching for, but maybe one day, it'll be clear. For now, the chanting and the beads Carla gave me are comforting.

It only takes a month for life in New York to feel right, like a full-circle feeling. I'm going to great shows like *Rent* and *Equus*, meeting people like Blake Lively and Haley Joel Osment, who I respect for leaving the business for college. New York is bringing me back to myself, like it always does.

And then Caleb comes back into my life. Just when I'm on a high, when I feel like I'm finally doing what I'm meant to do, he calls. He's visiting his family in Virginia and says he wants to drive up to New York that night to see me. Caleb somehow just keeps pulling me back in, even though I know it's not healthy. I can't help it, though. I tell him to drive up.

It's like some rom-com dream montage. Caleb drives all night to see me and gets to my place in Manhattan early in the crisp fall morning. It is so romantic and passionate from the minute we see each other. After two days of bliss and long talks about anything and everything, we're best friends again. Caleb tells me that we're going to Tiffany's to pick out a ring. I know I'm stronger now and that I keep saying no man will stand in the way of my career, but Caleb isn't like that. One of the things we understand so deeply about each other is our love for what we do, for creating.

We pick the ring and size it. It's very small, with one cushion diamond in the center. It's perfect. He hasn't officially proposed yet, but I know it's coming. We're walking through the cool September Manhattan streets, totally on a high, when Caleb stops and turns to me.

"I have something to tell you."

It's never a good thing when anyone says this. He tells me that after we broke up this last time (which was, what, breakup number five hundred?), he started seeing that local girl Tabitha again. When I get angry, he reminds me that I've dated guys like Chase when we're not together. But with Tabitha, I can tell it's not just a fling for him. The guys I dated didn't matter. I've always been emotionally tethered to Caleb. He swears it's over, but he had to come clean, to start our lives together in an honest way. He says she's reached out to him lately and that he doesn't know what to do. Through gritted teeth, I say, "I'll handle it." It's something my dad would say.

So later that day, when he's out, I find Tabitha on Facebook and send her a message. I tell her to leave him the fuck alone and not to reach out to him again because we're engaged. She immediately writes back this sweet note saying she's "so sorry" and just wanted to make sure he's okay after some storm that happened that week. Is that the Southern way of saying "fuck you," by being extra sweet? I tell her to "stop being cute" and to "drop the act." My inner East Coast tough girl is now in full defense mode, which is not very Buddhist of me. Hopefully, that's the end of Tabitha. The last thing she writes is *I'll pray for you,* which also weirdly feels like an insult.

Caleb stays in New York a week before he has to go back to Louisiana to work. I'm making the most of it. Right before Caleb leaves town, I'm supposed to ring the bell at the New York Stock Exchange. We stay up past midnight drinking, so when I wake up, I realize I'm going to be late to ring the bell. Fuck.

It's something my new fancy PR team set up for me, since ringing the bell is an honor and it keeps your name out there. I wake Caleb and get ready as fast as we can. We hop in the cab since he wants to come along. We run out of the cab and into the building, and an assistant leads us to the right floor. I keep apologizing for being late, since this is timed like clockwork, and you can't really be late to ring the stock bell. The assistant keeps telling me not to worry about it.

"It's a weird day," she says as she leads us out of the elevator and onto that iconic floor. "You'll see."

It's eerily quiet on the floor, and I'm immediately terrified that I have screwed the whole thing up by being late. This will piss off my managers and PR people.

I apologize again, and a tall guy in a suit comes up and tells us it's fine. He ushers us into a side room and hands me a large metal coin that reads NYSE and the date, September 17, 2008.

"We don't need to ring the bell today," he says. "The market just had a major crash. Trust me, no one is thinking about you being late."

When we get back outside, we find out that the stock market just experienced a massive collapse. If I had rung that stupid bell, that would have followed me forever: *Former Disney Star Christy Romano Rings Bell on Worst Day for Stocks in Modern History!*

When *Avenue Q* ends, I visit Caleb in Louisiana. I try to blend in with his crew and cast, smoking weed and drinking at local country bars like before. But I hate it. I also feel Tabitha's presence lurking around every small-town corner, even though I don't see her. I'm in a panic. I don't mention this to Caleb. I play the cool chick, the one who doesn't think about girls like Tabitha at all. I don't know how long I can keep up the act, though.

Caleb takes me to New Orleans for a night to celebrate our anniversary. We have a gorgeous room at Hotel Le Cirque. We're not fighting, and it feels like our early days of dating and falling in love. I feel so close to him, like we're meant to be. And then it happens.

We're walking in the French Quarter, and out of the blue, Caleb stops, turns to me, and gets on one knee. As people pass by, drunk and singing and joyous, he tells me he wants to spend his life with me, that I'm his best friend, that when you know, you know. He pulls out the Tiffany ring and slips it onto my finger. I say yes, and we kiss in the middle of all that revelry. He takes me to the restaurant Commander's Palace that night to celebrate, which feels especially sweet since Caleb hates to spend money. I feel like a princess. I feel lucky. This is nothing like my past relationships. It's everything I've dreamed about.

I don't love leaving New York for LA, but I'm still trying to land a TV show, so that's where I need to be since *Avenue Q* has ended. Plus, once Caleb is finished with Louisiana, he'll be back, and we'll settle into our life together. I'm much closer to Mom and Dad since all the Ravi drama, so my family is happy for us. We've worked on communicating and moving past everything that happened with our estrangement. They like Caleb so much more than Ravi, because Ravi was trying to separate me from them. My dad thinks Caleb is more down-to-earth, which he is.

Going back to Louisiana to visit him is always a little boring. I don't want to hang out on set all day while he's directing his latest movie, because unless you're in the film, it's like watching paint dry. So here I am, hanging out alone in Caleb's apartment, trying to force myself not to go through his shit.

But it's so tempting! And I am so bored. Plus, since I've been back here, he's seemed a little distant, a little off. So I start flipping through some of his papers, mostly script notes or storyboards for a horror movie about rabid sharks. I open his desktop and search keywords in the finder: Tabitha, sex, girlfriend. That's when I see it.

That's weird. In GarageBand, there's a song called "My Insta Girlfriend." I feel sick to my stomach as I click to listen.

"Baby, we both have other lovers . . . but one thing is true . . . when I hold your hand, I feel real love . . . and don't know what to do . . ."

The delivery is incredibly emotional, and I know this song is not for me. It's not about me. He's never played it, never shared it. The thing inside me that has already been broken is now on fire.

I ransack the room, throwing papers and files around, searching desk drawers, and opening books. I empty out bags and turn over lamps like I'm a detective in a bad movie. I know it's wrong, but so is writing a song about another woman when you're engaged! I know the song isn't old either. The file was dated weeks ago. I'm sweating by the time I empty out all the drawers. For some reason, I'm compelled to look under his desk. Why not? I've looked everywhere else. Taped underneath the desk is a manila envelope, which is obviously super weird and creepy. Is it a stash of money? Drugs? Love letters to Tabitha? What kind of name is "Tabitha" anyway?!

I tear open the envelope and find a camcorder tape. There's a date written on it. It's a familiar date, and I run through a hundred memories until I land on it. It's the date of our trip to Big Bear, when we'd only been dating a few months. I feel even more sick. I think I know what this is.

I find his camcorder and pop the tape in, bracing myself for what's to come. The tiny flip screen lights up with grainy footage. A bedroom. A cabin. Two bodies, naked. My body, naked. I let him film us on that trip because, well, he's a director, and he had a camera, and it felt kind of naughty and fun. So, because I trusted him and because he promised he'd get rid of it, I let it happen. And here it is. Hidden under a desk, like evidence he's keeping for the right time.

Enraged, I take the tape out of the camcorder and rush to the bathroom. I turn the shower on as hot as it'll go and start pulling the guts of the tape out, smashing it in my hands, putting it under the scalding water, and stringing it up around the shower like one of his horror movies come to life. I know I look deranged because I feel deranged, but I don't care. I want him to know how much this hurts. I want him to see it, to feel it.

"Christy, what the fuck?"

I turn around, my hair and clothes soaking wet, to see Caleb. He looks totally confused.

"You were supposed to destroy this! Why was it under your desk?! In an envelope?"

I'm screaming at him. I leap out of the shower and start charging at him.

"Stop! This is crazy," he yells. "I was keeping it safe, that's all! I didn't want it to get out."

I don't believe him. I can't. He pleads with me, but I pull the ring off my finger, just like I did with Ravi. My heart is broken. Again. I throw the ring at him, tell him it's over. As much as I want the dream and I want to believe he was really hiding it to protect me, I know it would be pathetic to stay. Why do I keep doing this to myself? Why can't I just figure it out, have a normal life? Maybe if I'd given up acting a long time ago, stayed in Connecticut at public school, and just gotten a regular job, none of this would be happening. But it is happening. And I'm devastated again. Maybe it's my fault, and I'm broken and unlovable.

The tape plays again in my head, the one that tells me I'm not good enough, not pretty enough or strong enough. I want to die. I grab my things and leave, slamming the front door.

When I go back to LA, everything feels lonely. Most days I feel numb, so I go out at night and drink. It doesn't help. I go shopping, even though I shouldn't. I go to any social event I can just to have a place to be. Work-wise, there's nothing on the horizon. No offers, no auditions. Money is tight. I'm even using some of the savings meant for college, as if I'll ever go back. I'm desperate, but not desperate enough to take my clothes off or let a guy pay for my bills like some of my friends do.

My agent has gotten me one interesting opportunity, which is a little crazy, but that's why I want to do it. I'm desperate for anything to shake me out of how low I've felt since leaving Louisiana. It's heartbreak, and also I just feel so scared about my career and my money, or the lack of it. So I'm going to Afghanistan as part of an Ambassadors of Hollywood tour to entertain and cheer up the troops over there. Yes, it's dangerous there right now, but they wouldn't send us if we weren't going to be protected. When I told Dad about the trip, he wanted to have a conference call with my reps to make sure they're being smart and to hear about their safety protocols. I know it sounds crazy, but I feel like going into a war zone is probably a pretty good way to get my mind off the fact that my life is a mess, that I'm heartbroken.

We start in Qatar and then take helicopters to Kandahar. The flights over were long and exhausting, and, yeah, I was a little scared, but being here, I don't feel as terrified as I thought I would be. I've always hated flying, especially after 9/11, but I make it over. There are a few of us actors: me, Maeve Quinlan, Paul Johansson, and Don McManus. We travel to different FOBs (forward operating bases), meeting soldiers, talking to locals, and experiencing this place that so many Americans are terrified of. I sing the national anthem, and it means a lot to me to do this for soldiers who're out here risking their lives for us. They're not making stupid horror movies or clubbing at Hyde. They're doing something meaningful. I really admire them. One day on the trip, they take us to see a little girl who had been burned across 90 percent of her body. As soon as I see her, I break down crying. All of the LA bullshit I'd been caring so much about disappears immediately. Talk about getting fucking perspective.

When I get back from Afghanistan, my brother forces me to go through all my finances with him. He says I can't spend more than one hundred dollars a day. I trust him more than I trust a business manager or my parents at this point. I scale way back. Beverly Hills Playhouse gives me a "scholarship" so I won't have to pay for classes, and I find a place on Craigslist that's affordable but also pretty rad. I'm renting a section of this beautiful house in the Valley from a lawyer named Han who's going through a divorce. There's a pool and a hot tub and a great view. I basically have my own wing, and I feel totally safe. Han and I are both pretty heartbroken, so I think we connect over that. I barely thought about Caleb at all when I was overseas, but being back in LA brings up so many memories.

Going to classes at BHP feels different now too. When I started, I thought I was on top of the world, career-wise. I was one of the bigger names in the room then, and now I'm barely working. The only real thing that I've gotten since moving back is voicing a *Kim Possible* Epcot ride, which paid pretty well, but I'm pissed that they didn't even offer to bring me to Orlando to try the ride. Maybe I should just be grateful they still want to use my voice and not replace me.

I've been partying a lot with my friends Edie and Hope. I met Edie at an industry party and instantly bonded with her. Through Edie I met Hope, who is a little older, like the mama hen of LA nightlife. She's a club promoter, so we get into every club because of her. Maybe it's a way to distract myself from Caleb and to forget that I am almost broke and very single. I date, but it's all meaningless. I feel vacant, like Los Angeles. This is supposed to be some golden land of opportunity, but some days it feels like a dungeon. I even go to the Scientology center, the Celebrity Centre in Hollywood, because a classmate from BHP invites me. She knows I'm heartbroken and lost and broke, and so I go. It's ornate and polished inside. I've tried crystals and psychics and Buddhism, so I figure, why not just give this a chance? There are some men in matching suits looking extremely serious. Going in, I figure that maybe this can help me with my career and with relationships. I'm desperate for community like I always find in theater in New York. But those communities are always temporary. The whole Scientology thing doesn't do it for me, though.

Most days I sleep until three in the afternoon, get ready for the night, and stay out almost until the sun comes up. I'm depressed and starting to feel a little untethered, and it scares me. I've become so numb, I've tried being bulimic just to feel something. I'm already a 00 in my pants size, and I love eating when my appetite isn't suppressed from anxiety. The drinking doesn't help, and I feel like if I sleep all day, I'll spend less money on food. It's fucked up, I know. I try scraping my nails against the insides of my arms to see if I can become a cutter. No such luck. I feel like a dumbass. How was I ever someone's role model? What would those little girls waiting for an autograph from Belle think if they could see the real me? I'm not even sure I know who that is anymore.

Since Edie knows *everyone*, she gets invited to a Halloween party at Paris Hilton's house, and she's bringing me and Hope. Edie is gorgeous and works as an assistant at a marketing firm. She's not even in the industry, and the girl knows how to network better than I do. There are six of us dressing as Roller Derby girls from *Whip It*. It was such a big thing this year and Drew Barrymore directed it, which got me thinking about directing. I've had ten thousand hours behind the scenes watching how directors work, right? I'm not saying it's an easy job at all, but I am curious, I guess. Plus Kathryn Bigelow was the first female to win a Best Director Oscar recently, and when I watched her speech after *The Hurt Locker* won, I was so fucking inspired. Not only did she win and then get an entire industry to start seeking out women directors, but she beat her ex James Cameron, who directed *Avatar*. I mean, if I say I have not fantasized about one day beating Caleb for a directing award, I'd be lying. Revenge would be sweet.

I've never been part of a group Halloween costume, so I'm loving it when Edie and Hope and I head to Paris's massive house with its killer view. There's security of course, but there are also, like, a hundred random people wandering around by her pool and all over her house. One of the rooms has been converted into an actual nightclub with a DJ booth and dance floor, and there are beefcake guys in tiny Chippendales costumes serving drinks. Paris is flitting around outside, but I don't really speak to her. I'm doing shots, and at some point, I look around the dance floor and realize Edie and Hope aren't there anymore, so I go look for them.

I'm pretty wasted as I weave through the crowded dance floor, calling their names. There's a half-open door with a light on inside, so I push the door open to find Edie, Hope, and a few other people hunched over a table in what looks like a music studio.

"Guys! I've been looking all over!" I yell, maybe a little too loudly. The music is ringing in my ears. "What're you doing in here?"

I walk toward them, and Edie turns around. Even though I've been to a million clubs, I've never seen cocaine before, never done it, but I know what the white lines on the table are. I've always sworn I'd never try it.

"It's coke! Come try!" Edie holds her hand out for me to join them. "It's strawberry flavored," she adds.

"How does that even work?" I ask, feeling lame for even questioning it.

"The drip afterward tastes like strawberries, I swear!" Edie says excitedly.

"Okay, fuck it. What should I do?!" I ask, wide-eyed in my slutty schoolgirl uniform with red fishnets and Heelys.

"Aw, I got you! Hold one side of your nose down and sniff. But do each side. Then put some water around the rim of your nose so you don't see the powder."

I promised myself for years I'd never do hard drugs, but what if I just try a *little*? I need to experience life, right? I have nothing to lose, quite frankly. I take the key loaded up with a bump from Edie's hands and inhale. There, it's done.

"Oh no! I got the Disney girl to do blow for the first time!" Edie and the small group around us laugh loudly.

I don't even remember leaving the music studio, but here we are on the dance floor, sweating in this mass of people, all gorgeous, all young, some famous. And it means nothing. I'm also swinging around a stripper pole in Paris Hilton's club/living room. Somehow I'm not falling on my ass, even though I'm in Heelys and not very coordinated. Edie and Hope and a few other people I recognize but can't name are dancing with their eyes closed, blissed-out smiles across their faces.

"I can't believe little Romano did coke!" yells one of the guys with large black-rimmed glasses who was in the music studio with us. He was my voice-over agent years ago and has watched me grow up. And now here we are. Fucked up on Paris Hilton's dance floor, surrounded by roided-out guys in Chippendales outfits serving champagne. This is the party that everyone in LA wants to be at, and as I look around, I know I should feel like I've finally made it, like I'm in the scene with my tribe. The misfit girl who pissed her pants; got barked off the bus; had buckteeth, small boobs, and no friends; was passed over by her peers who were making millions; and got trampled on by any man she dared give her heart to. But the only thing I feel is that none of this matters. The room is packed with people but feels totally, completely empty and on mute. I close my eyes, focus on the music, and keep dancing like a zombie.

It turns out that my bottom of the barrel isn't doing coke and feeling like nothing matters. It's answering the phone when Caleb calls, even though we've been broken up and haven't spoken. It's agreeing to do this stupid movie *Mirrors 2* because he says there's a part for me and he knows I could use the work. He won't be directing it, but a buddy of his will. I have been so desperate for work, and it's like he's serving me a role on a silver platter. The role requires nudity, which I swore I would never ever do. But I take it, because it doesn't really feel like I have a choice. I'm there, and it's Caleb, and I need to keep working.

We film back in Louisiana, and even though I'm nervous, I also feel like this is my chance to step out of the Disney little kid world and into adult roles for good. I even had lunch with a Disney exec before I said yes to the movie to get his blessing. He basically told me I'm too old to be cast as a kid, too young to be a mom, so go for it. So here I am, standing topless in front of the makeup artist, India, as she airbrushes my nipples bright pink "like they do with Playmates," according to her. The spray she's using is cold, so I'm glad when it's over. I feel confident because I know my boobs look good from my breast implants, and I haven't been eating much, so I know my body will look skinny. I'm too numb to feel nervous. I feel . . . nothing.

I put on a robe and walk into the closed set with the director and just a few crew members. They're all very respectful, so it doesn't feel sleazy. I step into the shower, and the director asks if I'm okay, which I guess I am. I hand the robe to India, and we start shooting. In my mind I just tell myself I'm a performer, and it's my job to perform. Just commit to the moment and do it. My character gets her head chopped off in the scene, so I try to think of it as something iconic, like the shower scene in *Psycho*. If anything, it feels a little rebellious. It's not like landing a *Maxim* cover, but hopefully, it does lead to more mature roles.

Caleb and I hook up casually while I'm shooting the movie for a few weeks, but I can tell he's distant, and I'm pretty sure he's now officially with Tabitha. I don't love the girl, but I also feel terrible that he's probably cheating on her with me. The day I head back to LA, I break down and beg him to just stop coming in and out of my life. I say, "I want to be number one on your call sheet," when he tells me he wants to date Tabitha *and* date me. It's so pathetic, but when you're hungover, being dramatic gets you attention fast. While I'm crying and begging this guy to just stay out of my life, he picks up his guitar and starts singing the Hootie & the Blowfish song "Let Her Cry." What a total asshole.

After six months back in LA, I have that familiar feeling: I need to go. I'm spiraling there, my career is less than nothing, and I can't keep sleeping all day and partying all night. After getting a taste for it the first time at Paris's party, I've been partying too much and trying coke more, and honestly, it's a way to try to make Caleb worry about me, which he is—but not enough. He and I have been on a roller coaster, and not a fun one, for over two years now. I can't take the shallowness of Hollywood and clubs anymore. It's going to kill me.

After speaking to this amazing woman in financial aid at Barnard, I work toward getting some grants so I can finish school. I move back home to Connecticut until school starts next fall. I'm lonely in this old house that's falling apart. Even with Mom and Dad here, it's cold and damp, and I feel disconnected from everything and everyone.

Still, we're getting along well enough. I think my family does like that they can help me when I'm struggling. Even with all their issues, they've always been ride or die about me. They cheer me on while I feel like I'm back to square one in so many ways. I'm nervous about *Mirrors 2* coming out, even though it's going straight to video. I don't know if I should have broken my long-standing rule of NO NUDITY ONSCREEN or if it'll just be a blip and no one will care. It's scary being so vulnerable in that way, but I have to take charge of my own career, my own mind and body. At least, I'm trying to. When I didn't want to cut my hair as a kid for that asshole hair guy in the *Follies*, I stood up for myself. I'm finding that harder and harder to do as I get older. It's always easier in the moment to be "agreeable," and my confidence is so low, I struggle to speak up, to even access how I really feel about something. It's tough, because I feel so lost.

Just like Louisiana, Connecticut has a tax credit that's bringing more filmmakers here. Dad is trying to get into producing, which drives Mom crazy. "He has no idea what he's doing. It's ridiculous," she always says. But he's partly retired and just consulting for businesses here and there, so I think producing—or trying to produce—is a way for him to stay busy. He's been through radiation and treatment for cancer, so the guy can do what he wants. It is a little embarrassing that he's trying to be, like, Mr. Filmmaker at this point in his life, but it's not like his movie career is taking off like a rocket or anything. He has always wanted to be famous—or at least seem important—and now this is just his latest attempt.

I'm ready to get out of the house, even if it means moving into the tiny student apartment I'll be going to when I start school.

Since there are so many indie films shooting locally around Connecticut while I'm there, I reconnect with some of Caleb's film buddies from Louisiana. One of them, Brian, is really sweet. So we start hooking up out of sheer boredom and loneliness. It's not like I'm doing it to get back at Caleb or anything. Or maybe I am. But it's fun, and it's casual, and it's not like Caleb cares anyway. He's with *Tabitha*, thousands of miles away, wrestling an alligator or something. Maybe she's baking him cookies and pies. I sigh heavily and try not to care, but he has such a hold on me still. I know it's ridiculous, but it's the way it is.

And then he calls. Of course he calls.

"I heard you've been hanging out with Brian and the crew up there," he says, barely even saying hello. "Are you hooking up with him?"

"Why do you even care, Caleb?" I ask, secretly excited that he does care. "You're happy with Tabitha, right? It's none of your business who I date."

"Christy, he's my friend. You can't do that. It's fucked up. I know you're doing it to get revenge on me."

"Oh wow," I say, shocked that he'd try to make me feel bad after everything he's done. "You've hurt me for three years. You have no say or control over what I do or who I do it with!"

"Fuck you, Christy," he says before hanging up. When I hear the silence on the line, my heart breaks all over again. I would have done anything for him, and it scares me that I still might. Even after all this. I'm depressed and tired, so I take a nap. In my old childhood room, in this drafty house, I fall asleep so I don't have to think. Or feel.

The day after our fight, I wake up to a text from Caleb:

> *Remember those photos I took of you in Big Bear? You didn't listen to me about Brian, so I'm selling them online, bitch. Just watch.*

Panic surges through my body, and my hands start shaking. I start to text back but then delete it. That's what he wants, right? And this is serious. Actresses have had nude photos of them leaked and sold online, and it's horrible. And now I might be part of this. For a brief moment, I have the sick thought that he's doing this to me because he still loves me, but I know, deep inside, that that is wrong.

> *Why are you doing this to me? I hate you! Leave me the fuck alone!*

I know I shouldn't reply, but I can't help it. I feel totally exposed and vulnerable, like nothing is in my control.

> *I'm selling to the highest bidder. I already sent the photos to multiple people, and they only offered $5,000 because you're not famous or pretty enough.*

I throw my phone across the room. I can hear voices coming from the big TV downstairs. Dad laughs at whatever show he's watching. I'm so nauseous, I might throw up, so I head downstairs and do something I know I *need* to do, even though the thought of it fills me with dread.

I find Dad alone on the couch, eating pasta and watching a Giants game. Mom must be out running errands. I stand in the kitchen doorway and take a deep breath.

"Dad? I'm in trouble."

He looks up, immediately worried. My fingers feel numb from fear. Dad stands and crosses his arms.

"What happened?"

He has that serious, time-to-take-care-of-business look that I've seen before when I've needed him to help me. Like I'm ripping off a bandage, I just blurt it out.

"Caleb has naked pictures of me that he's trying to sell online."

"Sit down and tell me everything," Dad says very calmly. He looks pissed, not at me but at Caleb. But he's also laser-focused. Whenever there's a crisis, he snaps to attention and takes care of shit. Just like he's done for me so many times in the past. I tell him everything that I know like he's my priest. I tell him the photos are private and intimate, which is not something you want to confess to your fucking father. I thought everything else—the coke, the moving back home, the two broken engagements—was rock bottom. Nope. This is it.

"We're calling the FBI," Dad says. "I have a contact."

He starts dialing a number.

"How do you just have the number for the FBI?" I ask.

"I just do."

It's a little weird that he has that number, but then again, he's always protected me. That's his thing. And I need his protection now, so I don't ask any more questions.

"They're transferring me to my contact," he says. "Just do as I say, you got it? I know how to talk to these guys. You can't keep pretending like the world is a party, Christy. This is serious."

I trust my dad since he's saved me so many times. But as he waits on the phone, I can't help but feel that the world is crashing down around me.

It's a freezing February day, so cold that I can see my breath as we drive to New Haven in Dad's Nissan. The FBI building is brick and rectangular and nondescript. I tried to dress as conservatively as possible, and I'm listening to everything Dad tells me, like "Don't mess this up, Christy."

"I'll do whatever it takes, Dad."

We hurry into the lobby and check in, and a receptionist tells us to take the elevator up. We meet two agents, one bald and tall and the other short with curly black hair. They're both wearing suits. We shake hands, and they lead us into a conference room with nothing on the walls. Just totally blank and boring. I let Dad take the lead since I trust him in these situations. He knows enough about legal issues, what to say and not to say, so I just listen.

The agents have me sign and date a form *February 23, 2010*. They ask me questions about what Caleb said over text, I show them the texts, and they ask some basic things about our relationship. I finish giving them a rundown of our relationship, and then they tell me to call Caleb on speaker so they can record it.

"We'll tell you exactly what to say," says the bald one.

"He won't pick up," I say, finding his number in my phone. "He hates me."

The phone rings a few times, and just when I'm about to hang up, Caleb answers. This fucking guy answers! I'm terrified, and I look to the agents, who write down things for me to say, so I just read their notepad and try to sound calm. I guess years of professional acting training come in handy in situations like this.

"I know you're trying to sell the photos," I say. "What would you have done if you'd caught me and Brian together?" I ask, not understanding why they're having me say this.

"I would have driven out there and gutted you both like O. J. did," he says. "If you're not scared for your life, you should be."

My blood goes cold. I've never heard him talk this way, so openly violent. The agents make an urgent signal for me to hang up, and as soon as I do, Dad sits back, crosses his arms, and gets quiet. When my dad gets silent, I know he's furious. I have that tingly sensation that I once felt on stage while standing in a puddle of piss, except this time I've stepped in shit and I can't just exit into the wings.

"We got him for threatening you over state lines," the agents say. They start making calls, devising plans, and shuffling papers. In this sudden whirlwind of activity, I'm totally confused and unsure of what just happened. Part of me feels vindicated for all the shit Caleb has done to me, and part of me feels horrible, like I may have just gotten a guy I once knew so intimately and loved so much into very serious trouble. I want to explode and disappear.

Dad can probably sense my fear, because he puts his hand on my shoulder and says, "You did the right thing, Christy."

"I did?" I ask, but Dad is out of the chair and talking to one of the agents before he can respond.

After the trial in Connecticut, I chop my long hair off. Caleb and his dad came to the East Coast, and my dad went to the hearing on my behalf. Caleb had the nerve to wear the Hugo Boss suit I bought him when he came to New York once. I know that wasn't an accident.

The day after my call with him, the FBI seized Caleb's computer in LA and arrested him at his house. Supposedly Tabitha, who is now living with him, was crying and screaming in the street.

After everything that happened with the assault and then with Caleb, cutting my hair feels like a way to flip the middle finger at femininity and men, especially LA men. I'm doing this play called *White's Lies* off Broadway with the great Betty Buckley, staying part-time with my old friend from PCS, Luka. He's a hairstylist now, so he cuts my hair for free, which is a perk, since I'm flat broke. When I stay over, we sometimes go out to this insane club called The Box, where they have burlesque dancers doing wild things. I'm not singing in *White's Lies* since it's a straight-up comedy, so I don't feel bad going out all the time and drinking. Plus it gets my mind off everything that happened. I can let my guard down, and it helps me forget Caleb. I know I'm probably drinking too much, but some days I just can't help it. I can't stop.

I keep on doing coke when it's offered because it seems like *everyone* is doing it, and it just obliterates any doubts or worries I have about my career or my future: if I'll ever get a big part again, if I'll ever find love. I love the cast I'm working with, and I have my little New York theater community back, at least for the few months the show runs, before I'm back in school.

I tell Luka everything, and he never judges me. He's always dragging me to gay bars near the theater in Midtown, which I love because I feel more comfortable there. There are no predatory straight men preying on me. I can just be free and have fun. Summer in Manhattan is the best, and I am taking full advantage.

Still, I'm scared about finances and about keeping my health insurance. I've been making just enough with small jobs to still qualify for benefits through SAG. I'm scared about a lot of things, and the tape in my head that keeps telling me I'm not pretty enough or talented enough gets louder at night, so I go out, hoping that loud, pulsing music will make it go away. I know I might look like I'm just another girl in Manhattan partying with her friends, but I feel myself closing up. That voice tells me I'm a piece of shit, that I should hurt myself. I feel my heart getting harder, my ability to connect getting rusty, like an old barbed-wire fence. "Just keep going, Christy," my family always says. "Don't give up on your dreams."

But what does that even mean anymore? What did it ever mean?

Dear Girls,

So . . . that was a lot.

Your mom has been through some shit. When I started this project, I was very unsure of just how much I was going to share about myself, of just how deep I was willing to go. Your father and I had some serious conversations about what you might have to hear when you come of age, when you got old enough to read this and to understand what it means. Know that I'm okay now and have been sober for a really long time, so we can unpack this whenever you're ready.

Every parent has a story, and nobody is perfect. That, however, doesn't excuse any of the insane, stupid things that I did to sabotage myself. My time with Caleb and the period after was a life lived without personal choice. And that's not because I didn't have *a choice, but because I didn't hold myself accountable for my actions and learn or grow. Oddly enough, if I had chosen myself long ago and gotten away from the industry to start over on another path, who knows what would have happened—whether I would have met your dad or if I would even have become a mom. It all led me here, to you, and so I'm grateful.*

They say hindsight is twenty-twenty, but I say it's also somewhat useless. The truth is that my addiction to alcohol started a long time before this multiyear spiral with Caleb. I'd known through years of Al-Anon meetings that I was addicted to people, places, and things, but I was in the wrong program. I wasn't ready to fully admit to my problem. Because of my sexual assault, I had no interest in going to meetings of any kind. I think that Paul just made me never trust those rooms again. Meetings work for so many people, but I had to find my own way. You have to do what works for you.

I believe addiction is in your family bloodline on both sides. That's why we have a dry house outside of having guests over for the occasional dinner party. Alcohol is not at the center of our life for good reason. While I don't think I was physically addicted and needed to dry out in rehab, I was most definitely a binge drinker. When I chose to drink, it was in excess: It was six to eight drinks a night on an empty stomach. I was drinking to get away from myself, from my thoughts and feelings.

If you should ever lose yourself, please know that the way back isn't through numbing the pain or running from it. The way through is sitting with discomfort until you remember who you are underneath all the performance. You find yourself by stopping—stopping the chaos, the substances, the toxic relationships, the constant motion that keeps you from feeling anything real.

I found myself by finally getting quiet enough to hear my own voice again. Not my mother's voice, not the industry's voice, not some man's voice telling me who I should be. Mine. And, girls, your voices are in there too, even when the world gets loud. Especially when the world gets loud.

The greatest gift I can give you is breaking this family pattern. You get to grow up knowing your worth isn't conditional. You get to feel your feelings instead of diverting, disassociating, or drowning them out. You get to ask for help without shame, since your parents have both been around the block. And if you ever find yourself reaching for anything harmful to avoid sitting with yourself, I need you to remember that you are enough, exactly as you are. If you need to reach out, you call me, and I'll drop what I'm doing to support you.

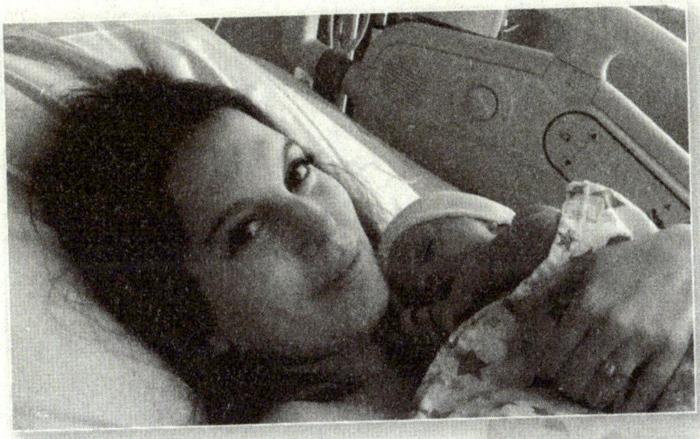

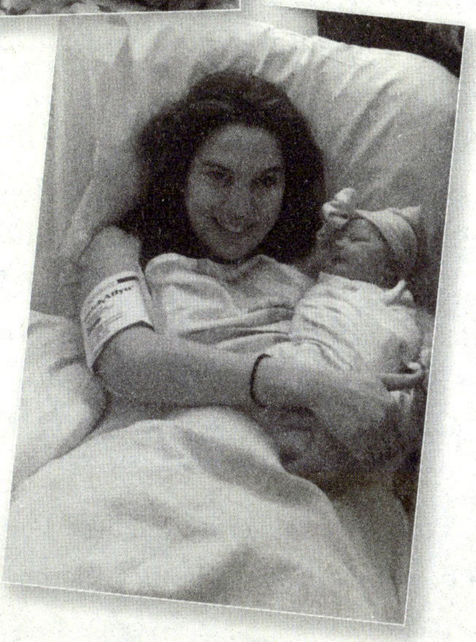

11

God's Plan

2011–2017

Ages 26 to 33

I order my third vodka soda, and my sorority sister Rachel gives me a weird look. I'm about to start my second semester since going back to Barnard, and maybe it's the freezing February weather, but things don't feel right. I don't feel right.

Rachel talks about how amazing Lady Gaga was tonight, and she's right. The entire crowd at Madison Square Garden was screaming for her. I was screaming. But I still feel empty and unfulfilled. Going back to school, I switched my major to film, and I love it. I do want to direct, but I can't help but feel like I've failed at everything. The tape plays in my head over and over: *You had your chance and you blew it . . . You're not good enough . . . Not pretty enough . . . Maybe you should just die . . .*

"What's up with you?" Rachel asks in the gruff way some New Yorkers talk. "You've been weird tonight."

I down my drink and order another one. Fuck it.

"I don't know what's wrong," I say. And I honestly don't. Maybe it's everything.

"You're not still thinking about that asshole, are you?" she asks. "Christy, he was fucking evil. He was going to sell nude photos of you."

"Thanks for reminding me."

The truth is, being rejected by Caleb almost feels worse than being rejected by the industry that I devoted my entire life to. Because I'm realizing that any chance at a so-called normal life was gone the minute I started doing pageants, the second I went on the road as a kid. I can't help but feel that I fucked up our whole family by not being home, by being on TV and taking Mom away. I deserve this, though. I did this all to myself. That day that I had to sit there with the guys from the FBI, knowing these strangers, these guys in suits, saw photos of me naked, it just killed something in me. And after all of that, nothing came of the investigation at all. The only act that seems halfway possible right now is to finish school. To wake up, go to class, try to direct. Because I am done with acting. Before I came back to school, I told my agent and managers I was quitting for good.

"Rachel, I don't know what to do anymore," I say. I'm not sure why I'm pouring my heart out to a sorority sister who barely knows me, but she's here now, I guess. "Some days I feel dead, like I could die. It's an unforgiving cycle. I guess I feel lost."

"You'll be okay," Rachel says, looking a little unsure. "God has a plan, Christy."

What does that even mean? I thought there was a plan, and look how that turned out. The last acting job I got was a low-budget horror movie shot in the fall, and I had my eye eaten by a zombie. I did it mainly so I could keep my SAG health insurance. The director and producers asked me to get naked in one scene, but this time I stood my ground and refused. At least there's that. For so many years, I felt accomplished, like a "shining star," like agents and managers used to say when I was little. Now, in 2011, I don't feel at all like a shining star anymore. I feel broken.

It's a little weird being an almost-twenty-seven-year-old junior in college, and I know some of the students give me the side-eye when I'm on campus. Like, *Look at that girl who was on a Disney show and now she's this older film studies major . . .* Maybe I'm projecting, but I just keep my head down, go to class, and learn as much as I can. I'm not here to be in a sorority or make eight hundred friends. I'm hanging out with some old PCS friends, though, which is cool. Linda is making documentaries, and Bianca is working with her mom's nonprofit. I still party with them, or else I just go to the restaurant down the street from my tiny apartment alone to eat and drink. The bartender knows me so well, he barely charges me anymore.

"Okay, class, you're going to partner up for critiques," says our Screenwriting 101 instructor, Professor O'Malley. She's always wearing a scarf around her neck, and she loves classic Italian cinema. She keeps telling us "all roads lead to Fellini."

I look to my right and smile at the hot guy who's been auditing the class the last few weeks. We haven't talked much, but since we're sitting next to each other, that means we'll be critique partners. He's so hot that he's way out of my league, with bright blue eyes and light hair, slicked back and stylish.

"Hi, I'm Christy," I say. "I guess we're partners."

"Hey, I'm Brendan," he says in a way that's totally genuine and not loaded or fake like so many LA guys sound, even if they're just saying hey. I know this guy is about my age and that he's a military veteran at Columbia on the G.I. Bill, because I asked my friend Vic, who also happens to be a vet. According to Vic, Brendan is kind of a big deal since he's the president of the campus veterans' association. I try to play it cool, even though inside I am not feeling cool at all.

We exchange scripts. Mine, called *Heart Phone*, is about two iPhones that fall in love, but in the end, it's their owners who come together to fall for each other.

"We should probably exchange numbers, right?" Brendan asks. My heart jumps in my chest. This guy is gorgeous, but we'll never hook up. I'm sure he has models fawning all over him when he goes out at night.

"Yeah, sounds good," I say as I take his phone and type in my number. He texts me right away so I have his. I know I'll see him later because I'm helping Vic film part of his documentary later in the anthro building, but I don't tell him that. This guy is intimidating, and I don't want to seem desperate.

I can't help myself, though. It's not like a game, like it sometimes felt with Ravi and Caleb. It feels different. Easy. Maybe *I'm* different.

About an hour after class, I text Brendan.

Hey, handsome ;)

I mean, what do I have to lose?

Vic is cool, but he can also be a dick. He's super sarcastic and puts me down sometimes with passive-aggressive comments, like he's trying to make me feel not smart or something. He also thinks he's going to be the next Michael Bay meets Steven Spielberg. But he's not all bad, and I'm not at school to be Miss Popular. I'm just here to finish. Plus Vic and most of the vets are my age.

He sets up his camera, and I assist however I can. The seats are all full since some students are pissed about the ROTC coming back. One even called some of the vets "baby killers," and they heckled an amputee, which is fucked up. The guy earned a Purple Heart. It's a rowdy group at the town hall, and I'm a little afraid it might get violent. Vic films a few speakers, and then it's Brendan's time to head to the podium. My stomach flips when I see him. He's so poised and confident, the exact opposite of how I feel these days.

Brendan clears his throat and launches into a speech that's passionate and eloquent. I try to focus on helping Vic, but all I want to do is watch this guy. He talks about repealing "Don't ask, don't tell," and tells the students that it's important to bring inclusivity to the military, that it's not like it used to be in the old days, and that it's healthy to have the ROTC on campus. He does get some jeers, but mostly people listen. I know I'm listening.

After his speech, I help Vic wrangle equipment and wrap up the shoot. Brendan walks up to us, and my cheeks go red-hot, so I pretend to be extremely busy putting away the camera tripod so he won't notice.

"Hey, we're going to this Cuban place on 116th after this if you want to come."

I know the place he's talking about. It used to be the West End, the bar that had so many bad memories of nights with my ex Giovanni, of nights with the hockey team, but those guys are ghosts to me now. Long gone, from what feels like another lifetime.

"Sure," I say, zipping the tripod into its case and smiling up at Brendan. "I'll help Vic with this stuff, and we can head over."

"Perfect," Brendan says.

I think this is an actual date. I mean, he texted asking me to coffee, not to some club or a group outing but just us. I loosened up around him at the Cuban place the day before, and then met him and his friends later at Haakon's Hall for drinks, but I freaked out seeing all these beautiful girls hanging around him like hummingbirds. I can't compete with girls who are younger, blonder, flirtier. I stayed for, like, twenty minutes and then left without saying goodbye. My insecurity got the best of me, I guess. But then he texted the next day, and here we are, meeting for coffee.

The Hungarian Pastry Shop on Amsterdam is a historic Manhattan eatery, but I've never been. After we get our croissants and chai it doesn't take long before we turn from small talk to him telling me about growing up in Orange County and the fact that his mom was only seventeen when he was born. He tells me about going into the Marines and being in Iraq, but mostly he asks questions about me. And for some reason, I don't hold anything back. I feel the floodgates open, and I tell him *everything*: I tell him about being a child actor, about my relationship with my mom and about my parents' toxic marriage, about being bullied and PCS and Disney and never really having a sense of community, of wanting to be normal but also "succeed" in acting. I'm honest about struggles I've had and how I quit acting, but I'm a creative person and want to direct. I even tell him about the FBI case and the fact that I've been in a pretty dark place. Throughout it all, he never judges or scolds or tries to make me feel bad like Ravi or Caleb would have done. He just . . . listens. I guess my problems don't seem so horrible to someone who's been in an actual war. He's not impressed by celebrity or Hollywood, which I love.

"Sorry," I say when I come up for air. "That was a lot."

"Don't ever be sorry for being honest," he says. I have to hold myself back from tackling him right there in the pastry shop. We look at each other for a few intense seconds, and then my phone beeps with a text. Thank God, because I was about to not be able to control myself around this guy.

"It's a friend," I say. "We went to PCS together."

RU coming to my party later?

I totally forgot it was her birthday tonight. Without second-guessing myself, I look up into Brendan's eyes.

"My friend Bianca is having a party tonight for her birthday," I say. "You want to come with me?"

My chest clenches while waiting for his answer. I probably got too excited, and now he thinks I'm some lame stalker. Fuck.

"Yes," he says. "Yes, I do."

Since that first cold and gorgeous February night when we went to Bianca's party and later kissed in a club, which led to making out in the Meatpacking District, surrounded by stacks of wooden crates, falling and literally rolling around together on the cobblestone, Brendan and I have been inseparable. I pretty much moved into his apartment that first weekend. It just felt natural and still feels that way a month later. We can't help ourselves. I love making him laugh and talking about art and creativity and our families. I feel like together, we can do anything. I don't think I've ever been so much myself with another person, whether it's with family or at work or in relationships. I've never met someone who makes me feel so in the moment, so present. He just accepts everything about me, and for the first time, I don't have to pretend. He's been to war. His mom was on welfare at one point and was a teenager when he was born. He's got a depth that no one I've ever dated has.

After a month, it feels right to introduce Brendan to my sisters and brother, and my brother's girlfriend, Tina. I'm nervous since they hated Ravi and Caleb, and my whole family thinks I am clueless and a loser when it comes to love, but this time I know in my heart that it's different. Plus they were right to hate my exes. I just couldn't see that at the time. Dad hasn't met him yet, but I can tell he's impressed that Brendan served our country, that he's a Marine and not some Hollywood trust-fund kid. He's about the furthest thing from that I can imagine.

We meet up with everyone at Rose Bar at Gramercy Park Hotel. I know my siblings are walking into this with skepticism, but they warm up to Brendan immediately. The place is packed and rowdy, and we're all squished together, shouting to hear one another and to order our drinks. I talk to Tina about her job, and I can overhear Brendan telling my brother about investing in minerals in Afghanistan or something. He's going off about lithium deposits and the history of the region, and I can hear my sister jump into their conversation, trying to change the subject.

"So, Brendan," she says. "What kind of girls did you date before Christy?"

My ears prick up, of course. I listen to Tina, but my focus is directly behind me on my sister. I hold my breath, scared of where she's going.

"I was in a relationship," Brendan says. I know this already because we've talked about our pasts. I can't help but feel a little jealousy like I always do, but something in me keeps pushing me to trust him and not fall into the same cycles I've been in with guys. "She was a German girl, but it wasn't a good fit."

"Oh, a German girl," my sister says, extra loud so I can hear. "I bet she was really pretty."

In the past, I might have turned around and confronted my sister for antagonizing me like this, but now it just seems sad to me. I refuse to take the bait, and it feels good.

"Uh, your sister's much more beautiful," Brendan says. I don't turn around. I just smile, keep the moment all to myself.

Brendan and I love New York, but his mentor gets him a job in LA starting right after he graduates in May. Why does that town keep luring me back? We're moving fast, but we're both in this 100 percent. He's met my whole family. The night I introduced him and Dad, Brendan was giving a speech to the Producers Guild of America about veterans in the entertainment industry. (I brought Dad on purpose because I knew he'd be impressed.) We all went to dinner after the event. I got up to go to the restroom, and Brendan told me later that Dad leaned across the table and said, "When things go sideways and she breaks your heart, don't talk to her about it. Just come straight to me."

Brendan said he just started laughing because what Dad said was so ridiculous. I've never brought it up to Dad because I know he wants to protect me, and I know he genuinely likes Brendan. But I want to get to a place in my life where I don't need to be protected from a man or from anyone else. I've spent so much of my life being "protected" by Mom as a kid in auditions or on sets, and then by Dad when relationships got toxic or outright dangerous. I want to break the patterns, end the cycles. But some days I don't know how. I don't know if I have it in me.

I swipe my badge to open the door and head up to the fifth floor of the ABC Studios building in Burbank. It's weird, I know, to be a former Disney child star now interning for a Disney-owned company and using my ID badge to answer phones and assist executives all day, but it's part of my plan. I applied for the position and got a reference letter from Mick Frost, plus the internship counts toward my degree at school. At the Beverly Hills Playhouse, they were always telling us to do "admin" and map out what things we can do to further our career, and this internship is a way for me to network not as an actor but as a woman who wants to direct. I've gotten some weird looks and side-eyes from people who recognize me, which can be awkward. But if I just focus on my end goal, I can shrug it off. Part of me does like having "normal" office clothes and commuting to a nine-to-five job, since I've never experienced anything like this before. What I don't love is feeling ancient, because all the other interns are about eighteen.

Brendan started a job on *The Biggest Loser*, and it's not his dream gig, but his mentor keeps saying it's his "foot-in-the-door experience." My internship pays a little and Brendan gets a salary, but we're only just scraping by. We're renting a tiny room in an apartment a friend of his owns, and we have roommates. It's a little different than me having my own huge place in West Hollywood, but I'd rather be happy and in love, pursuing my dreams, than back in that time when I was shopping on Rodeo every week and driving around in a G-Wagon. I mean, I don't love feeling broke, but I know there's a light at the end of the tunnel.

"Christy Romano?"

I look up from scrolling Facebook, which I'm not supposed to be doing, but I'm filling in for the receptionist, and my sole job is to answer the phone, which is not ringing since it's everyone's lunch break. In Hollywood, *everyone* goes to lunch meetings. The hour from one to two is like a ghost town.

"What are you doing here?"

My cheeks flush red. It's Tim, an executive I knew from my *Even Stevens* days. I'm slightly mortified, but I put on my sunniest Disney-kid smile and act like this is all totally normal. Inside I'm cringing—I mean, talk about a humbling experience.

"Hi, Tim! I'm back at Barnard, and I'm interning for the summer as part of my major. I'm pursuing directing now!"

He looks a little confused but quickly shifts gears into Hollywood networking mode.

"Do you know Anne Sweeney? You should take a meeting with her to talk about directing."

Of course I know who Anne Sweeney is. She basically runs everything at Disney–ABC TV. I try to keep my cool, but the prospect of having a meeting with her is the most exciting thing that's happened in the four weeks I've been at this internship. It's definitely better than scrolling through Facebook and rolling calls.

"I don't know her personally, but I know who she is, of course. That would be amazing!"

"You got it," Tim says. "I'm hurrying to a lunch, but I'll get it set. It's good to see you, Christy," he says. "You should eat something, kid. You look a little skinny."

Tim hurries off, and I'm torn. Half elated at the thought of meeting a powerful woman in the business, someone who might help me get a step closer to my goals. And half sick to my stomach about Tim's last comment. As happy as I am with Brendan, I know I'm not the healthiest. I still drink too much, party too much. But I'm having fun. I'm in love. I can quit partying anytime. Just not right now, because it's too much fun. I like it too much to stop.

Anne Sweeney's office is huge, with gorgeous views of the city. When I walk in, she looks every bit the high-powered businesswoman that she is. Michelle, the woman in charge of us interns, gave me a dirty look when I told her I needed to be excused to go meet Anne Sweeney.

"Fine," Michelle said, as if she were spitting out the word. "Just be back in thirty."

I know Michelle and the other interns think I'm using some sort of privilege to get ahead, but wouldn't they do the same if they'd been actors and had the connections? Plus I worked my ass off my entire childhood. I don't think a sit-down with Anne Sweeney is the same as the company handing me a hundred-million-dollar movie to direct. I'm just saying hello to the woman.

Unlike so many people in this town, Anne is genuine and kind. She asks about Barnard, about my goals of directing. I try to impress her by laying out my goals, telling her about my work-study job with the Athena Film Festival on campus, which promotes films by and about women. She has a vision for young people coming into the company to create in all sorts of roles, and she makes me feel valuable and not like some weird old intern who didn't make it in acting. She gives me some hope.

I spend about twenty minutes with Anne, which is an eternity to a busy executive. I thank her for the time, and she tells me to reach out anytime. When I get back to the reception desk, I add her contact info to the growing "bible" of Hollywood contacts I've been compiling. I don't know when or if I'll contact all these people, but I'm sure when the right moment comes, I'll know.

I drive home, excited to tell Brendan about the meeting. As much as I love being here with him and experiencing LA in a healthy relationship, it's hard sometimes being confronted with so many past ghosts. The bar where I was assaulted, the places I went to with exes, buildings I auditioned in for so many years. Places I lived in with Mom or alone. The Oakwood, the *Even Stevens* studios, The WB lot, where I'd see massive murals of *Dawson's Creek* or *Gilmore Girls* and feel like I'd never make it through those gates. I try to push away anything negative, anything that could distract me from where I am now. But it's not always easy.

Over drinks at a local pub, I tell Brendan about my meeting. He's happy for me and fully supportive of me directing. But he doesn't understand why I've given up on acting or singing, since I have so much "obvious talent" there. Ever since I came back to school and decided to focus on being behind the camera, I've been adamant that I'm finished with acting. It feels good to stand my ground, even if there is a tiny seed of doubt inside me. Isn't that true of any creative person, though? I believe in him, in us, but being in this city and grinding it out, living with random roommates, can be overwhelming. I just have to shut off that negative tape that plays in my head. I have to stay positive and stop second-guessing myself. I have to keep telling myself that this is right, and it's not like it used to be, and I am not like I used to be. So much has been fucked up over the last decade that I need to shift. I want to change, not just for Brendan but for me.

I had a hunch it would happen in Italy. Even though we've only been together about six months, we've been pretty much inseparable and even designed a ring (emerald cut). It's the most beautiful ring I've ever seen. Over the summer, I straight-up asked him what the future held for our relationship, since he was planning to stay in LA and I needed to know where things were going. Unlike how I was with Ravi and Caleb, I know that I can say what I really feel with Brendan and not pretend to be the "cool girl" who doesn't speak her mind. He told me not to worry. That he's serious about me for the long haul. We splurged on the Italy trip (aka went into more debt) to celebrate Brendan getting into the American Film Institute for grad school.

Italy in August is warm and quiet, since all the locals leave the cities for vacation, and most tourists are back to school or work. We have some wild nights in Rome, one where we get so wasted that Brendan has to be hospitalized. But he toughs it out, and when we get to Venice, he proposes in a gondola under the Rialto Bridge. I've been through this before, I've had rings before, but this is different, because I've decided to be different. I may have doubts about my career and money, but I have zero doubts about us. When we call our families, they are so excited for us. I know exactly where I want to get married. Years ago, during the *Follies*, we stayed in that magical town in Canada called Banff that looks straight out of a fairy tale. It's surrounded by a national park, and my dream is to get married there in the winter, on New Year's Eve. I have no clue how we'll afford it, but we'll find a way. I'm following my heart. I know it's gotten me into trouble in the past, but this time is different.

Right after the engagement, Brendan starts grad school in LA. The plan is that we'll spend two years here and plan the wedding, get married when he graduates, and then we'll head back to New York so I can finish college, finally. Being engaged to him is a dream, and I love hiking in Malibu with him and exploring the city, but nothing ever comes from my meeting with Anne at ABC or any of the contacts I made during my internship. I finish the short film I made back in New York, but student films don't exactly pay the bills. I feel so many echoes from Mom and Dad's money fights, but I'm just trying to work and plan the wedding and make something, anything, happen. This is what happens to child actors who're never taught how to manage money, I guess. We hustle to survive.

I'm getting sort of desperate, so I take a job with this guy Charles, who manages a modeling-and-talent agency for kids. It's been around since the 1920s, and the ads all say that super-famous people like Fred Astaire and Lucille Ball got their starts with the company, but I doubt that's true. Charles brings in former Disney and Nickelodeon stars to recruit families at malls around the country and then teach workshops and classes. It feels like I'm perpetuating this child-actor cycle that I know in my heart is unhealthy, but I need money, so I'm in no position to say no. My car got repossessed because I couldn't make the payments, and Brendan is driving Uber at night to make extra cash. On the weekends, I travel to random towns in North Carolina or Michigan, places that Charles thinks are "made of money," and I sit with these young kids, some as young as I was when I started, and I teach them what I know. The class packages sell for over a thousand dollars, and the company promises that *Your Child Will Be Discovered.* I try to give the kids confidence and praise, which makes me feel a little less guilty about the whole thing.

I know money is not the most important thing in life, but I just want to feel secure, at least, and not like my car or home will get taken away. It brings me back to a deep hurt in that drafty Connecticut house. Brendan and I are both working hard, but I know our families are worried. I do get a little bit of residual money from my shows still, but with each paycheck, the number dwindles bit by bit. It helps, but not enough. Something will come along. Because some days the tape in my head tells me that this is it for me. And I want to smash that tape to pieces.

After two years of being engaged, we get married on New Year's Eve 2013. We have the most beautiful, perfect wedding in Banff. Our families are there, and no one fights or gets too wasted and has a meltdown. The night after the wedding, Dad hosts a huge Italian feast for both families. There's snow outside, just like I imagined it. All I can do is try to make this relationship with a guy who sees *me* the healthiest and most honest relationship that I can. The whole night is magical, with our families and friends we've made over the years there. I've never felt surer of anything in my life than saying "I do" to him.

After the wedding, we head back to New York. We sublet our old apartment in LA, so we get a little money from that. I'm back at Barnard, and I am determined to graduate this May. Brendan finished graduate school, and he's been working with a writing partner in New York, going to meetings and pitching ideas. One bright spot has been that I'm being asked to travel to comic cons around the East Coast to talk about *Kim Possible* and sign autographs. Brendan comes with me, and the pay isn't amazing, but it helps us cobble together enough to get by on. It fucks with my head to hear some people say things like "Christy Romano? You're still alive? What have you been doing?" But, as always, I put on a smile and tell them I've been busy studying film and directing. It does feel good to connect with fans again, though. Even if they are asking where I've been.

As part of my minor in women's leadership, I'm in a small class with this professor, Judy O'Connell. She's always telling us to never have children and to just focus on our careers, which is weird, because she has two kids. But it's like her mantra: *DO NOT HAVE CHILDREN.* Brendan and I haven't really talked about kids; we're too zeroed in on ourselves and our careers. My whole focus is on graduating. Ever since I was young, I dreamed of college and getting a degree. It's just taken me a million years to get here.

"Today, as you're all thinking about your senior thesis topics, I want you to think about the idea of community," says Judy. "Who are your people? Not your family or friends but your community. Where do you self-identify?"

We're sitting in a circle around the table in a small room in Lehman Hall, since there are only about ten of us in the class. I'm a little hungover because Brendan and I went out with friends again last night, but I try to imagine what or who my community is through the thick fog of my brain. I don't know why I keep drinking so much when I know it makes me feel horrible the next day, but I can't help it. We're in New York, right? It's hard not to go out.

"Libby, we'll start with you," Judy says, looking at one of my classmates. Libby has always been pretty quiet in class, so I don't know a ton about her besides the fact that she plays trumpet and lives in Greenpoint.

"Well, I guess my community would be second-generation African immigrants, since my parents came here from Somalia. I'm interested in my heritage and connecting with other people whose parents have similar stories."

"That's great," Judy says. "As you're thinking about your thesis, dig into that."

My classmates all seem so confident in where they belong, who they belong with. For Rachel, it's Orthodox Jews who've broken with tradition, and for Claire, it's adoptees. My stomach tightens as we go around the circle and my turn comes up. I've been searching for my community forever. Whether it was in the theater or at "regular school," at PCS or at Disney, or with different relationships. Nothing ever felt completely right. I have no idea what to say until the moment Judy looks straight at me, the last one to go in the circle.

"And you, Christy? What's your community?"

I freeze for a second and feel like I'm going to break out in a cold sweat. Why is it so hard to say it? Because I've never realized or admitted it? Because it suddenly feels so right and true, even though for years I fought back against it? Finally, I decide to just spit it out.

"I think . . . I mean, I know it's . . . child actors," I say. And the minute the words come out of my mouth, I feel a massive rush of what feels like immense relief mixed with something like fear. I don't care if my classmates think it's dumb or lame. It's the truth. I suddenly remember Myra, that awful tutor who helped with my college essay so long ago. The one who made me feel like I'd never contributed anything to the world and had only done things to serve myself in life. I believed her then but not now. There have to be others out there like me. Not the Shias or Hilarys or Scarletts. The ones who were once the shining stars and who are now just trying to find out their places in the world.

"That's really interesting," Judy says. "You should lean into that."

For spring break, I travel to Los Angeles with Brendan to shoot interviews for my thesis documentary and to clean out our sublet. We're getting rid of it, so the tenants left, and we have to get it in shape so we don't lose our deposit. While we're there, I'm filming at SAG headquarters and talking to a few former child actors, plus some executives from SAG's Looking Ahead Program, which helps kids and parents navigate the crazy world of auditions and labor laws and work in the industry as a young performer. I wish they had programs like this when I was little.

As excited as I am about my thesis and about finally graduating, money is still a stress. I love Brendan, but we've been arguing a lot. It doesn't help things when we walk into the sublet. The place looks like the world's most disgusting frat house. Old food everywhere, beer cans, cigarette stains, and what look like sex stains on the bed and couch. There are roaches and the most awful smell. And it's up to us to clean it.

"We can do this," Brendan says, trying to reassure me. But I'm hit with an overwhelming worry. As hard as we are trying, will we ever catch a break? We put on gloves and get trash bags and start the horrible process of cleaning up someone else's filth. In the middle of it all, I break down in tears. How can I go from feeling like things are about to turn around to totally defeated within five minutes? I feel trapped financially, scared that we won't ever have kids, even if we want to, because we can't even take care of ourselves. I'm still teaching Charles's stupid acting workshops to kids when I can, which is so hypocritical, since I'm also trying to make this documentary about the dangers of being a child actor. I stuff old pizza boxes and a condom wrapper into the trash bag, trying not to lose it completely. I know Brendan is upset too, but he's been through worse than this cleanup.

I quit. Even though we needed the money, I told Charles I was done with the classes. I did it for almost two years, way longer than I'd planned to stay. I couldn't sell that toxic dream of child stardom to all those kids anymore. All the travel was putting a strain on my marriage too, so it was time. I was barely home, always tired, and when I wasn't traveling or working, I was drinking, which I know isn't healthy. The bright spot is that I also graduated. Not in four years, but I did it. Brendan was there, of course, plus my parents. I went to Michaels in Connecticut and made myself a silly hat with clock hands sticking up that said *ABOUT TIME* across the front. When I walked across the stage, Nanette, the kind financial aid advisor who helped me so much over the years, was there to shake my hand. I cried when I saw her. I was so grateful. And now the Van Wilder of Barnard has her degree at last.

Once I quit working with Charles, it helped, but my fights with Brendan didn't stop. For a while, it has felt like we're on two separate islands, which is painful to admit. From the minute we met, we felt so connected, but I may end up alone and divorced or married and miserable like Mom was for so many years. The one thing we've connected on is making a movie together. We cowrote a Christmas movie and cobbled together funds to shoot it in Connecticut. Dad got a coproducing credit, which felt nice to do for him because he helped us secure some locations. His cancer came back, so he's been getting weaker, and I wanted to give this to him. Plus he always has said that if Brendan and I can lift each other up and find ways to use our talents that support each of our dreams, we'll be okay. It wasn't easy, but we did it. And I got to direct. There were some teen actors on the set, so I went out of my way to make them feel safe and heard and not treated like cattle. I love directing and love working with my husband, but in the pit of my stomach, I don't know what the future holds for us. I hate admitting that, but there are so many unknowns. I know alcohol doesn't make things better, that it makes you feel *more* depressed, but it's just always there, and I'm finding that cycle to be the toughest one to break.

We've been back in LA, editing our movie. Brendan and I started couples counseling to make sure our relationship stays strong. He claimed that my jobs weren't hard work and that I needed to stop acting like a victim. Needless to say, I was furious that he couldn't see my efforts. We've tried all the communication techniques the therapist has been suggesting. We finished filming our movie in February. A few weeks after we get home, I start to feel more exhausted than normal. And then I feel nauseous. Then I know. Because of our situation and because I still have that professor's voice in my head telling us to NEVER have kids, I didn't even think it would happen.

I tell Brendan I think I might be pregnant, and I want him to be with me when I take the test. I'm scared. But also excited, nervous, and terrified but hopeful. As soon as I get two blue lines, I know that I don't want to just have *a* child. I want to have *his* child.

I show Brendan, and he's overcome with emotion like I am. We've been drifting apart, but all of a sudden, we're reminded of all the good, all the reasons we were stuck together like glue from the minute we had our first kiss in that club. We cry. We hug. We tell each other we're going to do this right. We're going to grow up and stop living our lives like two forever college kids. It's time. We'll never stop fighting for us, for our child. I stopped drinking a few weeks ago when I started acknowledging that I had a problem, and now this is even more of a reason to stay on that course.

We have a counseling session that afternoon, and as we sit side by side, hands clasped, and tell the therapist our news, I know there is something else I need to say, not just to her but to myself. Something I've been running from for years. But I can't run. Not anymore.

"I'm thrilled for you both," she says. "But how are you feeling about this pregnancy?"

Brendan squeezes my hand. He knows what I'm going to say, what I need to say. What I wish my parents could have said to each other and to my sisters.

"We're feeling so hopeful," I say before starting to cry. "But also . . ."

"Yes, Christy? What is it?" asks the therapist.

"I also have to admit something. I'm scared to say it."

"It's okay," she says. "Take your time."

I muster all my courage. I think about the life inside my body. My baby. *Our* baby.

"It's that . . . I'm powerless over alcohol," I say. "And I need to stop."

As soon as it's out, I break down, and Brendan holds me close. I know at that moment, after two years of marriage, that we're going to be okay. That I'm going to be okay if I break the cycles. I'm getting off the hamster wheel. I'm not running anymore. No matter how hard things get, I'm shutting off the tape in my head, this time for good.

Pregnancy pushes us both into full-blown protector mode. Brendan becomes hyperfocused on our daughter, and I become hyperfocused on taking care of myself. It's like we see each other with new eyes, almost as if we've remarried each other. We mourn the careers we thought we'd have together, we pray together, and we recommit fully to not being like our parents and not being part of some destructive cycle that makes our daughter ever think that she's not good enough or that she doesn't belong. We let out all the resentments and grievances that have been building up and hold nothing back. I may not be a perfect parent, and I know I'll make mistakes, but I know one thing with full certainty: Our kids will *not* become child actors. That, above all else, is nonnegotiable.

Each day is a choice not to drink. It's not always easy, and I have to remind myself that I'm an alcoholic, I am not perfect, and that is okay. For the first time, I don't live in the past. I let it go. I stay as present as I can. I look at our beautiful four-month-old baby girl, and I know I'll break the cycles. What came before is part of my story, it's part of me, but it doesn't have power over me. Not anymore.

The day we leave Los Angeles for good, I cradle our daughter Isabella before putting her into the car seat. After a lifetime of craving normalcy, I found an old Victorian house in the suburbs in Orange, California. The trees and foliage remind me of the East Coast, and it's peaceful and quiet. Once I announced the pregnancy, baby brands started asking me to post about products, and a whole new world opened for us. Whatever we do, we do it for the family. I've had insane highs in my life and in my career, like being on a giant billboard in Times Square and acting on Broadway and working with Disney, and I've also been incredibly humbled, like working as an intern when the red carpets stopped rolling out for me.

Brendan didn't save me, but he saw me. It took me so long to see myself.

I finish buckling Isabella in and give her a kiss.

"Ready?" Brendan asks as he gets into the car.

"So ready," I say, getting into the car beside him.

He starts the car and pulls away from Los Angeles, toward a new—and unknown—future. I've been scared of the unknown for so long, but not anymore. I keep my eyes straight ahead, and not once do I look back.

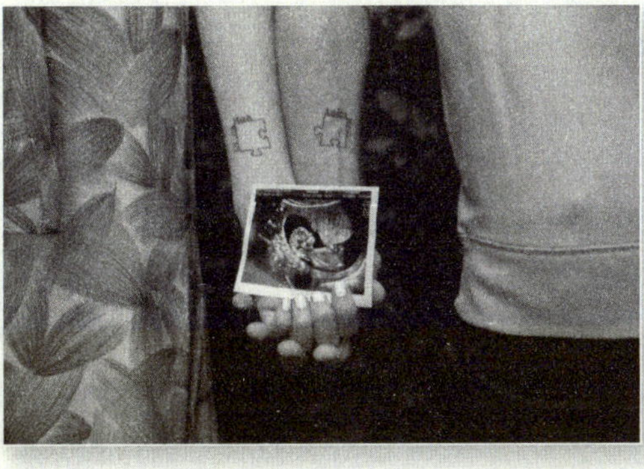

Mom,

Writing to my daughters throughout this book made me want to do the same for you, as both your daughter and a fellow mom . . .

How do I start this letter but with love? I love you deeply. But it's been complicated, if we're being honest with each other.

You have always been one of the most elaborate storytellers I have ever encountered. To this day, in your presence, there are always tales and anecdotes turned into grand voyages we've traveled together. Perpetual orations delivered to anyone willing to listen about the adventures you and your youngest experienced. So many of the details have been eroded over time, but the colors are still bright. The villains and heroes who came and went during our lifetime together exist vibrantly in your mind and have served as cautionary tales to those you meet and want to mentor.

For over forty years, there has been so much unsaid between us. Until now.

It may not seem like it at times, but this memoir is part love letter, an attempt to bridge the divide that's been wedged between us for decades. The dull ache between a mother and a daughter who veered off course and fell into a chronic cognitive dissonance, where you have your version of events and some days I struggle to look in the mirror to live with mine.

I know my story might upset you, because I would never want my daughters to write a book like this about me. But you are not weak, as I once saw you through angsty teenage eyes; you are, in fact, one of the scrappiest people I have ever met. You've endured so much sacrifice, abuse, and mental anguish, and yet you still fight another day. I've watched you literally fall, break your femur, and then fight with the doctors to release you home to take care of your beloved dogs. You are unsinkable and have therefore imbued me with one of the most invaluable lessons a mother could release to her child—the ability to survive hardship.

Since having the girls, I have grown to see you in a very different light. Not in the forgiving, pious way where I might let you push boundaries, but rather, in a way that holds a mirror up to your potential during this latter part of your life. What a blessing it has been to have been able to fly to Milford, to finally say goodbye to our home, to visit Dad's grave, and to hold your hand as you walked into your new place in Austin. I giggled helping you sign up for a dating app so you could end up finding an amazing companion these last few years. I never thought I'd live to see the day that you would find strength on your own. While your budget might be tight, deep down, you know I am waiting in the wings to rescue you without hesitation. But this time on my terms. Even though you can be prideful and stubborn, you are the epitome of resourcefulness, and I respect that most about you.

There was a time I thought you betrayed me. I thought you exploited me, a kid, because of a selfish desire to live freely away from an unhealthy marriage and the pressures of motherhood. I assumed that you benefited greatly from the lifestyle we built all those years. I held a deep grudge about some of your old-school disciplinary tactics.

But you are a special breed of parent. You are a stage mom. As much as you hate that title, that is what you are. Be proud of it. You shepherded a talented child into the arts and then relentlessly did your best to navigate the perilous waters of Hollywood. It's a battle and a tale as old as time, isn't it? Except stage parents are erased from the legacy of their children's accomplishments. You aim for greatness and often end up with nothing. Many times stage parents lose their marriages, their relationships to their children, and their autonomy in committing so deeply to THE DREAM. I can't begin to understand what level of commitment it takes to love your child that much and to want that much happiness for your child. Maybe that's what scares me most of all. As a little girl, I should have told you I wanted to quit. It's my fault. If I had had the courage to stand up for myself, I could have given you your life back.

But we can't change the past, so the stories are kept alive in detail by you, my matriarchal record keeper.

This memoir is my story, my record of things. It's a way to teach my daughters to be as resilient, gritty, and passionate as the women who came before them. We aren't perfect, but we're still here, fighting.

I finally realized while writing this that every time you told me to never give up, you weren't pushing me to stay in Hollywood—you were begging me to believe in myself.

I finally do.

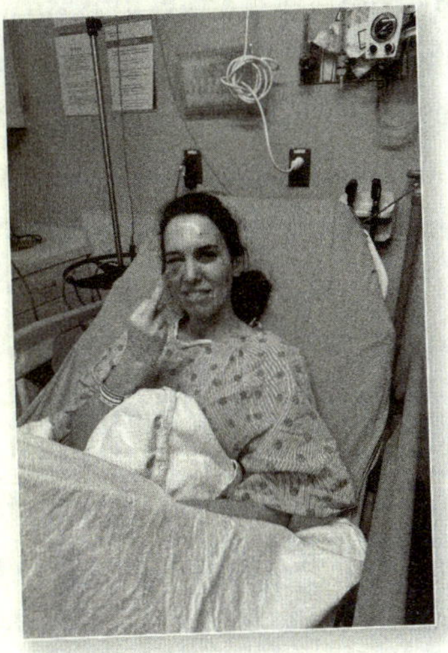

Epilogue

2025

Age 40–41

"Are you hit?!"

I can hear my husband's voice call out in an intense tone. I can feel my knee gently throbbing from hitting the scratchy ground of the Texas shooting range we've been at all afternoon for his birthday. I place my loaded shotgun ten feet away from me and stumble to my current resting spot. He's turning forty-two today. Surprise!

The field is quiet now. No more jokes and anecdotes. No more congratulatory shouts when an object is hit in the air and falls to the ground. The object is now me, and all at once, I feel the rush of attention I've known during many periods of my life. I'm immediately important. People are beelining toward my small frame, which has now crumpled into a ball. Am I dead?

Just the night before, I had finished watching myself in a "badass" reality TV show for a big network. One where you're shipped off to a remote location and you consent to getting "trained" by former elite military operators.

Even before signing my contract the previous spring, I knew that being put in a tear gas chamber, jumping out of helicopters into oceans, being buried alive, and getting perpetually demoralized by tough men would be a ratings bump for my social media and a great paycheck. So I did it—telling myself it was about personal growth and pushing boundaries, but if I'm honest, I was still chasing that familiar high of external validation. Old habits. That confidence is what led me here today. But that's not what got me accidentally shot.

On that show, you would throw up your thumb to show the spec ops team you were unharmed. For some reason, I decide to answer my husband's question like that, which only confuses him more. I thought I was back in Wales on the reality show for half a second.

"Oh, wait—are you good?!" I can still hear him in the distance. He has always had a handsome voice. This might be the last time I hear it. Oh God—my girls.

My face has been buried, but my vision is now blurred with a dark liquid. It seems to be getting worse, and it stings my contact lenses. I begin to laugh darkly.

"NO—I'm fucking hit! I'm not okay!"

"FUCK!" I haven't looked up and around, but I hear him running to me.

But I hear him stop mid-run while the person who accidentally shot me begins to run toward me as well. I need Brendan by my side NOW, or I'm gonna lose it. I don't have time for him to attack my accidental shooter.

"WHERE ARE YOU, BRENDAN? GET OVER HERE NOW!" God, why do I have such a mom voice? I gotta pull myself together. I look up at my husband of over ten years. It's been a good run, right?

"Okay, I'm here. Look at me." He takes a knee but is elevated over me. I begin to feel woozy. But I'm still trying to laugh it off. Tears are starting to surface on my face.

I've been handed a shirt, and as I gently dab my undereye area, which feels like a large, puffy foreign object, my husband repeats, "Can you see? Can you see?" I find out later it's because he thought for certain I would lose my sight any second from nerve damage. I work up the will to cry. Feelings don't come easily to me anymore.

"AM I UGLY?!" I snort a perfect mix of a laugh and a sob.

"Stop, you're gonna be fine. You just look like Tyson punched you." My husband has proven to be good at many things, but I never knew he could remain this calm under an emergency situation. I can tell he is assessing my wound as if he were back in the military, and I am now pressing on my forehead with the fabric of a man's shirt. That man is now gone, shirtless and running to his car for ice. Brendan also gets up and begins to run off to our truck.

"She's gotta get to the hospital!" Brendan says. "Christy, stay with him. DON'T LET HER FALL ASLEEP!"

That's when I know I could very well die here today, based on the fact that I was just shot in the face at close range. To be exact for all those "fun" people needing specifics out there—I caught bird shot fragment scatter because a shotgun was fired in my direction from two hundred feet away.

I'm now sitting on my butt, watching Brendan run away. My shooter, who is very dear to me, is sitting motionless with his hands around his knees. I can tell he's trying to act casual, because he's from where I'm from, and we're all fucked up in times like these.

"Are you good?" he asks.

"Um, I think so . . . I think I'm . . . Oh, wait, I think I'm dizzy. I just need to lie down." My eyes begin to roll into the back of my head.

"NO, no, no. Don't do that." He lunges for me and sits at my side. This would be a bonding moment for us if I weren't almost certain I was going to die.

"I'm okay. I'm okay." I rest my head on his shoulder so my eyes can readjust. I have to stay awake, or I may not wake up.

The Texas sky is big and beautiful today. Cicadas haven't quite woken up from their long winter's nap this February, and it's not too hot or humid. It's a beautiful day to die.

"I forgive you. I love you. It's okay," I say to him, quickly and meaningfully.

"No, it's not fucking okay. It's fucked up." He begins to choke up and immediately pushes his feelings down.

"I still love you."

"Just don't fall asleep, okay?!"

Brendan flies into our area like a bat out of hell with the truck. A cloud of dust scatters throughout the air. He rushes out the door and lifts me up under his armpit.

"Am I going to die?! Who will take care of the girls?!" I begin to cry more as he places me in the front seat gently.

"You're going to be okay! We're going to the closest hospital. It's, like, forty miles, but we'll get there fast."

Waves of emotions that I've learned to fear feeling without monetary profit come up in spurts. A part of me is proud at how "easygoing" I am at this moment.

My beloved shooter sits in the back seat with us, and I try to break the tension as we fly down an empty freeway, going well over the speed limit—112 miles per hour, to be exact.

"They say you miss one hundred percent of the shots you don't take." The guys try not to laugh in spite of the gruesome moment.

"Can you still see?" Brendan asks again.

I nod, smirking because I'm satisfied with my delivery of my joke.

Girls, here's what I learned from getting shot in the face: In the moment when everything stops, you find out what actually matters.

Lying in that Texas dirt with blood in my eyes, I wasn't thinking about my career or my past or whether I'd made the right choices. I was completely, terrifyingly present. All I could think about was my girls—whether I'd see you grow up, whether you'd know how much I love you.

The good girl who spent her whole life performing would have worried about ruining someone's birthday, about being dramatic, about looking ugly. But she wasn't there anymore. What remained was just a mother who wanted more time.

Brendan got me to that hospital fast by speeding on Texas back roads. The doctors said the bird shot missed my eye by one millimeter. I'd have a scar and two pieces of bird shot permanently in my head, but I'd live. That's all that mattered.

Girls, that little girl who peed onstage because she was too afraid to ask for what she needed? She finally grew up. Not into someone perfect or without scars but into someone who knows what matters.

The bird shot is still in my head. The scar is still on my face. And I'm grateful for both, because they remind me to stay present. To snap back to reality and give thanks for it. I received nothing short of a miracle in what could have been my final act.

When you read this book someday—all the mistakes, all the attempts at survival, all the masks I wore and slowly learned to put down—know that every hard lesson brought me to that Texas dirt, where everything finally became clear. I spent my whole life looking for the love that always existed inside me, until I had you both. You two are my heart, torn in half, walking around in this world. Live a good life and protect it.

Dear Girls,

One of the many gifts of sobriety is never having to be hungover again. I cannot imagine what it must be like to have a young child and endure a migraine-induced haze while potty training them in the middle of the night. High on my own pregnancy hormones with you, Izzy, I didn't feel the full weight (or weightlessness) of sobriety until years later, after having Sophia in February 2019.

It hit me during the heart of COVID. When we were writing down what we had in stock in our deep freezer and using paper towels for toilet paper, I realized I would never be able to go back to my old habits of self-sabotage. Not when my kids needed me present and clearheaded in this new world. My life has changed for the better, as the girls from Wicked *would say.*

As your dad and I navigated this new world with young kids, we also had to face questions of how we would make money and provide for you. We still had to keep the lights on, and as your late Grandpa Romano (who passed from cancer in 2017) would always say, "The baby needs shoes."

Comic cons helped us financially before we had you two. We traveled with you, Izzy, and went as far as flying to Australia while I was nauseous and pregnant with your sister because we wanted you to see kangaroos. But what changed our family's lives was creating cooking content for YouTube from home. We combined our skills, collaborated, and found a way to be creative and also to make money for the family. The cooking videos we made together opened the door.

Your dad became every bit the life partner I'd hoped to have, because we came together to use our strengths (his filmmaking eye, my on-camera presence, our shared understanding of storytelling) to build a successful life free of debt and fear while still being artists. This is what a real partnership looks like: two people coming together to protect what matters most.

After Grandpa Romano passed away, I flew to Connecticut alone and relocated your grandma to live closer to us. She's my ride or die, after all. Despite everything, despite all our complicated history, family shows up. She always showed up. That's what I'm teaching you.

As you both know, your dad and I work nonstop, 365 days a year, to keep the lights on and to course-correct the financial damage from our earlier years. I'm a working mom who happens to work in a very public way: online. The smartest thing I could do for our family was to never stop, never quit, and take back my narrative. I've made more in recent years than I made my entire time working for Disney by repurposing my skills to fit our needs and reconnecting with those kids who grew up with me and who still see me as a bit magical. I think they're magical too.

Here's what I want you to understand: Your dad and I built this life intentionally. We chose sobriety, we chose partnership, and we chose to stay creative while also being practical. We chose to move to Austin because we wanted you to have childhoods that felt like childhoods. Lake days, tacos, and stability rather than auditions and chaos. Every choice we've made has been about breaking the patterns I grew up with and creating something healthier for you.

You will see me work. You will see me create content, do sponsored posts, travel for appearances. Some people might judge that, might think it's too much or too public. But I hope you'll understand that this work allows me to be present for you. I'm not choosing my career over your needs. I'm integrating these things, because that's what modern working motherhood looks like, and I refuse to apologize for it.

Your dad and I are a team. We're not perfect. We might bicker about dishes and who is picking up groceries and whether we're too hard or too soft with discipline. But we show up for each other. We show up for you. And that's the magic I want you to remember.

So we end where I began, in that letter I wrote you at the start of this book. I still believe in magic. Not the franchise kind that sells merchandise and requires performance. The real kind. The magic of showing up every day for the people you love, of building something meaningful from broken pieces, of choosing presence over perfection.

I'll never give up on keeping that magic alive for you. It's worth the work.

Acknowledgments

To Simon Element, for empowering voices like mine that have been so quiet for years that they barely know how to speak their truth until you show them it's possible.

To my editor, Ronnie—you are the entire reason this book exists. After my YouTube videos years ago, when I was still figuring out how much of myself I was allowed to share, you saw the book living inside me before I did. You guided me with the kind of care, acceptance, humor, and patience of a family member. I will never forget that.

To Dina, my cowriter, who spoke my truth to life in years of conversations. You've held my hand through the hardest parts and then (diligently) led me right back to the computer to write them down with joy for their closure. This book has both of our fingerprints on it.

To Meg Thompson, whose time and attention I never had to fight for. In a world where I've spent my whole life waiting for the phone to ring, you simply believed in me. Your dedication means more than you know.

To my husband Brendan, my soulmate, my light in the darkest night. You have saved me more times than I can count. Thank you for giving me the eternal gifts of our daughters. My only hope is that we may continue to run toward each other with reckless abandon even when we are too old to walk. I will love you forever.

To my mom. I am so grateful for our relationship. It's taught me that love isn't linear.

For my family members—may you get to know me better by sitting down with this book, and may we chat deeper someday about my lived experience documented here. You were not forgotten but rather respected.

To my fans—you will always be more than that to me, as I believe I've never been a "celebrity" in your eyes. After years of confusion, I now know that I was never meant to be the girl you aspired to be but rather the one you knew you could sit at a table and be human with. I'm sorry if you ever thought I was trying too hard, and it frustrated you. I've only been hustling to provide for my family, and I didn't come from money. But I am so grateful to fully know now what I mean to you, and I truly hope this book brings us closer together.

About the Author

CHRISTY CARLSON ROMANO is an actress, singer, and author best known for her roles as Ren Stevens on Disney Channel's *Even Stevens* and the Emmy-nominated voice of Kim Possible. She went on to star on Broadway and build a devoted following of fans through her social media, podcasts, and beyond. *Once Upon a Trainwreck: The Fall and Rise of a Child Star* is her debut memoir, a candid account of fame, reinvention, and finding yourself on the other side of it.

She lives with her husband and two daughters and is probably boiling pasta for them somewhere as you read this.